# Europe Unites

Fifteen EU Members

# Europe Unites

*The EU's Eastern Enlargement*

PETER A. POOLE

PRAEGER

**Westport, Connecticut**
**London**

**Library of Congress Cataloging-in-Publication Data**

Poole, Peter A.
 Europe unites : the EU's eastern enlargement / Peter A. Poole.
  p. cm.
 Includes bibliographical references and index.
 ISBN 0–275–97704–8—ISBN 0–275–97705–6 (pbk.: alk. paper)
 1. European Union—Europe, Eastern. 2. Europe—Economic integration. I. Title.

HC240.25.E77P66 2003
341.242′2′0947—dc21        2002193022

British Library Cataloguing in Publication Data is available.

Library of Congress Catalog Card Number: 2002193022
ISBN: 0–275–97704–8
    0–275–97705–6 (pbk.)

First published in 2003

Praeger Publishers, 88 Post Road West, Westport, CT 06881
An imprint of Greenwood Publishing Group, Inc.
www.praeger.com

Printed in the United States of America

The paper used in this book complies with the
Permanent Paper Standard issued by the National
Information Standards Organization (Z39.48–1984).

10 9 8 7 6 5 4 3 2 1

To Rosemary Poole

# Contents

# Illustrations

**FIGURES**

## TABLES

# Preface

The unification of Europe after a century of war and cold war marks a major change in the international system. Europe is regaining its influence in world affairs, and the eastern enlargement will leave its imprint on all the important social, economic, and political changes that are taking place there.

One of the main themes of this book is that enlargement influences and encourages the process of regional integration in Europe. Fortunately, I have had some opportunities to witness this process, while serving in American embassies abroad and as a teacher of international relations at the Naval War College and Old Dominion University. This is an attempt to analyze and describe how the eastern enlargement is changing and will change Europe. And, of course, the greatest changes are taking place in the eastern states themselves.

I am grateful to Desmond Dinan for encouraging my interest in this subject both personally and through his books and articles, which helped fill large gaps in my knowledge of the EU. Other writers whose books have helped me understand how enlargement and integration fit together include Michael Baun, Heather Grabbe, John Redmond, Christopher Preston, Glenda Rosenthal, and Helen and William Wallace. In one of her articles, Glenda Rosenthal provided a timely reminder that the eastern enlargement needed to be seen from the accession countries' perspective.

For background purposes, I have been privileged to interview officials of the accession states, EU member states, the European Commission, and Americans specializing in European affairs. For taking time to share their insights, I want to thank Karen and Niels Abrahamsen, Ivo Daalder,

Jonathan Davidson, Andras Dekaney, Nicolas de Riviere, Bo Ericksson, Philippe Errera, Claudius Fischbach, Cristina Gaginsky, Ambassador Robert Hunter, and Cecilia Julin.

I also want to express my appreciation to Zlatin Krastev, Priit Masing, Nikolaus Meyer-Landrut, Richard Morford, Michael O'Neill, Anna Pankiewicz, Andre Querton, Borut Repansek, Stelian Stoian, Andre Sapire, David Summers, Tamas Toth, Ambassador Vygaudas Usackas, Klaas van der Tempel, and Ambassador Andrew Vershbow.

Putting out a textbook is a team effort. My thanks to the staff of Impressions Book and Journal Services who saw the book through production and to Marcia Goldstein and Jim Sabin at Praeger and Michelle Horne and Bob Pierce at Cavallino Graphics for drawing the maps. Most of all, I am grateful to my wife, Rosemary Poole, for her insights and encouragement.

# Abbreviations

| | |
|---|---|
| Benelux | Belgium, the Netherlands, and Luxembourg |
| CAP | Common Agricultural Policy |
| CEES | Central and Eastern European States |
| CFSP | Common Foreign and Security Policy |
| EAGGF | European Agricultural Guidance & Guarantee Fund |
| EC | European Community |
| EEA | European Economic Area |
| EFTA | European Free Trade Area |
| EMS | European Monetary System |
| EMU | Economic and Monetary Union |
| ERM | Exchange Rate Mechanism |
| ESDP | European Security and Defense Policy |
| EU | European Union |
| EUROPOL | European police agency |
| FDI | Foreign Direct Investment |
| GDP | Gross Domestic Product |
| GNP | Gross National Product |
| IMF | International Monetary Fund |
| JHA | Justice and Home Affairs |
| MEP | Member of the European Parliament |
| PHARE | Poland-Hungary: Actions for Economic Reconstruction |
| TEU | Treaty on European Union |
| WEU | Western European Union |

# CHAPTER 1

# Enlargement and Integration

The European Union (EU) traces its history back to the founding of the European Coal and Steel Community in 1950, and that small community of six nations has been growing ever since. By 2004, there will be twenty-five members, and they are already much more closely joined than the original six. By 2010, it is likely that the community will be even larger and more tightly integrated. What is the connection between enlargement and integration?

People who favor a stronger union have tried to link each intake of new members to a more federal approach to decision making, for example, by limiting the right of member states to veto legislation. However, when countries first enter the union they usually want to enjoy the voting rights and other powers that membership confers, so they tend to favor a loose, intergovernmental approach to decision making.

Nevertheless, the presence of new faces around the table and the airing of new interests and viewpoints invigorate the community and force it to rethink its goals. In time a new political dynamic takes hold and the member states decide to create new common policies, which will mean yielding some of their national sovereignty to the EU's central institutions.

The eastern enlargement has been a lengthy process. It began in 1989 and has coincided with an intensive period of European integration, including the start of a common currency and monetary policy, an EU foreign and security policy, policies for maintaining order within the Union, and the prospect of a European constitution. This book examines how the eastern enlargement relates to each of these new common policies. A good place to begin is with the observations of Joschka Fischer, one of Europe's most visionary statesmen.

Figure 1.1   In his May 2000 speech in Berlin, German Foreign Minister Joschka Fischer said the EU
must honor its commitment to the candidate states
without delay, and it must make the EU more
democratic. Credit: Embassy of the Federal Republic of Germany, Washington, D.C.

## JOSCHKA FISCHER AND THE "FINALITY OF EUROPE"

In a May 2000 speech, German Foreign Minister Joschka Fischer said the
European Union must accomplish two great tasks. First, it must honor its
promise to bring the countries of central and eastern Europe into the
Union without delay. They had been waiting for more than a decade, and
Fischer warned that the people in those countries were beginning to ques-
tion the sincerity of the EU's commitment.[1]

Second, the EU must address the growing confusion and cynicism of
ordinary citizens in both halves of Europe about the remoteness of EU
institutions and the secretive way in which they arrive at decisions. Fischer
warned that adding the eastern countries would create a crisis by over-
loading the EU's institutions, but he thought this was exactly what was
needed to force the Union's cautious leaders to turn it into a "lean" and
democratic federation. Although he avoided suggesting the German constitution as a model, many people believed this was what he had in mind.

Fischer's main point was that Europe must be united politically as well as geographically. That is what he meant by the "finality" of Europe. To those who feared it would be too difficult to achieve both aims at once, Fischer replied that there was no other choice. The people of Europe could not go back to the era of extreme nationalism that led to two world wars. One look at the recent wars of ethnic cleansing in former Yugoslavia should be enough to remind them what their own past was like. They could only move ahead toward greater unity, and the sooner they did so the better.

## Federalists and Intergovernmentalists

Fischer's speech was a major contribution to the ongoing debate about Europe's future, a debate between people who hold two broadly conflicting points of view. One group known as "federalists" seeks to create a closely integrated political and economic federation with power concentrated in the central institutions. Fischer considers himself a federalist, although he would strictly limit the powers of the central government, and he is more enthusiastic about enlargement than many federalists. Most Dutch and Belgian leaders have been federalists, because such a system would allow their small countries to become part of a major world power without losing their distinctive national identities.

Another group called "intergovernmentalists" have tried to preserve as much of their nations' sovereignty as they could. Many British and Scandinavian officials favor this approach; they want the EU to be run by intergovernmental committees. There have been highly influential French and German leaders in each of the two groups, but the French are now more inclined to be intergovernmentalists, in part because they fear that Germany will increasingly dominate the central institutions of the European Union.

As the organization evolved over the years, it underwent several name changes, but the terms European Community and European Union are used interchangeably in this book, even though the latter term was only added in 1992.[2]

Most German leaders believe it is in their country's basic interest to be part of a European federal union, because this arrangement is least likely to frighten or antagonize their smaller neighbors. Chancellor Gerhard Schroder has called for an EU constitution similar to Germany's, which limits the power of the central government and gives substantial power to the member states. Inevitably, some politicians in neighboring countries criticized Schroder for seeking to impose a "German model" on the EU.[3]

### Widening and Deepening the Union

Often, the intergovernmentalists have been in favor of enlarging the Union, partly to gain wider markets for their exports, but many federalists believe that enlarging the Union tends to delay or block the process of integration, and they have accused the intergovernmentalists of wanting to do just that. Baroness Margaret Thatcher, former British prime minister and one of the most vocal anti-federalists, never hesitated to speak her mind in favor of enlarging the community, in part because it would make the federalist goals more difficult to achieve.[4]

Federalists such as Jacques Delors, who served with great distinction as president of the EU Commission from 1985 to 1995, have been more interested in deepening the Union than enlarging it. Delors sought to delay the eastern enlargement (and the accession of several western European countries) because he believed it would interfere with his project to create a common currency. Nevertheless, Spain, Portugal, East Germany, Austria, Finland, and Sweden all joined the Union during Delors's presidency, and substantial progress was made in preparing for the eastern enlargement.

### "Flexibility" or a Two-Speed Europe

At first glance, the conflicting views of federalists and intergovernmentalists seem to offer little room for compromise, but in reality, the EU has evolved through constant bargaining between proponents of these two viewpoints. Both sides have come to see the advantage of letting like-minded countries take the lead in pioneering new forms of integration and allowing the other member states to catch up at their own pace. In EU jargon, this is called "flexibility" or "enhanced cooperation," but both sides have some very inflexible conditions that they like to attach to it.

Federalists insist that countries applying to join the EU must not be allowed to pick and choose what EU laws and policies they will subscribe to, as Sweden did when it chose not to join the common currency. Intergovernmentalists emphasize that the pioneer group must not become an exclusive inner circle that controls the community. For example, Britain chose not to join the common currency but insisted on being allowed to attend all meetings at which EU financial policy was made.

### EU INSTITUTIONS

The EU's four main institutions are the Commission, the Council, the Parliament, and the Court. They have evolved from the institutions of the European Coal and Steel Community, and their powers are defined in a series of treaties. The Commission is the administrative arm of the EU. With a staff of about twenty thousand people drawn from all the member states, it has the power to initiate laws and directives. The president of the Commission is nominated by the heads of member state governments and approved by the Parliament.

The Council of Ministers, composed of senior representatives of the member states, decides which laws and directives to approve. It is the EU's main decision-making body, although it sometimes defers to the EU heads of government, who meet several times a year as the European Council. The European Parliament began life as an advisory body, but it now shares real legislative powers with the Council of Ministers. Finally, the Court of Justice interprets EU laws and reconciles differences with the laws of member states.

## HOW HAVE PAST ENLARGEMENTS CHANGED THE EU?

The EU's history has been marked by an almost continuous process of enlargement. It began in 1950, with the decision by France and Germany to create the European Coal and Steel Community. Belgium, the Netherlands, Luxembourg, and Italy became founding members of that body in 1951, and Paul-Henri Spaak, Belgium's foreign minister, took the lead in designing the European Economic Community, which joined the same six countries in a common market for manufactured goods in 1957. The European Atomic Energy Community (Euratom) was created in the same year.

### The First Enlargement

In 1973, Britain, Ireland, and Denmark joined the European Community. As table 1.1 shows, this brought the largest increase in the EU's population and wealth of any enlargement, including the eastern enlargement. The first intake of new countries broadened the EU's influence worldwide because of Britain's close links with the Commonwealth and the United States, and Britain eventually became a leading advocate of a strong European Security and Defense Policy (ESDP). The new members also insisted on a more open approach to decision making in the Council and a stronger role for the European Parliament in EU affairs.

However, polls showed that neither the British nor the Danish people shared the EU's aim of creating a closer economic and political union. Britain and Denmark opted out of monetary union, and the British sought major reform of the Common Agricultural Policy. However, the Irish were much easier for the EU to accommodate. They welcomed EU economic aid and advanced rapidly from one of the poorest countries in Europe to one of the wealthiest, although they too began to show some skepticism about the goal of closer integration.[5] So the first enlargement helped to ensure that the intergovernmental approach to decision making has prevailed, and as a result the EU's central institutions have remained relatively weak.

**Table 1.1**
**Enlarging the European Union**

| Entry Date | New Members | Total Population (millions) | GDP (% increase) |
|---|---|---|---|
| 1951 | France, Germany, the Netherlands, Luxembourg, Belgium, Italy | 185 | |
| 1973 | U.K., Ireland, Denmark | 273 | 29 |
| 1981-1986 | Greece, Spain, Portugal | 338 | 15 |
| 1990 | East Germany | 354 | 1 |
| 1995 | Austria, Sweden, Finland | 375 | 8 |
| 2004 | Poland, Hungary, Czech Republic, Slovakia, Estonia, Latvia, Lithuania, Slovenia, Cyprus, Malta | 450 | 9 |
| 2007? | Romania, Bulgaria | 481 | 2 |

*Source:* European Commission

## The Southern Enlargement

Greece joined the community in 1981, with Spain and Portugal following in 1986. The three southern countries had rid themselves of dictatorial regimes in the 1970s, but they were much poorer than most European Community (EC) members. The Greek government was allowed to delay implementing some of the more stringent economic rules by claiming this would strengthen public support for democracy in their country. The Spanish also sought special concessions from the EU, and the Portuguese had to wait until Spain completed lengthy negotiations over agricultural subsidies and fishing rights before the two Iberian countries were admitted together.

## Cohesion Fund

In the 1980s, the Commission found that poor countries were unable to benefit nearly as much as rich ones from the free movement of goods and capital, because they lacked the necessary infrastructure. So Commission

President Delors persuaded the rich EU countries to provide aid to help the poor countries catch up. The resulting Cohesion Fund is perhaps the most obvious case of enlargement leading to closer integration. It set an important precedent for the eastern enlargement, because the central and eastern European states were much poorer than the western European EU members. Inevitably, Spain and the other southern states resisted transferring any of the aid they were receiving to the eastern candidates. The southern enlargement also set in motion a process by which the Mediterranean region has become an important focus of the EU's Common Foreign and Security Policy.

### East Germany

The eastern enlargement of the EU began in 1990 with the unification of Germany and the granting of EU aid to Poland, Hungary, and Czechoslovakia. The *lander* (states) comprising East Germany were added to the Federal Republic in October 1990, bypassing the usual process of negotiating a treaty of accession. In many ways, however, East Germany's transition to democracy and a free market economy has been just as difficult as that of the other candidates, and the heavy costs have been borne mainly by taxpayers in western Germany, making them less willing to pay such a disproportionate share of the EU's expenses. In addition, extending the Common Agricultural Policy (CAP) to farmers in eastern Germany proved to be such a drain on the EU budget that it led to the first major reform of the CAP.

### The Northern Enlargement

Austria, Sweden, and Finland joined the EU in 1995. Because they are located close to the former Soviet Empire, they have helped Hungary, Slovenia, and the Baltic states prepare for EU membership. They have also tried to make EU institutions more open and democratic, particularly when they have held the rotating Council presidency, and despite their countries' neutral status, leaders of Austria, Sweden, and Finland have made important contributions to EU policy in the Balkans and played important leadership roles there.

### THE PROCESS OF ENLARGEMENT

The 1957 Treaty of the European Economic Community says that any European country may apply to join the community, and there has never been any shortage of applicants, even though membership means giving up control over some important areas of policy. Now that the EU has formed a monetary union and is increasingly responsible for the security of member states, some of the most crucial aspects of national sovereignty are becoming shared responsibilities. Membership also involves considerable expense to bring the applicant's laws and institutions into line with those of the EU. For each of the central and eastern European states, the cost of meeting EU environmental standards will run into the billions of euros, although the EU will help foot the bill. These costs are not excessive when measured against the benefits of membership, which include increased security and financial stability, more trade and foreign investment, and improved relations with neighboring countries.

## Commission Opinion

After a country applies to join the EU, the next step is for the Commission to issue an opinion on its qualifications for membership. Morocco was not accepted as a candidate because it is not located in Europe. The Commission's opinion on the application submitted by Greece, which indicated that it was not ready to be accepted as a candidate, was overruled by the Council of Ministers. When Hungary, Poland, Czech Republic, Estonia, and Slovenia applied, the Commission recommended that they be allowed to begin accession negotiations, and the Council agreed. The Commission recommended accepting Slovakia, Latvia, Lithuania, Romania, and Bulgaria as candidates, but added that they had not fully met the basic criteria for membership and should be allowed to begin accession negotiations only after they had done so. The Council also approved this recommendation.

## Copenhagen Criteria

At a 1993 summit in Copenhagen, EU leaders established the basic political and economic criteria for membership. A candidate country must have stable institutions guaranteeing democracy, the rule of law, human rights, and protection of minorities. It must also have a market economy capable of coping with competitive pressures within the EU, and finally, the candidate must accept all of the EU's laws and policies (known as the *acquis communautaire*). Moreover, applicants are expected to resolve any outstanding disputes with their neighbors before joining the Union.

In 1999, the Turkish government was told that while it did not meet these criteria, it could move on to the next stage in the enlargement process (the negotiation of an accession treaty) when it did so. EU leaders were well aware of the importance of having good relations with Turkey because of its strategic location. They also knew that the prospect of membership in the Union was a powerful inducement to the Turks to reform their institutions. Therefore, the EU has encouraged Turkey to pursue the goal of EU membership, and Ankara is making a strong effort to respond. In December 2002, Turkey was told that if it met the Copenhagen criteria by December 2004, it could begin accession negotiations "without further delay."

## The Right to Veto Applicants

Any member state can veto any candidate for EU membership. For example, Greece essentially blocked Turkey from being accepted as a candidate for EU membership until 1999, although other member states shared their position. Greece warned that it would block the entire eastern enlargement unless Cyprus was allowed to join the EU along with the first central and eastern European countries.[6]

In the 1960s, the first enlargement of the EU was delayed for several years because President de Gaulle of France vetoed Britain's application in 1963. De Gaulle said he did not believe Britain fully accepted the goals of the European Community, thereby helping to establish the principle that an applicant must accept the entire body of EU laws and policies. Ironically, de Gaulle's own reservations about European integration were very similar to Britain's, but for most of the EU's history, France has tried to manage the process of integration, while Britain has sought to limit its participation in programs like the common currency. Britain was finally accepted as a candidate for membership (along with Ireland, Denmark, and Norway) after de Gaulle left office in 1969.

## The Accession Treaty

When an applicant is judged to have met the Copenhagen criteria, it is allowed to move to the next stage of the accession process, which is the negotiation of an accession treaty. Six countries were allowed to begin negotiations in 1998: Poland, Hungary, the Czech Republic, Estonia, Slovenia, and Cyprus. Six more were allowed to begin in 2000: Slovakia, Latvia, Lithuania, Romania, Bulgaria, and Malta.

The accession treaty is divided into thirty chapters, each covering an important issue, such as agriculture, external relations, or the environment. The applicant country is expected to adopt all of the EU's laws and policies in each of these areas, and it must also demonstrate that it can implement them. When it has done so to the EU's satisfaction, that chapter of the negotiation is considered closed and the negotiators move on to the next chapter. The size of the task can be judged by the fact that the entire body of EU laws and policies that must be adopted covered eighty thousand pages by the year 2000, and it continues to grow month by month.

## Transition Periods

If an applicant country is unable to adopt all of the EU's laws or policies in a particular area (e.g., environmental policy), it will almost certainly not be allowed to opt out indefinitely. At most, it may be granted a transition period of a few years in which to adopt and enforce that particular set of rules. For example, the Polish government was afraid that Germans would buy up much of their country's best farmland (some of which belonged to Germans before the map of Europe was redrawn after World War II). Hungarians were also afraid that their land prices would be inflated when foreigners entered the market. So both countries sought (and were granted) a transition period in which non-nationals would be denied the right to buy farmland. Poland was granted an exceptionally long transition period of twelve years to protect farmland in certain areas. Normally, transition periods are much shorter.

EU countries can also request a transition period before certain EU rules apply to the new members, and the decision is usually made by the other member states. For example, the German government sought a seven-year transition period before central and eastern European workers could apply for jobs in Germany. (Other EU countries were allowed to set shorter transition periods, and both Sweden and Britain opted for none at all.) EU members are usually in a much stronger bargaining position than the candidate countries during the accession negotiations, but all parties know they will have to live together, so it is in everyone's interest to avoid creating a situation in which the new members feel they were treated unfairly.

### Ratifying the Accession Treaty

When agreement is reached with a candidate on all thirty chapters in the accession treaty, the document must be ratified by each of the member states, the European Parliament, and the parliament of the candidate country. Some of the candidate countries, including Poland, have a constitutional requirement that the accession treaty must be submitted to a national referendum. Even if this is not a constitutional requirement, the leaders of a candidate country may decide that accession is so important it must be put to a referendum. Table 1.2 shows how long the enlargement process took for each of the countries that were previously added.

Although the process is lengthy and difficult, the new relationship that is being created will be permanent, and considerable mutual adjustment is required. This is true even if the candidate country closely resembles the existing member states and has a long history of interaction with them, as was the case for Austria, Sweden, and Finland.

### Commission's Role in Enlargement

In addition to giving EU leaders its opinion on the applicants' qualifications, the Commission also plays a major role in the enlargement negotiations. When the applicant country and the member states disagree on a point, it is often the Commission's role to propose a compromise. In the eastern enlargement, more than any previous one, the Commission has

**Table 1.2**
**Length of Each Phase of EU Enlargements**

|  | Preparing Commission Opinion (months) | Decision to Open Negotiations (months) | Duration of the Negotiations (months) | Length of Enlargement Process |
|---|---|---|---|---|
| Britain | 5 | 33 | 19 | 5 years, 7 months |
| Denmark | 5 | 33 | 19 | 5 years, 7 months |
| Ireland | 5 | 33 | 19 | 5 years, 7 months |
| Norway | 2 | 33 | 19 | 5 years, 7 months |
| Greece | 7 | 6 | 34 | 5 years, 6 months |
| Portugal | 14 | 5 | 80 | 8 years, 9 months |
| Spain | 16 | 2 | 76 | 8 years, 5 months |
| East Germany | (joined EU by reuniting with West Germany in 1990) | | | |
| Austria | 24 | 18 | 13 | 5 years, 5 months |
| Sweden | 13 | 6 | 13 | 3 years, 6 months |
| Finland | 8 | 3 | 13 | 2 years, 9 months |

*Note:* Hungary, Poland, the Czech Republic, Slovakia, Slovenia, Lithuania, Latvia, and Estonia will be admitted to the EU in May 2004 if all the parties concerned ratify the accession treaties. The time elapsed since the first of these countries (Poland and Hungary) applied for membership in March 1994 will be ten years and two months. However, the enlargement process for Britain, Ireland, Denmark, and Greece was even longer if one counts from the time of their first applications in the early 1960s.

*Source:* Christopher Preston, *Enlargement and Integration in the European Union* (London and New York: Routledge, 1997), 14. The period of time shown in the right-hand column is greater than the sum of the other three columns because other delays occurred.

done most of the actual negotiating with the applicant countries. A major reason for this was that the negotiations involved many technical details that the Commission staff had mastered.

Commissioner for Enlargement Gunther Verheugen was highly regarded by both the member states and the candidates, and he was trusted by all the parties to mediate the most sensitive issues. For example, he was asked to intercede when politicians in Austria, Hungary, and Germany argued that the Czech Republic should not be allowed to join the EU until it repealed the Benes decrees by which Germans and Hungarians were expelled from Czechoslovakia after World War II.[7]

### Enlargement and Institutional Reform

It has become almost a tradition before each enlargement for the Commission to argue that the EU's decision-making process must be reformed before new states are taken in or else all EU business will grind to a halt. Reforming the voting system in the Council of Ministers is usually the main focus of attention, with federalists arguing for a greater use of majority voting (to deny individual states the right of veto). Yet each of the past enlargements has left the EU's institutional structure essentially unchanged. If anything, the growing number of member states has confirmed the practice of decision making by intergovernmental committee.[8]

As momentum increased for the eastern enlargement in the 1990s, EU leaders agreed that certain institutional reforms were essential before so many countries were added to the Union. The Treaty of Nice, embodying these reforms, was negotiated in 2000, and EU leaders declared that it must be ratified before accepting any accession treaties with the central and eastern European countries. Irish voters rejected the treaty in a 2001 referendum, but they finally approved it in a second Irish referendum in 2002.[9]

## HOW DOES THE EASTERN ENLARGEMENT DIFFER FROM PAST ONES?

During the 1990s, most analysts agreed that the eastern enlargement was unique because it was the largest one in the EU's history and the candidates were so much poorer than the member states and still bore some of the scars of forty years of communist rule.[10] As noted earlier, however, the eastern enlargement actually brings a smaller increase in the EU's population than the first enlargement. And the ten countries that will enter the Union in 2004 all have stable democratic systems. Moreover, by the late 1990s, the eastern states were beginning to experience strong economic growth, some fast enough to overtake the poorest EU members within a few years.

The eastern enlargement may place a greater strain on EU institutions than past enlargements, but the prospect this time is for significant reform. EU leaders waited until 2000 to address the subject of institutional reform, and the Treaty of Nice amounted to little more than tinkering at the margins. However, the constitutional convention that began work in February 2002 is likely to recommend a thorough overhaul of the system.

The central and eastern European candidates were invited to take part in the debate on the EU's future even before joining the Union. Having so recently regained their freedom, most of them seemed to favor a Union of sovereign states rather than a highly centralized Europe. President Alexander Kwasniewski of Poland probably expressed the views of many eastern European leaders when he said, "Polish experience speaks in favor of respect for the national factor, for building a Europe of father-lands."[11] This suggests that the eastern enlargement, like those that came before, will reinforce the EU's tendency toward intergovernmental deci-sion making.

### Unique Aspects

Nevertheless, the eastern enlargement is qualitatively different from past enlargements. As already noted, the growing range of EU rules and functions has made this enlargement much more complex and technical. As a result, the Commission rather than the Council of Ministers has been the EU's main interlocutor with the candidate states. The process has taken longer than previous enlargements not only because of the com-plexity, but also because EU leaders were determined to launch the mon-etary union first. Once that was achieved, enlargement negotiations began to move fairly quickly. Finally, since the enlargement is taking place against a backdrop of closer economic union and EU security coop-eration, the new states will be involved in the development of these new functions.

### Monetary Union

The eastern European states will adopt the common currency, the euro, as soon as they are ready. This is now a requirement for new EU members. Most of them are eager to do it quickly because it will encourage foreign investment, but the timing of their entry into monetary union will be determined by when they meet specific criteria in the Treaty of European Union. Their economies must converge as much as possible with those of other EU members, because the European Central Bank will set interest rates that meet the needs of the majority of member states.

When the eastern Europeans adopt the euro, it will increase the stability of their economies and attract investment from older EU member states and from outside the eurozone. It is possible that the entry of central and eastern European states into the eurozone will coincide with the entry of several of the western European holdouts, including Britain, Denmark, Sweden, Switzerland, and Norway (although the latter two would first have to join the EU).

The eastern and western halves of Europe complement each other eco-nomically. The linkup between western European capital and technology and the skilled eastern European workforce has already helped to speed economic growth throughout Europe, but such a large increase in the size and diversity of the eurozone will make it even harder to adopt monetary policy decisions that suit as many states as possible.

### European Security

Early in the 1990s, EU leaders used the prospect of membership in the Union to persuade the eastern Europeans to resolve outstanding differences with their neighbors. This strategy helped spare them from engaging in the kind of ethnic conflicts that have raged in the Balkans and parts of the former Soviet Union. All of Europe benefited from this wise policy.

As the EU became more deeply involved in stabilizing the Balkan conflicts, the eastern European states played an important role, supporting peacekeeping efforts with their troops and allowing their territory to be used to mount peacekeeping missions. After they join the EU, the new members will have the task of managing its eastern and southern borders. Part of this job will consist of reducing the flow of illegal immigrants and criminal gangs that have created problems within the EU, but the EU does not want its external border to become a new dividing line in Europe. The new members will play an important role in developing strong economic and political relations with the EU's neighbors in the former Soviet and Yugoslav republics.

### The Next EU Enlargement

In fact, the external border established after the first group of central and eastern European states joins in 2004 will almost certainly be temporary, because this will not be the EU's final enlargement. The Union has indicated that Romania and Bulgaria are likely to be ready to join by 2007.

Indeed, all of the countries of southeastern Europe—including Croatia, Macedonia, Albania, Bosnia, Serbia, and Montenegro—are potential candidates, and the EU is in the process of assuming major responsibilities for the security of that region, thus illustrating the close relationship between enlargement and integration.

### NOTES

1. Fischer's speech, entitled "From Confederacy to Federation: Thoughts on the Finality of European Integration," was delivered at Humboldt University in Berlin on May 12, 2000, three days after the fiftieth anniversary of French Foreign Minister Robert Schuman's announcement of the European Coal and Steel Community. Excerpts from Fischer's speech, provided by the press office of the German Permanent Representation in Brussels, appear in the appendix of this book.

2. The European Community (EC), which was originally called the European Economic Community, was established by the Treaty of Rome in 1957. The European Union was created by the Treaty of European Union, which was signed in 1992 and ratified (after much difficulty) by the end of 1993. The EC still exists as a

major component of the European Union and includes all of the functions that are managed on a community basis, including trade policy and the Common Agricultural Policy.

3. Chancellor Schroder's proposal was put forward as a Social Democratic Party policy paper on April 30, 2001, and was summarized (with the reactions of other EU governments) in the *Financial Times* (May 1–3, 2001).

4. Margaret Thatcher, *The Downing Street Years* (New York: HarperCollins, 1993), pp. 545–48.

5. In 2001, Irish government leaders expressed irritation when the Commission warned them that their fast-growing economy was in danger of overheating. In the same year, Irish voters for the first time rejected an EU treaty in a referendum.

6. Judy Dempsey, "UN Tries Again to Reach Cyprus Accord," *Financial Times* (July 12, 2002).

7. Stefan Wagstyl, "Holding Back," *Financial Times* (April 3, 2002).

8. See Desmond Dinan, "The Commission and Enlargement," in *The Expanding European Union,* ed. John Redmond and Glenda G. Rosenthal (Boulder, Colo.: Lynne Rienner, 1998), pp. 17–40.

9. Irish opponents of the treaty argued that it would violate Ireland's neutrality, and this was one of the reasons Irish voters rejected it in the first referendum. To counter this argument, EU leaders passed a resolution at their June 2002 summit affirming Ireland's right to remain neutral.

10. Michael J. Baun, *A Wider Europe: The Process and Politics of European Union Enlargement* (Lanham, Md.: Rowman and Littlefield, 2000), pp. 4–8.

11. John Reed, "Polish President Sets Out Vision of 'Europe of Fatherlands,'" *Financial Times* (February 19, 2002).

# CHAPTER 2

# The Pattern of Previous Enlargements

In the aftermath of World War II, Europeans found themselves struggling to rebuild their battered nations in a world dominated by U.S.-Soviet rivalry and the cold war. Idealists saw the need for Europe to unite if it was to regain its influence, but the old Franco-German rivalry threatened to reemerge as French leaders struggled to prevent the rebuilding of German industry and the rearmament of the German people.

On May 9, 1950, in a dramatic reversal of his government's policy, French Foreign Minister Robert Schuman announced that France and Germany would place their main war industries under the control of a supranational organization. The European Coal and Steel Community (ECSC) was supposed to make war impossible between the two rivals. It was soon joined by Belgium, the Netherlands, Luxembourg, and Italy. The ECSC was inspired by Schuman's friend, Jean Monnet, who was a key advisor to Allied leaders during World War II.[1]

The dream of Monnet and Schuman was that Europe would gradually be united, sector by economic sector, until the nations would see the logic of forming a close political union. Monnet's vision was primarily of a French-led union of western European states, but Schuman foresaw the eventual reunification of both halves of Europe. In 1963, he said, "We must build the united Europe not only in the interest of the free nations, but also in order to be able to admit the peoples of Eastern Europe into this community."[2]

In 1957, the same six countries that formed the Coal and Steel Community signed treaties in Rome creating the European Economic Community and the European Atomic Energy Community. Soon, their economic success began to attract new applicants for membership. In this chapter, we look at how each enlargement has changed the European Community (EC) and influenced its development. While new member states generally favor intergovernmental decision making when they first join, the new interests and viewpoints that they bring tend to reinvigorate the community and force it to rethink its goals. Thus, in time, the new political dynamic created by enlargement encourages closer integration.[3]

## BRITAIN, IRELAND, AND DENMARK JOIN THE EC

When Britain first applied to join the European Community in 1961, British leaders had been weighing the question of establishing closer ties with Europe since the Coal and Steel Community was formed a decade earlier. To Monnet's disappointment, the Labour Party government of Clement Atlee had decided not to join the ECSC because they did not believe Britain's economic interests should be so closely tied to Europe. Winston Churchill supported this decision when he became prime minister for a second time in 1951. "I love France and Belgium," he said a few months later, "but we should not allow ourselves to be pulled down to their level."[4]

### EFTA versus the Common Market

The European Community had a common external tariff that kept most foreign food products out of Europe. The EC's Common Agricultural Policy subsidized farmers and made food expensive for European consumers. Britain's policy was to import food cheaply from Commonwealth countries like New Zealand and pay much lower subsidies to its own farmers. Thus, Britain's initial response to the creation of the EC was to organize a rival group known as the European Free Trade Area (EFTA). This group—which included the Scandinavian countries plus Austria, Switzerland, Spain, and Liechtenstein—had no external tariff or common policy on farm subsidies.

However, by 1961, British government and business leaders realized they had made a mistake. The EC countries were enjoying faster economic growth than the EFTA group, and their plans for integration were moving rapidly. Therefore, the longer other countries waited, the harder it would be for them to join. Also, with 185 million people, the EC was a much larger market than the EFTA's 90 million. When Britain applied for EC membership in 1961, Denmark, Ireland, and Norway followed because their economies were closely linked to the United Kingdom. Figure 2.1 provides a chronology of events related to the first enlargement.

In 1963, President Charles de Gaulle of France vetoed Britain's application to the EC on the grounds that he did not believe the British were

**Figure 2.1**
**The Accession of Britain, Denmark, and Ireland**

---

1957    European Community and European Atomic Energy Community (Euratom) treaties signed in Rome by France, Germany, Belgium, the Netherlands, Luxembourg, and Italy.

1960    Britain takes the lead in forming European Free Trade Area.

1961    Britain, Denmark, Ireland, and Norway apply to join the European Community.

1963    President de Gaulle of France vetoes U.K. application.

1966    De Gaulle again rebuffs Britain's application.

1969    De Gaulle resigns. Britain, Denmark, Ireland, and Norway reactivate their applications to EC.

1969    EC summit in The Hague links enlargement to monetary cooperation and a new budgetary system for funding the Common Agricultural Policy.

1973    Britain, Denmark, and Ireland join the EC.

1974    To make the EC more popular with British public, EC leaders create European Regional Development Fund.

1978    Commission President Roy Jenkins proposes European Monetary System (EMS) to cope with turbulent exchange rates. EMS is backed by French and German leaders.

1979    First direct elections for the European Parliament help to revitalize that institution.

---

prepared to give up their close ties with the United States and the Commonwealth and adopt all of the EC's rules and policies. (Acceptance by the candidates of the *acquis communautaire* became the central principle of the enlargement process.) But de Gaulle also wanted Europe to be more independent of U.S. military support, and he was particularly irritated when British Prime Minister Macmillan accepted President Kennedy's offer of Polaris missiles as the delivery system for U.K. nuclear warheads.[5]

Denmark, Ireland, and Norway allowed their applications to lapse when Britain's did, but all four countries reactivated their applications together in 1966, when Britain decided the time was right. However, the British were having serious economic difficulties, and de Gaulle rebuffed their application on the grounds that Britain's economy could not compete within the EC. Whether or not de Gaulle's judgment was fair in

Britain's case, economic competitiveness became an important criterion in deciding if an applicant was ready to begin negotiating a treaty of accession.

After de Gaulle left office in 1969, the four countries tried again, and de Gaulle's successor, Georges Pompidou, welcomed their applications. Pompidou believed they would strengthen the EC at a time of considerable economic and political turmoil in the international system. EC leaders meeting in The Hague linked their acceptance of the four nations' candidacies to monetary cooperation and a new system for funding the Common Agricultural Policy.[6]

### European Monetary System

In 1978, Commission President Roy Jenkins proposed the European Monetary System (EMS), the first major step toward monetary union. France and Germany strongly supported this initiative, which included an Exchange Rate Mechanism (ERM) that limited the fluctuation of member states' currencies within a certain range. Britain opted not to join the ERM until 1990, but was forced out two years later, when its overvalued currency was attacked by currency speculators. This experience contributed to Britain's decision not to join the common currency. Denmark also opted out, but both countries reserved the right to join later.

### Common Fisheries Policy

The EC's creation of a Common Fisheries Policy (CFP) late in the enlargement negotiations angered the candidate countries. Under this new policy, all EC members would gain the right to fish in the new members' previously restricted coastal fishing grounds. This seemed highly opportunistic, because the candidates controlled more extensive fishing grounds than the existing six EC members. The candidates demanded and were given a transition period before the CFP came fully into effect. Nevertheless, the Norwegian people rejected membership in the EC when it was put to a referendum in 1992 and again in 1994.

### European Political Cooperation

The EC countries also began in the 1970s to develop a common foreign policy by a process they called European Political Cooperation. Member state officials formed working groups at various levels to try and hammer out common positions on various issues. However, at this stage in their history, the EC members disagreed on many issues, and since any member state could veto a common position or force the others to water it down by threatening a veto, they produced mostly bland and ineffective declarations.

The main value of the process was that EC diplomats learned to work together and trust each other, and the member states gradually brought their foreign policies into line with each other on certain key issues such as relations with Russia, but they remained far apart on others. In the 1990s, the renamed Common Foreign and Security Policy (CFSP) would become an important facet of European integration, and the United Kingdom would play a leading role in CFSP, in contrast to its opting out of the common currency.

## European Council

In 1974, shortly after Britain joined the EC, the heads of member state governments began the practice of holding summit meetings several times a year. These meetings, known as the European Council, gave the EC much greater visibility in the media, and allowed their heads of government to steal some of the Commission's thunder as initiators of policy. U.K. leaders strongly favored this kind of intergovernmental decision making, and Prime Minister Tony Blair proposed in 2000 that the European Council should set the EU's annual agenda and that it be given a secretariat to track progress on major projects.

## Regional Aid

The EC's largest program for aiding member states, the European Regional Development Fund (ERDF), was initiated by French President Georges Pompidou as a direct result of the Community's first enlargement. Pompidou wanted to help Prime Minister Edward Heath mobilize support for the EC in Britain. Although Britain was one of the richest countries in Europe, some of its regions had high unemployment because their traditional industries were no longer competitive. Although the ERDF was created to provide aid to all EC member states for redevelopment of their poorest regions, the poorest EC members received the largest allocation of funds.

## Addressing the "Democratic Deficit"

In 1979, the first direct elections for the European Parliament provided another sign that the EC was emerging from its long period of stagnation caused by de Gaulle's nationalism and the economic crises of the 1970s. A surprising 65 percent of eligible voters turned out to choose the first elected members of Parliament (called MEPs). The Parliament, which was located in Strasbourg in eastern France, had been known mainly for lackluster debates and high rates of absenteeism by the members, but after the first direct election, the MEPs began to take their jobs seriously and demanded a voice in shaping EU policies. The Parliament has steadily increased its powers, and it now has a role to play in the EU's major projects, including enlargement.

### Political Dynamics

The entry of Britain, Ireland, and Denmark into the Community (raising its membership from six to nine) changed the political dynamics among member states. British leaders became the EC's resident skeptics and intergovernmentalists, constantly irritating their partners by questioning the need for a closer union. Britain and Denmark favored free trade and reform of the Common Agricultural Policy, which was by far the costliest item in the EU budget. Ireland, being the first of several poor countries to enter the EC, helped develop the case for giving special cohesion aid to poor member states.

### Enhanced World Influence

Britain had relinquished its global empire by the time it joined the EC. However, its political, economic, and cultural influence was extensive and helped transform the European Community from an essentially inward-looking group of continental countries into an organization with worldwide influence.

## THE ENTRY OF GREECE, SPAIN, AND PORTUGAL

Since Greece joined the EC in 1981, five years before Spain and Portugal, the two events are usually described as two separate enlargements of the Community. However, the three southern countries had much in common in terms of their location, underdeveloped economies, and recent political history. In these respects, they somewhat resembled the central and eastern European states, and their accession served as a kind of rehearsal for the eastern enlargement.

### Rebuilding Democratic Institutions

By coincidence, all three southern countries emerged from periods of right-wing dictatorship between the years 1974 and 1976. The newly elected governments in these countries were weak and unstable, particularly in Portugal, and they faced a multitude of economic and other problems with very limited capabilities for dealing with them. Membership in

**Figure 2.2**
**The Accession of Greece, Spain, and Portugal into the European Community**

---

| | |
|---|---|
| 1974 | After Portuguese dictator Marcello Caetano is overthrown, Portugal enters period of instability. |
| 1974 | Turkish invasion of Cyprus leads to collapse of the military junta in Greece. Greek voters opt for a parliamentary republic. |
| 1975 | Greece applies to join the EC. |
| 1975 | Death of Spanish dictator Francisco Franco; King Juan Carlos pledges return to democracy. |
| 1976 | Commission suggests a pre-accession period to rebuild the Greek economy. EC Council rejects the idea and begins accession negotiations with Greece. |
| 1977 | Spain and Portugal apply for membership in the EC. |
| 1977 | Commission's Fresco Papers link enlargement to EC reform and continued integration. |
| 1979 | Accession negotiations begin with Spain and Portugal. |
| 1981 | Greece is admitted to the EC. |
| 1985 | Jacques Delors becomes President of Commission; presses for completion of single market and funds to reduce disparity between rich and poor members. |
| 1986 | Single European Act approved by member states; sets timetable for single market, funds for poor states, and reforms voting method in Council of Ministers. |
| 1986 | Spain and Portugal are admitted to the EC after issue of Mediterranean agricultural products is resolved. |

---

the EC offered a means of obtaining political, financial, and technical support for bringing their countries up to EC standards. Figure 2.2 outlines the accession process for these three southern countries.

EC leaders were anxious to shore up Europe's weak southern flank by helping Greece, Spain, and Portugal build stable democratic institutions and healthier economies. The EC had signed association agreements with Greece and Spain in the early 1960s; Portugal joined the EFTA in 1960. However, for political reasons, the EC had suspended relations with the three countries in the years prior to the collapse of the dictatorships. In addition, to balance its association agreement with Athens, the EC signed a similar one with Greece's rival, Turkey, in 1964.

## Commission Opinion on Applications

Greece applied to join the EC in 1975, followed by Spain and Portugal in 1977. In 1976, the Commission issued an opinion that halfheartedly welcomed the Greek application, but essentially argued that the country was not yet ready politically or economically for membership and should undergo a period of convergence before accession negotiations could begin.[7] Greek leaders were particularly upset by the Commission's emphasis on the EC preserving a balance in its relations with Greece and Turkey. However, the Council of Ministers rejected the Commission's proposal for a pre-accession period and decided to begin negotiations with Greece immediately. Throughout the lengthy enlargement process, the Greeks generally succeeded in keeping their negotiations with the EC separate from Spain's, which were complicated by Spain's greater size and economic importance and by its demands for special treatment.

## The Fresco Papers

In 1977, the Council asked the Commission to produce a study of how the EC would be affected when the three southern countries joined the Community. The resulting Fresco Papers argued that enlargement could cause major problems for the EC's integration projects—completing the common market and launching monetary union. The study also warned that integrating the three southern countries into the Common Agricultural Policy and regional aid programs would be a major challenge.[8]

The Commission paper also proposed reforming the weighted voting system in the Council of Ministers to preserve the existing balance between small and large countries. Additionally, the Commission urged that more Council decisions be made by majority vote rather than allowing member states the power to veto them. For once, the member states addressed these issues in the Single European Act (SEA), which was agreed in 1986.

## Delors's Contributions

The SEA was the first major achievement of Commission President Jacques Delors, and it laid the foundation for a series of bold initiatives by Delors, who is widely regarded as the most effective leader the EU has produced. During his decade in office (1985–95), he pressed for completion of the single market, put the EU's finances on a firmer footing, championed major social legislation, and brokered the adoption of the Treaty of European Union which set a timetable for launching the common currency.[9] Despite his concern that integration should take precedence over enlargement, Spain, Portugal, East Germany, Austria, Sweden, and Finland joined the Union on Delors's watch. Also, he persuaded the rich member states to provide cohesion funds to help the southern states and Ireland catch up.

## SOUTHERN ENLARGEMENT: A PREVIEW OF THE EASTERN ENLARGEMENT

The addition of the three southern countries established a number of precedents for the eastern enlargement, which began in 1989 with the reunification of Germany. Each of these enlargement processes offered an opportunity to strengthen democracy and free market principles in countries that had been run as one-party dictatorships with state-controlled economies.

In both enlargements, the Commission played an important role as an "honest broker" in negotiations between the member states and candidates. However, it played a much broader role in the eastern enlargement, because the candidates faced the task of adopting and implementing a greatly expanded body of laws and policies. In both enlargements, the Commission also urged the member states to link enlargement to closer integration and reform the voting procedures in the Council of Ministers before the new countries came on board.[10]

The free movement of workers from the southern states was delayed by a transition period of seven years, the same transition period German leaders demanded before central European workers could seek jobs in Germany. After joining the Community in 1981, Greek leaders promptly threatened to block Spain's entry unless they were given a huge aid program. Spain would issue a similar threat in regard to the eastern enlargement. In both enlargements, the French government's concern with protecting its farmers' interests caused major delays and difficulties in shaping a common EU negotiating position.

The timing of the removal of trade barriers between the candidates and the Community was similar in both the southern and eastern enlargements, and the candidates were allowed some extra time to protect their infant industries. In both enlargements, the candidates' pleas for an admission target date went unheeded for years, but although EU negotiators held most of the cards and refused to deal with the candidates as equals, the candidates could and did remind the EU that their countrymen might reject a treaty that did not serve their interests.[11]

### Political Dynamics

The entry of the southern states changed the internal dynamics of the Community. A north-south divide emerged, with mainly rich Protestant countries in the north and much poorer Catholic or Orthodox countries in the south. France sought, not always successfully, to gain the new members' support by presenting itself as the protector of their interests. The eastern enlargement was almost certain to have an even greater impact on internal EU politics, because most of the central and eastern European states were far more closely tied to Germany than to France. They would also increase the voting strength of poor countries on budget issues.

### Monetary Union

The three southern countries gained a significant increase in foreign investment after joining the EU, and all of them qualified for membership in the common currency. They received some warnings from the Commission when their budget deficits threatened to breach the 3 percent limit, but in general their financial management and economic performance improved steadily. This augured well for the prospects of the central and eastern European states, which were eager to join the common currency as soon as they could qualify.

### AUSTRIA, SWEDEN, AND FINLAND JOIN THE UNION

The northern enlargement (also called the EFTA enlargement) was the quickest and least contentious in EU history because the candidates had already adopted more than half of the *acquis communautaire* when they joined the European Economic Area (EEA) in 1992. The EEA allowed these countries to participate in the single market for goods, labor, services, and capital without making a commitment to join a political union.

From the Commission's perspective, the EEA was a device to accommodate the EFTA countries' desire for closer association with the EU without involving the Union in another full-scale enlargement at a time when EU leaders wanted to concentrate on integration. However, when the governments of Sweden, Finland, Norway, and Austria realized the EEA would not give them access to the full range of EU programs or a voice in EU decision making, they applied for full membership in the Union. Figure 2.3 lists major events in the northern enlargement process.

### EU Concessions to the EFTA Candidates

Although the EU claimed to be holding the candidates to the exact letter of the *acquis*, in fact it made important concessions to them during the negotiations. For example, the candidates had higher environmental standards than the EU, which might have been viewed as an obstacle to free trade with the EU members. Instead, the candidates were allowed to maintain their standards for a four-year period during which the enlarged

**Figure 2.3**
**The Accession of Finland, Sweden, and Austria**

| | |
|---|---|
| 1989 | Collapse of communism in central and eastern Europe; Austria applies for membership in European Community. |
| 1990 | EC begins negotiations to form European Economic Area with Austria, Sweden, Finland, Norway, and Switzerland. |
| 1991 | EC members complete the single market and agree terms of Treaty on European Union, including plans for monetary union. |
| 1991 | Sweden applies to join the EU as a full member. |
| 1992 | European Economic Area (EEA) negotiations complete. Swiss voters reject EEA in referendum. Finland and Norway apply to join the EU as full members. |
| 1993 | EU members complete ratification of EU Treaty, opening the way for the northern enlargement. |
| 1993 | Accession negotiations begin with Austria, Sweden, Finland, and Norway. |
| 1994 | Accession negotiations are completed, but Norwegians reject EU membership in a referendum. |
| 1995 | Austria, Sweden, and Finland join the Union. |

EU would consider raising its own standards. Austria was given a similar right to limit truck traffic through its alpine passes. Finland and Sweden were allowed to maintain their state monopolies on the retail sale of alcohol, and they were also allowed to keep their free trade agreements with Estonia, Latvia, and Lithuania, which were aimed at stabilizing the Baltic region.

As in the southern enlargement, the three most difficult issues were agriculture, fisheries, and regional aid. The EU agreed to provide aid to regions with a population density below eight people per square kilometer. This would help keep the northern regions of the Scandinavian countries populated, which was important for their security. The EU's agreement to this concession would also help win support for EU membership in the most Euroskeptic areas of Scandinavia.

## Fisheries

Norway's coastal villages depended heavily on fishing, and the government sought to manage the country's fishing grounds so they would produce indefinitely without becoming exhausted. This policy was hard to

Figure 2.4   Jacques Delors, former president of the
European Commission, oversaw the early stages of
the eastern enlargement process. *Credit:* European
Commission Audiovisual Library.

reconcile with the EU's Common Fisheries Policy, which aimed at opening
all EU fishing grounds to the fishing fleets of member states. Spain, with
the largest fleet in the EU, was eager to access Norway's coastal areas. An
agreement was reached which allocated specific catch quotas to member
states, ensuring that they would all ratify the Norwegian accession treaty.
The Austrians, Finns, and Swedes voted to join the EU in their referenda,
which were held before Norway's in an attempt to influence the outcome
of that country's vote, but the Norwegian people rejected the treaty by a
vote of 52.3 percent opposed and 47.7 percent in favor. Once again, the
issue of fishing rights was a major reason for Norway's decision.

### Implications for the Eastern Enlargement

The accession of Finland, Sweden, and Austria in 1995 helped pave the
way for the eastern enlargement, first of all by moving the EU's borders
closer to the former Communist states. Finland was a strong supporter of
Estonia's application, the two countries being closely linked culturally
and historically. Sweden also developed close ties with the Baltic states.

Austria supported Hungary and Slovenia, with whom it had once been closely associated in the Austro-Hungarian Empire.

### The "Northern Dimension"

To balance the EU's focus on southern Europe, Finland proposed a "northern dimension" to EU policy, with emphasis on broadening EU relations with Russia. Among other issues, Finland and Sweden sought to resolve the status of Kaliningrad, a Russian military enclave on the Baltic Sea, which will be surrounded by EU territory after the eastern enlargement. The issue was resolved in 2002 during the Danish presidency.

### Addressing the "Democratic Deficit"

The three new member states have also tried to make EU institutions more open and accessible, especially when they held the presidency of the Council of Ministers, which has often been criticized for the secrecy of its deliberations. As a result of their efforts, a great deal more information about EU policies and decisions is now released by the Union and posted on the Commission's website.

An episode involving Austria's far-right Freedom Party produced a controversy in the EU about whether members have the right to intervene in each other's domestic affairs. During Austria's 1999 election campaign, Jorg Haidar, leader of the Freedom Party, made inflammatory statements supporting Hitler's policies. When his party was included in the governing coalition, Austria was subjected to diplomatic isolation by the other EU countries. The boycott ended, however, when EU leaders decided there was no threat to human rights in Austria. Besides raising questions about the sovereignty of EU member states, the incident showed how right-wing politicians could exploit widely held concerns about the eastern enlargement and immigration unless mainstream politicians showed more leadership on these issues.[12]

### Peacekeeping

Finland, Sweden, and Austria had remained neutral during the cold war, but with the collapse of the Soviet Union in 1991, their neutrality ceased to have a clear purpose. Although they still held back from joining NATO, their military forces played an active role in Balkan peacekeeping operations after they joined the EU. Carl Bildt, a former Swedish prime minister, and Wolfgang Petrisch, an Austrian, each served as the EU's High Representative in Bosnia, and the former president of Finland, Martti Ahtisaari, played a leading diplomatic role during the war in Kosovo.

## NOTES

1. When France was about to surrender to Germany in 1940, Monnet tried to persuade Churchill that Britain and France should form an "indissoluble union." See Desmond Dinan, *Ever Closer Union*, 2d ed. (Boulder, Colo.: Lynne Rienner Publishers, 1999), p. 14.

2. Schuman's statement was cited by Foreign Minister Joschka Fischer in his May 12, 2000, speech at Humboldt University, Berlin. Excerpts from the speech appear as an appendix at the end of this book.

3. Christopher Preston, *Enlargement and Integration in the European Union* (London: Routledge, 1997), pp. 18–22, and 189–91.

4. Alfred Grosser, *The Western Alliance: European-American Relations Since 1945* (New York: Vantage, 1982), p. 121. Shortly before World War II, Churchill said Britain was "with Europe but not of it. We are interested and associated, but not absorbed." Cited in Arnold Zurcher, *The Struggle to Unite Europe, 1940–58* (New York: New York University Press, 1958), p. 6.

5. Charles de Gaulle, *Memoirs of Hope: Renewal and Endeavor* (New York: Simon & Schuster, 1971), pp. 219–20. Dinan, *Ever Closer Union*, pp. 37–56, summarizes de Gaulle's role in the European Community from 1958 to 1969.

6. Preston, *Enlargement and Integration*, p. 31–32.

7. The Commission's opinion on the Greek application appeared in the *Bulletin of the European Communities*, February 1976. The Commission's opinion of Portugal's application was contained in a May 1978 *Bulletin* supplement, and the Commission's opinion on Spain appeared in the September 1978 *Bulletin*.

8. European Commission, "The Challenge of Enlargement," *Bulletin of the European Communities*, January 1978 Supplement.

9. See Jacques Delors, address to the European Parliament, January 14, 1985, *Bulletin of the European Communities*, January 1985 Supplement; and Jacques Delors et al., *La France par l'Europe* (Paris: Bernard Grasset, 1988), pp. 50–51.

10. Desmond Dinan, "The Commission and Enlargement," in *The Expanding European Union*, ed. John Redmond and Glenda G. Rosenthal (Boulder, Colo.: Lynne Rienner, 1998), pp. 17–40.

11. John Reed, "Worried in Warsaw," *Financial Times* (January 10, 2002).

12. In April 2002, Jean-Marie Le Pen, leader of France's right-wing National Front espoused a line similar to Haidar's in the French presidential election. Le Pen received enough votes in the first round of the election to go on to compete against Jacques Chirac in the second round.

# CHAPTER 3

# The Eastern Enlargement: Politics and Process

The collapse of communism in eastern Europe created a historic opportunity for Europeans to unite their continent and achieve a level of freedom, security, and prosperity that they had never known before, but unification did not happen automatically. It was necessary to overcome major political and economic obstacles in both halves of Europe. Unless the leaders of western and eastern Europe were willing to make the necessary effort, there was a danger that all of Europe might drift back into its fail-safe mode of national and ethnic rivalries, economic protectionism, and armed conflict.

The most difficult tasks were those facing the governments and people of central and eastern Europe, as they struggled throughout the 1990s to build democratic institutions and market economies. Some of these countries had sounder bases to build on than others, but by the end of the 1990s, all ten central and eastern European states were politically stable, growing economically, and beginning to meet EU standards in many key areas, including the protection of their citizens' basic rights.

The reforms that EU member states needed to make in preparation for enlargement were far from revolutionary. Although they had made no plans before the collapse of communism in 1989 to admit the eastern states, they soon found themselves under pressure to do so—from the central and eastern European states themselves, from a few leaders of northern EU member states, and from the U.S. government, which was in part responding to pressures from its own citizens of eastern European descent.

**Figure 3.1**
**Twelve EU Candidates**

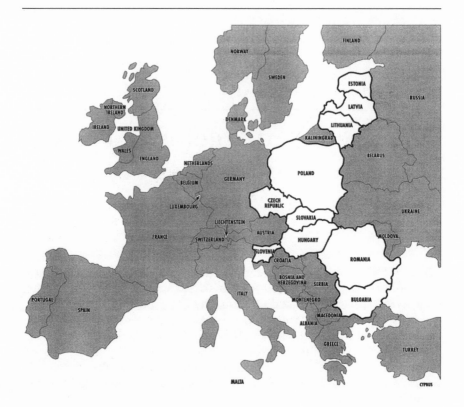

This chapter begins by looking at the politics of the eastern enlargement and why EU leaders waited so long before giving the project their full support. The Commission partially filled this leadership vacuum and helped the candidates prepare for enlargement. Finally, we review the accession negotiations and the agreement reached at Copenhagen in December 2002.

## THE POLITICS OF THE EASTERN ENLARGEMENT

The collapse of communism in central and eastern Europe in 1989 caught EU leaders off guard. They were aware of reform movements in Poland and Hungary, and they knew that Gorbachev, the Soviet leader, was loosening Moscow's grip over central and eastern Europe, but the leaders of the EU were focused on completing the single market and preparing for monetary union. They had no plans for adding any of the eastern countries, but the rapid unification of Germany more or less forced them to accept East Germany as part of the Community in 1990.

## Farm Subsidies and Regional Aid

The addition in the 1980s of Spain, Portugal, and Greece had taught EU leaders that adding countries with weak political and economic systems was expensive and difficult. The Common Agricultural Policy (CAP) and regional aid were the crux of the problem. Together these two programs took up 80 percent of the EU's annual budget—and, unless the rules for distributing these funds were changed, the candidate countries would qualify for all the money that was currently available for farm subsidies and regional aid, leaving nothing for the member states.

On the face of it, this did not sound like an impossible problem to solve. The EU's annual budget was the equivalent of less than $100 billion, only a fortieth of the combined national budgets of the member states. However, the countries that were net contributors to the EU budget refused to contribute more and insisted on reforming the Common Agricultural Policy, which enriched the least needy EU farmers, raised food prices for EU consumers, distorted world markets, and harmed the efforts of poor countries to develop their agricultural sectors.

Naturally, the EU countries that were major recipients of CAP funds (France, Spain, Greece, Portugal, and Ireland) resisted reform with strong support from their farm lobbies. They were backed by many federalists in the EU who revered the CAP as the EU's first common program and did not want to see farm policy renationalized (i.e., returned to the control of the member states). At their Berlin summit in March 1999, EU leaders rejected Commission proposals for a major reform of the Common Agricultural Policy in preparation for enlargement. France led the resistance to change. President Chirac refused to consider any major reform of CAP until 2006, although he agreed that the subject could be "reviewed" after French and German elections in 2002.[1]

## Lack of a Common Strategy

Although the EU member states were slow to develop a common strategy for admitting the eastern European states, individual member governments supported the candidacy of one or another of them. For example, Finland had close cultural and historical ties with Estonia, while Germany backed Poland partly out of remorse for the horrors inflicted on that country during World War II. Denmark adopted Lithuania, and Sweden supported Latvia. The British government, led by John Major, was more supportive of admitting the eastern states than most EU governments, but Major's Conservative Party was heavily Euroskeptic, which led many federalists to believe they favored enlargement mainly to block closer integration of the Union.

While few EU members openly opposed the idea of an eastern enlargement, some set a very high price on their support for it. Greece threatened to block enlargement unless Cyprus was admitted with the first east European candidates. Spain insisted that there must be no reduction in the amount of regional aid it received. And French leaders resisted any change in the Common Agricultural Policy. The French had little interest in enlargement because they feared it would enable Germany to greatly expand its influence in the EU. Belgian federalists were quite willing to delay enlargement as long as possible, because they saw it as competing with their cherished goal of monetary union. Delay became the easiest strategy for all to agree on, particularly when polls showed that most EU citizens did not consider the eastern enlargement a priority.[2]

### German Unification

Ironically, the most divisive political issue concerning enlargement was settled quickly and with a minimum of controversy. As soon as Berliners tore down the hated wall, Chancellor Helmut Kohl stunned his EU partners by announcing plans to reunify Germany. President Mitterrand of France instinctively opposed the idea, as did other European leaders, but Commission President Delors was astute enough to see that the Germans could not take this bold step unless they gave their full support to European integration. Otherwise, they would unite their EU partners against them.

When Chancellor Kohl's Christian Democratic Party won the first free election in East Germany, President Mitterrand bowed to the inevitable and joined Kohl in calling for the eastern *landers'* admission to the EU. By doing so, he gained Kohl's gratitude and a close bond was formed between them.[3] East Germany bypassed all the usual procedures and entered the EU when Germany's unification took place in October 1990. Figure 3.2 summarizes the main events leading to the eastern enlargement.

### Consequences of East Germany's Entry into the EU

Bringing East Germany's infrastructure up to western standards would cost the West German taxpayers a fortune, and this would make the federal government much less willing to bear the disproportionate share of EU expenses it had in the past. The EU contributed the equivalent of several billion dollars, mostly in the form of subsidies for East German farmers, and this shocked EU leaders into backing the first major reform of the Common Agricultural Policy.

Although German leaders have consistently supported the eastern enlargement, many of the country's citizens, particularly in the eastern *lander*, have opposed it because they feared a large influx of workers from the east competing for their jobs. Thus, Chancellor Schroeder was compelled to insist on a seven-year transition period (after the enlargement takes place) before workers from eastern Europe could seek employment in Germany.

**Figure 3.2**
**Chronology of the Eastern Enlargement**

---

| | |
|---|---|
| 1988 | Soviet leader Gorbachev repudiates Brezhnev Doctrine, which justified military intervention in eastern Europe. |
| 1989 | Collapse of communist regimes in central and eastern Europe. European Community (EC) launches PHARE aid program. |
| 1990 | German reunification brings eastern *lander* into EC. |
| 1991 | Europe agreements with Poland, Hungary, and Czechoslovakia. |
| 1994 | Hungary and Poland apply for European Union (EU) membership. EU summit approves pre-accession strategy for central and eastern European states. |
| 1995 | Pact on Stability in Europe signed in Paris. |
| | Commission issues its Single Market White Paper. |
| 1996 | Ten eastern European states have applied for EU membership. |
| 1997 | Commission issues opinions on eastern applicants; proposes "Agenda 2000," including budget for enlargement. |
| 1998 | EU begins accession negotiations with Poland, Hungary, the Czech Republic, Estonia, Slovenia, and Cyprus. |
| 1999 | Berlin summit adopts "Agenda 2000" and 2000–2006 budget. |
| 2000 | EU begins negotiations with Latvia, Lithuania, Slovakia, Romania, Bulgaria, and Malta. |
| 2000 | EU leaders adopt institutional reforms in Treaty of Nice, but Irish voters reject treaty in 2001 referendum. |
| 2002 | French and German elections clear the way for agreement on common EU positions on agriculture and regional aid. |
| 2002 | Ireland ratifies Treaty of Nice in second referendum. |
| 2002 | Copenhagen summit achieves final enlargement agreement. |
| 2003 | Accession treaty to be ratified by all parties. |
| 2004 | New members join EU in time for EU Parliament elections. |

---

## French Opposition to Enlargement

In France, support for the eastern enlargement was lower than in any other EU country. (In a fall 2001 poll by the *Eurobarometer* organization, France was the only country in which opponents of enlargement outnumbered supporters.) The far-Right National Front Party exploited French fears that a large influx of foreigners would add to the problems of crime and unemployment. As noted earlier, French support for the eastern enlargement was also weakened by the fact that it would expand Germany's influence in the EU and reduce French influence.

### European Stability Pact

In 1993, French Premier Edouard Balladur set out to prove that France could play a constructive role in the enlargement process by proposing that the eastern European states normalize relations with all of their neighbors. As table 3.1 shows, most of the candidate countries had large ethnic minorities. Wars and border changes throughout the twentieth century had left millions of eastern Europeans stranded in countries that did not necessarily want them, and the EU was concerned that this could lead to ethnic conflicts.

The prospect of EU membership proved to be a strong incentive to eastern European governments to resolve outstanding differences with their neighbors. After a year of intensive negotiations, the European Stability Pact was signed in Paris in 1995. Attached to the main document were ninety-two separate agreements resolving differences between pairs of eastern European states and between them and other neighbors. Besides making a major contribution to the enlargement process, Prime Minister Balladur's initiative was one of the first substantial achievements of the EU's Common Foreign and Security Policy.

## THE COMMISSION TAKES THE LEAD ON EASTERN ENLARGEMENT

In 1989, the Commission accepted responsibility for coordinating aid to eastern Europe from all of the western industrial nations, and the EU created the PHARE program. (PHARE is the French acronym for aid to Poland and Hungary, and it also means "lighthouse" in French.) This program was initially focused on Poland and Hungary, but it was later extended to all the central and eastern European states. Funding began at $500 million per year, but it was soon doubled.

### Europe Agreements

The EU also began signing what were called "Europe agreements" with the east European countries, starting with Poland, Hungary, and Czechoslovakia in 1991. Eventually, similar agreements were signed with ten eastern European countries. These documents were not very different from the association agreements the EU had signed with western European countries in the past. Although they were clearly a step

**Table 3.1**
**Ethnic Composition of the Countries of Central and Eastern Europe**

| Bulgaria | Bulgarian 85% | Turkish 9% | Other 6% | |
|---|---|---|---|---|
| Czech | Czech 94% | Slovakian 3% | Other 3% | |
| Estonia | Estonian 65% | Russian 28% | Ukrainian 3% | Other 3% |
| Hungary | Hungarian 90% | Roma 4% | German 3% | Other 3% |
| Latvia | Latvian 57% | Russian 30% | Belarusian 4% | Other 9% |
| Lithuania | Lithuanian 81% | Russian 8% | Polish 7% | Other 4% |
| Poland | Polish 98% | German 1% | Other 1% | |
| Romania | Romanian 89% | Hungarian 9% | Other 2% | |
| Slovakia | Slovakian 86% | Hungarian 11% | Roma 1% | Other 2% |
| Slovenia | Slovene 91% | Croatian 3% | Serbian 2% | Other 4% |

*Source: The Economist, Pocket Europe in Figures,* 4th ed. (London: Profile Books, Ltd., 2000), 38–39.

toward closer relations with the eastern states, the Europe agreements did not commit the EU to accepting these countries as members of the Union.[4]

The agreements also imposed limits on eastern European exports to the EU of coal, steel, textiles, and farm products. Since they had a comparative advantage in precisely these products, the Europe agreements would have been more valuable to the eastern countries' economic growth without these restrictions. The Commission was aware of this, and in a 1992 paper, it advised the member states that their eastern neighbors had needs that went beyond the Europe agreements. They wanted to be treated as "equal partners in the dialogue concerning Europe's future."[5]

## Copenhagen Criteria

In April 1993, the leaders of the four countries known as the Visegrad group (Poland, Hungary, the Czech Republic, and Slovakia) bluntly informed the EU that they were frustrated by the limitations of the Europe agreements and wanted to join the Union as full members. At their June 1993 summit in Copenhagen, the leaders of the member states indicated that the eastern European countries could become members of the Union if they met the following criteria:

Membership requires that the candidate country has achieved stability of institutions guaranteeing democracy, the rule of law, human rights and respect for and protection of minorities, the existence of a functioning market economy as well as the capacity to cope with competitive pressures and market forces within the Union. Membership presupposes the candidate's ability to take on the obligations of membership including adherence to the aims of political, economic and monetary union.[6]

EU leaders also called for a broad dialogue with the eastern countries on all issues of common interest and promised to speed up the removal of EU barriers. The Commission suggested that the dialogue should include such matters as integrating the eastern Europeans into the single market and dealing with organized crime, drugs, and security issues. At their December 1994 summit, EU leaders adopted this plan and asked the Commission to negotiate Europe agreements with Estonia, Latvia, Lithuania, and Slovenia. The heads of EU governments also agreed that EU institutions would need to be reformed before enlargement could take place.

### Single Market White Paper

The most urgent task facing the candidates was adopting the huge body of regulations governing the EU's single market in goods, labor, services, and capital. To help them get started, the Commission drew up a voluminous white paper listing all the measures that had to be adopted and indicating the most logical order in which to tackle them. Adopting all the single market regulations made the eastern enlargement far more difficult than previous ones. When Greece, Spain, and Portugal joined in the 1980s, the common market was far from complete. And when the EFTA countries joined in the 1990s, they had already adopted more than half of the regulations when they entered the European Economic Area.

In addition to the white paper, the Commission gave the candidates considerable financial and technical assistance, but it did not tell them when they could expect to join the Union or even when they would be allowed to begin accession negotiations. EU officials maintained that giving them a timetable would remove the incentive to reform their economic and political systems. Eastern European leaders complained that this lack of a firm commitment on the EU's part made it hard to mobilize support in their countries for the difficult reforms the Union required.[7]

### Commission Opinions on the Candidates

In July 1997, the Commission issued separate opinions on the applications of each of the ten candidates. However, instead of evaluating their current qualifications, the Commission tried to judge whether they would be advanced enough to join in 2002, which was thought to be the earliest any of them would be ready. This was a departure from the Commission's previous practice of judging applicants' current qualifications, but it probably allowed the candidates to begin negotiations sooner than if they had to wait until they met all of the criteria.

The Commission opinions recommended beginning accession negotiations with Poland, Hungary, the Czech Republic, Estonia, Slovenia, and Cyprus, which was a major step forward for those countries. The Commission also recommended beginning negotiations with Slovakia, Latvia, Lithuania, Romania, Bulgaria, and Malta, "as soon as they have made sufficient progress" in meeting the Copenhagen criteria for membership.

The Commission opinions said that none of these countries had fully established the rule of law or provided adequate protection of human rights, including those of minorities. Slovakia received by far the most negative opinion, because Prime Minister Vladimir Meciar had repeatedly abused democratic principles in his treatment of political opponents, including the president of Slovakia.[8]

The Commission found that six of the candidates—Poland, Hungary, the Czech Republic, Slovenia, Estonia, and Slovakia—qualified as market economies or came close to doing so. Poland and Hungary were judged likely to be able to withstand competitive pressures in the EU by 2002. The Czech Republic, Slovakia, and Slovenia were considered likely to meet this test if they increased their reform efforts, and Estonia was regarded as close to meeting this standard.

### Agenda 2000 and Budget Perspective

Along with its opinions on the candidates, the Commission produced a report called "Agenda 2000," which claimed that it would not be necessary to raise the current level of budget contributions from member states in order to pay for the enlargement. For the period from 2000 to 2006, the Commission projected total EU expenditures of 684 billion euros, of which 21.84 billion euros would be provided to the candidate countries as pre-accession aid. The Commission obviously hoped to build support for the enlargement in the member states by avoiding an increase in their budget contributions during this period. (The euro-dollar exchange rate fluctuates, but it tended toward parity in the first four years after the euro was launched in 1999.)

However, the "Agenda 2000" report also recommended substantial reforms in the Common Agricultural Policy and regional aid programs. Unless the rules for allocating these funds were drastically revised, the candidates would qualify for most of the money budgeted for these programs after they joined the Union.

At their Berlin summit in 1999, EU leaders cut the projected expenditures to 640 billion euros but left the sum for aid to the candidate countries unchanged. Because of resistance to CAP reform from France and other major recipients of CAP funds, EU leaders adopted much less drastic reforms of the Common Agricultural Policy than the Commission proposed; however, they agreed to a mid-term review of the subject, which was to be held in the final months of 2002 after the French and German national elections.

### Luxembourg Summit

Meanwhile, at their December 1997 Luxembourg summit, EU leaders accepted the Commission's recommendation to begin accession negotiations with Poland, Hungary, the Czech Republic, Estonia, Slovenia, and Cyprus. In spite of its divided status, Cyprus was included because Greece had threatened to block the enlargement if it was not. The six candidates that were chosen were all well qualified, but politics entered into their selection as well. For example, German leaders insisted that Poland must be in the first group because Germany needed to atone for the way it treated the Poles in World War II.

### NATO and EU Enlargement

Since Poland, Hungary, and the Czech Republic had just been chosen to join NATO, EU leaders wanted to encourage the other candidates that might feel they were being shut out of both NATO and the EU. Estonia was chosen as the most advanced of the Baltic states, and Slovenia was recognized as the Balkan applicant that was most qualified to join the Union.[9] Both the EU and NATO insisted that new members be committed to democracy and support for human rights, but the EU's requirement that candidates adopt and implement the entire body of EU laws was much harder than meeting NATO's military criteria.

## NEGOTIATING THE ACCESSION TREATIES

On March 31, 1998, a ceremonial meeting of the foreign ministers of the eastern European countries with their EU counterparts launched the accession negotiations. As in previous enlargements, the candidates were not negotiating with the EU members as equals because the scope of the negotiations was limited to their acceptance of Union laws and policies.

An intergovernmental committee that included representatives of each member state conducted negotiations with each individual candidate. However, because of the complex technical nature of this enlargement, the Commission proposed common EU negotiating positions to the member states and also did much of the actual negotiating with the candidates. Another new feature was the EU's insistence on verifying that candidates had not only adopted EU laws but also had the bureaucratic machinery in place to implement them.

## The Screening Process

Actual negotiations on a few of the least controversial issues began in November 1998, but the main activity for the first year consisted of screening each of the thirty chapters (or issue areas) that had to be covered. The chapters represented the main components of the body of EU laws and policies, known as the *acquis communautaire*. The screening process was carried out by senior representatives of the candidate countries and members of the Commission's Task Force for the Accession Negotiations.[10]

The purpose of the screening exercise was to determine how closely the laws of the candidate countries matched those of the EU, and to identify areas where the candidates might have to ask for a transition period before they could fully comply with the rules. On the basis of the screening process, the country holding the rotating EU presidency would decide (in consultation with the Commission) which chapters each of the candidates could open for negotiations. A chapter was considered closed when the EU agreed that the candidate country was in compliance with EU rules in that area, so the chapter could be opened and closed on the same day. Table 3.2 illustrates this process by showing the chapters that Hungary and Poland had opened and closed by May 2002.

## Transition Periods

The Commission made it clear that it would not allow the candidates to opt out of complying with any part of the *acquis*. A candidate could request a transition period in which to bring its system into compliance with EU rules, but this would require negotiation, and the EU was unlikely to agree to a transition period of more than a few years. EU members could also request a transition period before certain rights or privileges (such as the free movement of labor) would apply to the candidates. In November 1998, the presidency country, Austria, opened seven chapters that had been screened and did not appear to offer major difficulties for either side. No transition periods were requested.

## German Presidency

In January 1999, Germany took over the presidency and opened eight additional chapters that had been screened: company law, free movement of goods, consumer protection, fisheries, statistics, external economic relations, customs union, and competition (i.e., antitrust) policy. German lead-

**Table 3.2**
**EU Accession Negotiations with Hungary and Poland (May 2002)**

| Chapter | Hungary Chapter Closed | Poland Chapter Close |
|---|---|---|
| Free movement of goods | March 01 | March 01 |
| Free movement of persons | June 01 | December 01 |
| Free movement of services | March 01 | November 00 |
| Free movement of capital | June 01 | March 02 |
| Company law | March 01 | November 01 |
| Competition | opened May 99 | opened May 99 |
| Agriculture | opened June 99 | opened June 99 |
| Fisheries | May 99 | opened April 99 |
| Transport | December 01 | opened December 99 |
| Taxation | June 01 | March 02 |
| Monetary union | December 99 | December 99 |
| Statistics | April 99 | April 99 |
| Social Policy | November 00 | June 01 |
| Energy | October 00 | June 01 |
| Industry | April 99 | May 99 |
| Small & medium enterprises | November 98 | November 98 |
| Science & research | November 98 | November 98 |
| Education & training | November 98 | November 98 |
| Telecommunications | April 99 | May 99 |
| Culture & audiovisual | opened November 98 | December 00 |
| Regional policy | opened April 00 | opened April 00 |
| Environment | June 01 | October 01 |
| Consumer & health protection | May 99 | May 99 |
| Justice & home affairs | November 01 | opened May 00 |
| Customs union | June 01 | March 01 |
| External relations | October 00 | November 99 |
| CFSP | April 00 | April 00 |
| Financial & budgetary provisions | opened May 00 | opened May 00 |
| Institutions | opened April 02 | April 02 |
| Chapters opened | 30 | 30 |
| Chapters closed | 24 | 23 |

*Note:* Of the thirty chapters listed above, the next to last one (Financial and budgetary provisions) could only be closed at the end of the negotiations, when the EU offered its financial package to each of the candidates.
*Source:* European Commission

ers were eager to move the negotiations along. They said their goal was to close the first seven chapters by June, and they suggested that some of the second group of eight chapters could be closed almost immediately.

However, all six of the candidates asked to be allowed transition periods before implementing some of the chapters the Germans had opened.

For example, Poland and the Czech Republic wanted to maintain state aid schemes for their poorest regions, Hungary wanted to maintain special tariffs on so-called sensitive (highly competitive) products from non-EU countries, and Estonia sought a transition period for the chapter on fisheries. By October 2000, the Commission had recorded hundreds of requests for transitional arrangements.[11]

After the candidates presented their position papers, the Commission began drafting the EU's common positions on these chapters. In March 1999, Enlargement Commissioner Hans van den Broek announced that the EU would deal with the applicants individually, and that they each could close chapters whenever they were ready and join the Union without waiting for the others. The applicants welcomed this approach, but they were finding that many of the chapters were interrelated and could not be closed until related chapters had been dealt with. The applicants were also beginning to stake out their positions on some of the toughest issues that lay ahead. For example, Hungary and Poland asked to maintain restrictions on the sale of farmland to non-nationals during lengthy transition periods, but they were frustrated by the member states' slowness in developing common positions on the major issues.[12]

### Distracted Member States

One reason for this slowness was that member states faced major distractions in 1999, and senior ministers found they had little time to focus on the enlargement process. The war in Kosovo during the first half of that year led to important decisions by EU leaders to develop their own security policy and defense capability. Soon after the euro was launched in January 1999, its value fell sharply in relation to the dollar, and EU leaders were concerned about the European Central Bank's management of monetary policy. Moreover, the forced resignation of the commission led by Jacques Santer made it necessary to appoint a new group of commissioners, who had to struggle to reestablish the Commission's credibility.[13]

### New Negotiating Rules

The credibility problem may have been one reason that in late 1999 the EU adopted tough new ground rules for the negotiations. These rules were spelled out in the Commission's annual status report on the enlargement in October 1999, which said it would reopen all chapters that had been "provisionally" closed, and that recently adopted EU laws would have to be addressed in the negotiations. Most importantly, the Commission insisted that a stronger link must be established between the negotiations and the candidates' actual preparations for EU membership.[14]

In other words, the candidates would have to demonstrate that they not only accepted the EU's laws and policies, but also were able to implement them in practice. This was a much higher standard than Greece, Spain, and Portugal were held to in the 1980s, but the Commission report noted dryly that it would provide a "strong incentive for the candidates to intensify their preparations" for membership. The Commission added that the candidates must implement all laws related to the single market fully and promptly, and that transition periods allowed in this area would be "short and few."

### The Strategy Works

The Commission insisted that these rules were designed to serve the candidates' interests as well as those of the EU. Each candidate would be encouraged to progress through the negotiations at its own speed, which would allow those that began negotiations in 2000 to catch up with the first group. Although the negotiations were conducted with candidates individually, there was a strong tendency for the EU to favor admitting groups of countries in the same region together. The three Baltic states formed one regional group, and the five central European states comprised another. Bulgarians tended to feel they were being held back by being linked with their neighbor Romania.

Slovakia, having replaced the Meciar regime with a reform-minded government, soon caught up with Poland, Hungary, and the Czech Republic. Latvia and Lithuania also raced to catch up with neighboring Estonia, while Romania and Bulgaria (the least advanced of the candidates) both began to make progress in their negotiations thanks to the more determined reform efforts of their newly elected governments.

In 2000, the outlook brightened when Gunter Verheugen, the newly appointed commissioner for enlargement said he hoped by the end of the year to announce a timetable for completing the negotiations and to give the most advanced candidates specific entry dates. By midsummer, Verheugen was saying he hoped that the four Visegrad countries could join as a group, partly because this would simplify the movement of the EU's eastern border. He also encouraged the Lithuanians and Latvians to hope they could join at the same time as Estonia. Verheugen told reporters he would judge his own success as a commissioner by the number of candidates that had joined the EU by the end of his five-year term.[15]

In his October 2000 status report on the enlargement, Verheugen was not authorized by the EU members to specify entry dates for individual candidates, but he did lay out a timetable for completing the negotiations by the end of 2002. If the accession treaty was ratified during 2003, the candidates could join the EU in time to take part in elections for the European Parliament in 2004.[16]

Figure 3.3    Enlargement Commissioner Gunter Verheugen said the new member states would implement EU laws even more completely than the older members. *Credit:* European Commission Audiovisual Library.

## Treaty of Nice

This timetable received the blessing of the heads of state and government at their December 2000 summit in Nice. They also adopted some institutional reforms in preparation for enlargement, and these were embodied in the Treaty of Nice. Despite many inadequacies, the treaty was important because EU leaders had repeatedly stated that these institutional reforms must be in place before the enlargement could proceed; each member state had to ratify the treaty before it could go into effect. In May 2001, Irish voters rejected the treaty in a referendum, partly because treaty opponents claimed it would compromise Ireland's neutrality. However, a second referendum was held in October 2002, and Ireland became the last EU member to ratify the treaty, with 63 percent of the voters in favor.

## Swedish Presidency

During the first half of 2001, the EU presidency was assumed by Sweden, where public and governmental support for the enlargement was very strong. Under the forceful leadership of Prime Minister Goran Persson and Foreign Minister Anna Lindh, the member states finally adopted common positions on some of the more difficult issues, including the free movement of people and the right of non-nationals to buy farmland in the candidate countries (which was covered in the chapter on "free movement of capital"). Sweden also emphasized environmental issues, and most of the candidates had closed this chapter by the end of the Swedish presidency. President Chirac of France and Chancellor Schroder of Germany issued a statement saying the eastern enlargement was "irreversible."

At last it seemed to be so. In his November 2001 report on the enlargement process, Commissioner Verheugen said that all of the countries that fulfilled the accession criteria (i.e., the Copenhagen criteria) should be able to complete their negotiations by the end of 2002 and join the EU in 2004. The Commission report described all the candidates except Romania and Bulgaria as meeting the criteria. Romania and Bulgaria were judged to have met the political criteria, and Bulgaria was considered close to meeting the economic standard, but Romania still had much work to do in that regard, and they both were judged likely to enter the Union by 2007.

## Institutional Reform

Belgium's presidency in the second half of 2001 succeeded in launching a Convention on the Future of Europe, which could lead to an EU constitution within a few years. The institutional reforms being considered by the convention were much more ambitious than those covered by the Treaty of Nice. The candidate countries were active participants in the convention, and they will be full members of the Union when the next intergovernmental conference decides whether to adopt a constitution.

## Common EU Positions Adopted

The French and German elections in 2002 cleared the way for EU heads of government, led by France and Germany, to adopt common negotiating positions on farm subsidies and structural (regional) aid at a special summit in October 2002. The terms that EU leaders decided to offer the applicants generally followed the recommendations of the Commission. Union leaders decided that when the candidates joined in 2004, they would receive 25 percent as much farm aid as the other fifteen members were receiving. The support payments would then increase in annual increments until 2013, at which time the new members would receive the same

Figure 3.4    EU Environmental Commissioner Margot Wall-
strom helped develop major environmental cleanup programs
for the former communist states. *Credit:* European Commission Audiovisual Library.

amount of aid as the older member states. Spending on the Common Agricultural Policy would be capped at 2007 levels. Structural and cohesion
funds in the amount of 23 billion euros (approximately 23 billion dollars)
would be divided among the candidate countries.[17]

### Romania and Bulgaria

The Commission and leaders of member states also reaffirmed support
for the goal of admitting Romania and Bulgaria to the Union by 2007 and

indicated that the two countries appeared to be generally on track to be ready to join by that date. Increased pre-accession aid was approved to advance the accession process with those two countries.

## Turkey

At their October 2002 summit, EU leaders congratulated Turkey on the measures recently enacted to bring the country's support for human rights up to EU standards. However, both the Commission and the EU heads of state and government concluded that Turkey had not yet met the criteria for membership, so they did not set a date to begin accession negotiations. They also called on Turkey to help resolve the political division of Cyprus before the December 2002 EU summit in Copenhagen.

## Enlargement Agreed at Copenhagen

At the December 2002 Council meeting in Copenhagen, entry terms were agreed by the leaders of EU member states and eight central and eastern European candidates, plus Cyprus and Malta. After intense last-minute negotiations, the EU provided about 400 million euros (approximately 400 million dollars) in additional aid to the candidates and allowed them to transfer some funds for regional aid that would not be disbursed quickly (if at all) to categories such as aid to farmers, where the impact would be felt much sooner. Negotiations continued up to the last possible moment between Poland (on behalf of itself and the other candidates) and Germany, the largest contributor to the EU budget. Danish Prime Minister Anders Fogh Rasmussen and Gunter Verheugen, the enlargement commissioner, played key roles in the final negotiations.[18]

The newly elected Turkish leaders were not given a precise date for the start of accession negotiations, but were told that if they were judged to have fulfilled the Copenhagen criteria for membership by December 2004, the negotiations would begin "without delay." Recep Tayyip Erdogan, who was in line to head the Turkish government, swallowed his disappointment and put the best face on this commitment by the EU, calling it a step forward. He agreed to end Turkey's opposition to the "Berlin Plus" agreement, which would allow the EU to use NATO assets for peacekeeping operations under its European Security and Defense Policy. The EU promptly made plans to take over the small NATO peacekeeping operation in Macedonia.

## Cyprus

At Copenhagen, the Turkish Cypriot authorities failed to endorse the UN proposal to unite their divided island. They were given a new deadline of February 28, 2003, and the Turkish government in Ankara promised to press for an agreement, but the crisis over Iraq made it difficult for all of the interested parties to concentrate on the issue of Cyprus. Unless an agreement was reached between Greek and Turkish Cypriots, only that portion of the island that was under Greek Cypriot rule would enter the EU in 2004.

## RATIFICATION OF THE ACCESSION TREATY

During 2003, the candidate countries would each have to ratify the accession treaty according to their constitutional provisions, which in some cases included a public referendum. The first referendums would be held in March in Malta and Slovenia. Hungary's would be held in April 2003, because Hungarians were believed to be the most enthusiastic supporters of EU membership. It was hoped that the outcome of this referendum would influence voters in Poland, Latvia, and Estonia, where support for Union membership was not as strong. Table 3.3 shows how prospective voters said they would vote in each of the candidate countries (although a referendum might not be held in some of the countries). The political and economic issues affecting public attitudes toward the EU in each of the candidate countries are examined more closely in the following chapters.

### Ratification by EU Member States

The final hurdle in the accession process will be ratification of the treaties by the existing member states. This is normally done by the member states' parliaments, where mainstream political parties support enlargement and would be unlikely to reject the treaties. Many interest groups will have already obtained the concessions they sought before the treaties were signed, so it will be in their interest to support the treaties. In February 2003, President Chirac of France threatened to veto the enlargement because the candidate countries had publicly supported the U.S. position on Iraq.

In a poll of fifteen thousand EU citizens conducted in November 2002, two-thirds of the people polled said they were in favor of enlargement, and nearly three-quarters said they thought it was important for their country. Poland, the Czech Republic, and Turkey were most widely identified as candidates, but 40 percent of the people polled could not name a single candidate country. Eighty-four percent thought it would open up new markets for their countries and 80 percent said the EU would gain a stronger voice internationally, but 76 percent of the people polled thought enlargement would make the EU's decision making more difficult. Germans were particularly concerned that enlargement might lead to

**Table 3.3**
**Support for EU Membership in Applicant Countries**

|                | For Joining EU (%) | Against Joining EU (%) |
| -------------- | ------------------ | ---------------------- |
| Romania        | 97                 | 3                      |
| Bulgaria       | 95                 | 5                      |
| Hungary        | 87                 | 13                     |
| Slovakia       | 72                 | 14                     |
| Czech Republic | 75                 | 25                     |
| Slovenia       | 72                 | 28                     |
| Lithuania      | 71                 | 29                     |
| Poland         | 67                 | 33                     |
| Latvia         | 59                 | 41                     |
| Estonia        | 59                 | 41                     |

*Note*: Includes only respondents eighteen years old and over who said they would vote in a referendum on EU membership.
*Source:* European Commission *Eurobarometer Poll,* Autumn 2001.

increased unemployment and lower standards of social welfare in their country.[19]

### Economic Growth Favors Integration

Europeans tend to favor closer integration during periods of strong economic growth. All of the candidate countries weathered the global economic slowdown in 2001 much better than most emerging market economies and better than their western EU neighbors. As the enlargement process drew to a close, foreign direct investment was on the rise in the countries of eastern Europe in anticipation of their becoming full EU members. In April 2002, the International Monetary Fund's *World Economic Outlook* predicted that most eastern European candidates would achieve higher economic growth in 2003 than in 2002, with the Baltic states averaging 5.3 percent, the central European candidates averaging 3.5 percent, and Bulgaria, Cyprus, Malta, and Romania averaging 5 percent. Unfortunately, the prospect of war in Iraq had already led to a slowdown in economic growth in most European countries by March 2003, and this could make the process of ratifying the accession treaties more uncertain.

Although the possibility of war in Iraq created some economic uncertainty, the generally favorable outlook in eastern Europe should help Germany achieve higher economic growth, and it should reduce the possibility of a no vote in one or more of the candidate countries' referendums on the accession treaty.

## NOTES

1. President Chirac was a former French minister of agriculture, and farmers' unions formed an important part of his political base. After winning reelection in 2002, he and Chancellor Schroeder of Germany agreed that CAP subsidies should continue until 2013 but EU expenditures for agriculture should be frozen in 2006. The British and most other net contributors to the Union budget were furious at Schroeder for giving in to Chirac on this issue, but the Franco-German deal formed the basis of the EU's position.

2. A *Eurobarometer* poll carried out in early 1999 showed that 42 percent of EU citizens favored enlargement, but only 27 percent considered it a priority for the Union. However, 90 percent of EU citizens regarded unemployment and European security as priority issues for the EU to address.

3. Lily Gardner Feldman, "The EC and German Unification," in Leon Hurwitz and Christian Lequesne, *The State of the European Community: Politics, Institutions, and Debates in the Transition Years* (Boulder, Colo.: Lynne Rienner, 1991), pp. 310–29.

4. Christopher Preston, *Enlargement and Integration in the European Union* (London: Routledge, 1997), pp. 198–202.

5. European Commission, "The Challenge of Enlargement," *Bulletin of the European Communities,* March 1992 Supplement, p. 18.

6. European Council, *Conclusions of the Presidency,* Copenhagen, June 1993.

7. Preston, *Enlargement and Integration,* p. 203.

8. Michael Baun, *A Wider Europe* (Lanham, Md.: Rowman & Littlefield, 2000), pp. 78–81.

9. Desmond Dinan, *Ever Closer Union,* 2d ed. (Boulder, Colo.: Lynne Rienner, 1999), pp. 193–94.

10. In the November 1999 reorganization of the Commission, a special directorate-general was created for the enlargement process, whose tasks included managing and coordinating the screening process, coordinating the preparation of EU draft common positions, and preparing draft legislation relating to the negotiations.

11. Cezary Banasinski, "The Negotiations Decision-Making Machinery," in *Poland's Way to the European Union,* ed. Wladyslaw Czaplinski (Warsaw: Scholar Publishing House, 2002), p. 85.

12. Baun, *A Wider Europe,* pp. 199–212, provides a detailed description of the negotiations from the beginning of 1998 to February 2000.

13. The episode is described by Dick Leonard in his *Guide to the European Union,* 7th ed. (London: The Economist/Profile Books, 2000), p. 62.

14. European Commission, *Regular Report from the Commission on Progress towards Accession of Each of the Candidate Countries: Composite Paper,* Brussels, October 13, 1999, pp. 1–4.

15. See "Balancing Act for Enlargement Broker," *Financial Times* (October 24, 2000): p. 6.

16. European Commission, *Enlargement Strategy Paper,* Brussels, October 2000, pp. 30–31.

17. Brussels European Council, "Presidency Conclusions," October 24–25, 2002.

18. Copenhagen European Council, "Presidency Conclusions," December 12–13, 2002.

19. EU Commission, "Enlargement: Weekly Newsletter," December 17, 2002, pp. 5–6.

# CHAPTER 4

# Poland Joins the EU

For Poland, joining the European Union means gaining enhanced security and support for its democratic values, greatly increased economic prospects, and a voice in deciding Europe's future. For the EU, helping Poland prepare for membership has been a major challenge because of the country's size and the complex problems that have had to be solved. However, the success of European reunification has always depended most of all on bringing this great nation back into the mainstream of European society.

In this chapter, we begin by looking at the reasons why Poland has worked so hard to join the EU and examine how the main obstacles to membership have been overcome. Then, we look ahead and try to predict how the inclusion of this large and dynamic nation will change the EU and what membership will mean for Poland.

## POLAND SEEKS SECURITY AND INDEPENDENCE

When the Poles finally freed themselves from Soviet domination, their main reason for wanting to "join Europe" was to make sure the West would stand up for them when and if they again faced the danger of foreign invasion. This was not such a remote or theoretical possibility. In 1990, Russian troops opened fire on unarmed civilian demonstrators in neighboring Lithuania, and tried to intimidate the Latvians and Estonians as well. Russia's political and economic instability remained a major problem for its neighbors all through the 1990s, so Polish leaders made joining NATO their first priority, probably in part because Moscow strongly opposed it.

Joining the European Union was also a major goal because the Poles were determined to rebuild their nation on the Western model, and for that they needed strong political and economic ties with western Europe. They could see how fast the EU was evolving, and the gap between Poland and her western neighbors was getting wider all the time. Unless they set about quickly to transform their political and economic system, they might miss the opportunity to link Poland's development to that of the West.

History has taught the Poles to be among the most nationalistic and self-reliant people in Europe. Often in the past two centuries, their country has been partitioned and occupied by foreign troops because of its location between the empires of Germany, Russia, and Austria. During World War II, only a third of the people of Warsaw survived the horrors of Nazi occupation, and before liberating Warsaw in 1944, Soviet troops stood by and let the slaughter and destruction run its course.

After the war, the Poles rebuilt their demolished cities stone by stone, and during almost half a century of Soviet occupation, they were the most difficult nation in eastern Europe to suppress. In 1980, they formed Solidarity, the first free trade union in the Soviet bloc, and in June 1989, the Poles elected the first noncommunist parliament in the region.

### Political Reform

In 1990, Lech Walesa, the founder of Solidarity, was elected president of Poland. Since then, political power has been transferred by democratic elections with Left and Right coalitions of parties alternating in control of government. The major parties share a commitment to democracy and support EU membership, but two small Euroskeptic parties—the League of Polish Families and Self-Defense—entered parliament for the first time in 2001, winning 20 percent of the seats between them.

### Economic "Shock Treatment"

While some former communist states opted for gradual change, Poland's "shock treatment" reforms in the early 1990s led to an annual economic growth rate of 5.4 percent in the second half of the decade. Young, well-educated Poles in urban areas were the main beneficiaries of this reform program, which has attracted more than $40 billion in foreign investment, but elderly people living on fixed incomes and large numbers of people in rural areas received few direct benefits. The reform program began to lose steam at the end of the decade, although much restructuring of the economy still remained to be done. Under the Solidarity-led government, the program to privatize state industries was sometimes exploited for the personal gain of politicians and their cronies, leading to growing public cynicism about politics.

The global economic slowdown in 2000 led to declining foreign investment and reduced profits from exports. Poland's economic growth slowed, and the unemployment rate increased. However, the 2001 election brought a return to power of the Socialist and Peasant Party coalition, which had launched many of the earlier reforms, and the new team set to work immediately to stabilize Poland's finances and get the economy moving again. The Socialists strongly favored EU membership, and despite some resistance from their junior coalition partners, they began to press hard for early completion of the accession negotiations.

## Impact of Reform on the People

During the 1990s, the changes taking place in former communist countries across Europe were so vast and so stressful they were reflected in the health statistics and life expectancy rates of the population. Poland and the other eastern candidates for EU membership were spared the bloody ethnic wars and wholesale displacement of people that took place in the Balkans and some former Soviet republics, but even in more fortunate countries like Poland, living standards and health care facilities were hard hit by the rapid transition to a market economy, particularly in the first years of the decade.

In 1990 and 1991, a drop in life expectancy rates was recorded and as many as 40 percent of the children reportedly suffered from various illnesses, but in the second half of the decade, the picture changed dramatically. By 1996, the infant mortality rate was less than half what it was in 1980 (the best year of the communist period), and the average life expectancy rate was 72.7 years, up more than 2 percent since 1987. (The EU average was 77.1 years, and the rate was 67.4 years in neighboring Ukraine.) Thus, while some people benefited more than others from Poland's reform process, the population as a whole began to enjoy better health in the 1990s,[1] and living standards should continue to improve because the ongoing reform program and EU membership were likely to attract a large increase in foreign investment.[2]

## Relations with Germany

Poland's admission to the EU was championed by German leaders who felt a sense of remorse for the horrors inflicted by the Nazis during World War II. Relations between the two countries have improved steadily, beginning with the chancellorship of Willy Brandt in the 1970s. In 1990, the legislatures of East and West Germany recognized the Oder-Neisse line as the border between Germany and Poland, and in a 2001 meeting with Polish Premier Jerzy Buzek, Chancellor Gerhard Schroder reaffirmed German support for Poland's membership in the EU. However, for political reasons, Schroder insisted on a transition period of "up to seven years" before Polish workers could seek employment in Germany. He indicated that Germany might reduce the waiting period at its discretion.[3]

### Obstacles to Membership

From the EU's perspective, Poland's size greatly complicated the task of integrating it into the Union. With more than 38 million people, it would be the sixth largest country in a Union of twenty-five member states. Under existing EU rules for distributing farm subsidies and regional aid, Poland would qualify for a large share of the funds budgeted for these programs. A growing number of EU citizens also feared that a large influx of Polish workers might threaten their jobs. In addition Poland's close ties to the United States caused some EU officials, particularly the French, to question Poland's support for EU goals, such as the European Security and Defense Policy. More than other countries negotiating for EU membership, Poland was likely to change the political dynamics between member states, create pressure for institutional reform, and have a major impact on issues in which it had an interest.[4]

## NEGOTIATING FOR EU MEMBERSHIP

### Poland's Approach to Negotiations

In 1998, Poland entered into negotiations to join the EU. Commission officials soon learned to respect the tenacity and thoroughness of Poland's chief negotiator, Jan Kulakowski, who had won acclaim for negotiating the release of political prisoners in Latin America. He did not seem particularly worried by the fact that Poland was one of the slowest candidates to complete the thirty chapters (issue areas) into which its EU accession treaty was divided. "We're not treating this as a game," he said. "Closing quickly is not always the best tactic. It's better to prepare good membership."[5]

Commission members interviewed in Brussels tended to agree that slow and steady was the best approach. They noted that when Greece joined the EU, it was granted some excessively long transition periods in which to implement EU rules. Britain also spent years after joining the EU haggling over a revision to its budgetary contribution. In both cases, a great deal of trouble could have been avoided by getting it right the first time. Poland was the last of the candidates to sign an agreement on agricultural trade liberalization, but it was much more comprehensive than the agreements signed by the other states.

Nevertheless, by the summer of 2000, Poland lagged far behind most of the other candidates, and Polish leaders feared they might not be in the first group of countries to join the Union. Part of the problem was the slow pace of adopting all the EU laws and policies that made up the *acquis communautaire*. The Polish parliament formed a European Law Committee headed by a former foreign minister, and began channeling packets of bills for fast-track approval. In his first annual report on the enlargement process in November 2000, Commissioner Gunter Verheugen praised this initiative, but warned that Poland (and the other candidates) also had to create administrative structures to implement the laws.

### Economic Slump

Poland was in the midst of an economic slowdown that was partly due to economic problems in the rest of Europe. Foreign investment in Poland's economy was down, and so was the demand for the country's exports. Moreover, Poland's economic reform program seemed to be losing momentum. In the October 2001 elections, the center right government was replaced by a coalition government led by Prime Minister Leszek Miller and the Democratic Left Alliance (Socialist) Party, with the Peasant Party as its junior partner. The new team managed to avert a financial collapse and restore momentum to Poland's negotiations with the EU, but it still faced huge tasks in restructuring state-owned steelworks, railways, and coal mines.

In January 2002, Finance Minister Marek Belka presented a plan aimed at creating jobs, developing infrastructure, and restoring rapid economic growth within two years. The plan would amend Poland's restrictive labor code, reduce bureaucratic obstacles to business, and mobilize the equivalent of $45 billion to finance new infrastructure. To encourage employers to hire the one million young Poles who enter the job market each year, the plan would subsidize their social security contributions.[6] Unfortunately, the government's ability to revive the economy was weakened by the departure of Belka and other ministers.

### Free Movement of Persons

The new Polish government was also willing to take more political risks than its predecessor in order to complete the accession negotiations. In November 2001, they closed the chapter on "free movement of persons" by agreeing to a transition period of up to seven years before Polish workers could seek employment in Germany, while other EU countries were free to set shorter transition periods or none at all. The Polish government agreed to these terms with great reluctance, and of course their political opponents immediately accused them of allowing Poles to be treated as second-class EU citizens.

Despite the high rate of unemployment in Poland, most Polish workers would probably be reluctant to relocate abroad for the same reasons that inhibit other European workers (e.g., language barriers, unfamiliar culture). In any case, most analysts agreed that abridging the basic EU right to free movement of persons was bad policy, and that making a success of economic and monetary union called for greater labor market mobility rather than blocking it for purely political reasons.

### Free Movement of Capital

In March 2002, the Poles reached a far more satisfactory compromise with the EU on free movement of capital. The main issue was the right of non-Polish nationals to buy Polish farmland. Since Poland's borders were moved westward after World War II, encompassing land that had been part of Germany, many Poles feared that wealthy Germans would rush to buy back this land as soon as Poland's restrictions on foreign ownership were removed. In the agreement reached with the Commission, Poland was granted a twelve-year transition period before certain lands in western and northern Poland could be bought by foreigners. Non-Polish citizens who already leased land in these areas would be allowed to buy it seven years after the date the lease began, while elsewhere in Poland, foreigners who leased land could buy it three years after the lease date.

The issues of free movement of capital and free movement of persons were not linked in the accession negotiations. However, Poland's success on the land purchase issue helped make up for the fact that it had been forced to accept a very bad deal on free movement of persons. By the end of April 2002, Poland still had seven chapters open: competition, Justice and Home Affairs, transportation, fisheries, agriculture, regional policy, and financial and budgetary provisions. The government concentrated on closing the first three or four of these chapters quickly because the EU would only be able to negotiate on agriculture, regional policy, and financial and budgetary provisions in the fall of 2002 after the French and German elections. The EU had deliberately saved these issues for last because they involved by far the largest budgetary outlays.

### Competition Policy

Commissioner Verheugen had urged Poland to speed up privatization of state enterprises and get rid of indirect forms of state aid that hindered the functioning of market forces. He also noted that competition policy was one area where Poland had adequate administrative capacity but was not using it aggressively enough.[7] However, the new government was inclined to move more slowly on privatizing state enterprises than Poland had in the 1990s. Polish leaders were also beginning to have some reservations about foreign direct investment, although their announced aim was to reduce the state sector of the economy in accordance with EU guidelines.[8]

Some Polish economists suggested that the Commission might be asking Poland to meet a higher standard on competition policy than the member states, and others raised questions about whether the EU's competition policy was appropriate for transition economies like Poland's.[9]

### Justice and Home Affairs

Poland wanted to maintain its economic ties with former Soviet republics, Ukraine in particular, but to meet the EU's requirements in the area of Justice and Home Affairs (JHA), Poland was planning to introduce visas for citizens of Russia and Belarus by the end of 2002. In 2003, Ukrainians would also have to obtain visas for entry into Poland. This would mean that Poland would have to open new consulates in those countries and employ about three hundred additional people at considerable cost to Polish taxpayers.[10]

Polish officials estimated that it would take five to eight years before their country could fully implement the Schengen agreements, which call for a strong external border so that internal borders between member states can be eliminated. Inevitably, the inconvenience of tight border controls will reduce Poland's trade with its eastern neighbors, which amounts to about $7 billion per year, but Poland has no choice. It now conducts nearly 70 percent of its trade with the EU, although the 10 percent of its current trade that is with the former Soviet republics is very important to the economy of eastern Poland.[11]

### Agriculture

Farmers made up 18 percent of the Polish workforce and were the most Euroskeptic group in Poland, so the Polish government needed to get the best possible terms they could on farm subsidies in order to be sure of winning the national referendum on the accession treaty. The EU members only agreed to a negotiating position on agriculture at their October 2002 summit in Brussels. Polish negotiators fought up to the very last moment at the Copenhagen summit in December 2002, and they won a reasonably generous package that should help persuade some farmers to vote for EU membership.

Polish negotiators argued that their farmers would be at a competitive disadvantage in the EU unless they received the same production subsidies as other EU farmers. The EU only agreed to start the new member states with 25 percent of the full EU subsidy in 2004 and raise it in annual increments to the full amount, but the Poles won (for themselves and the other candidates) the right to "top up" this subsidy from other EU aid money for a certain period and thereafter with their own national funds. The Polish government professed to be pleased with this concession.

## Regional Policy

Under existing guidelines, every EU country receives some regional aid funds, but the poorest countries receive by far the most. One of Poland's objectives was to make certain that each of their country's sixteen regions qualified to receive regional aid from the EU. The task of defining the regions was difficult, because every Polish city wanted to be the center of a region in order to attract as much EU aid and foreign investment as possible.[12]

The regions were finally laid out in 1998, but many of them lacked the administrative capacity to apply for available EU aid, and some types of projects they could apply for did not have any immediate impact. Therefore, Polish negotiators sought and were granted the right to transfer some of the EU aid they were offered to categories where it had a more direct political impact. This was done with the aim of maximizing the prospects for a favorable vote on the accession treaty in the Polish national referendum, which was likely to be held in mid-2003. After the Copenhagen summit in December 2002, it seemed highly likely that Polish voters would ratify the treaty and that all the EU member states would do the same.[13]

## POLAND'S POSITION IN A UNITED EUROPE

Poland has a third of the population and 40 percent of the GNP of the central and eastern European countries. It will have the same number of votes as Spain in the Council of Ministers and European Parliament and the right to nominate one commissioner. On defense issues, Polish leaders will almost certainly side with the Atlanticists, who favor close ties with the United States, and on constitutional issues, they will probably vote with those states that favor an intergovernmental approach to decision making and a loose federation of nation-states. However, they are eager to join the eurozone, and they support the EU's common security and defense policy. In foreign affairs, Poland will want to play a role in shaping EU policy toward Russia and Ukraine.

### A "Europe of Fatherlands"

In February 2002, just before the opening of the constitutional convention in Brussels, Polish President Aleksander Kwasniewski addressed a forum in Warsaw on the future of Europe. Speaking particularly to Poland's delegates to the constitutional convention, President Kwasniewski said, "Polish experience speaks in favor of respect for the national factor, for building a Europe of fatherlands, for appealing to the fundamental values from which our civilization arises." He called for a tighter federation of EU structures, but rejected the creation of a centralized "superstate." His speech marked the start of a campaign to persuade undecided Poles to support Union membership.[14]

Figure 4.1    President Aleksander Kwasniewski of Poland
called for a "Europe of fatherlands," in which the nations
would continue to play a vital role in the EU. *Credit:* Polish
Embassy, Washington, D.C.

There were echoes of a speech Prime Minister Tony Blair had given in
Warsaw less than two years earlier, in which Blair argued that Europe
must become "a superpower but not a superstate." After joining the EU,
Poland seemed likely to side with states like Britain and Denmark that
favor an intergovernmental approach to decision making. Poland lobbied
hard to be included in the EU's constitutional convention, which began in
February 2001. The Poles and other CEES candidates would be able to
take part in the debates, but they would not have the right to block consensus decisions until they ratified their accession treaties.

## An "Eastern Dimension"

Addressing the same forum in Warsaw in February 2002, Polish Foreign Minister Wlodzimierz Cimoszewicz said Poland would seek to add an "eastern dimension" to EU foreign and security policy. This would focus on Ukraine, and it would be comparable to the "northern dimension" championed by Finland, which emphasized relations with Russia. According to Cimoszewicz, Ukraine would require "special attention" because of its importance to the security and stability in the region.[15]

Following the visit to Poland by Russian President Vladimir Putin in January 2002, Polish leaders accepted Russia as a "strategic partner" and supported the decision in May 2002 to establish a NATO-Russia Council to discuss issues of common concern. At the same meeting, NATO foreign ministers also agreed to establish a new relationship with Ukraine, a move that Foreign Minister Cimoszewicz undoubtedly supported.[16]

## ESDP and NATO

Poland became a full member of NATO in 1999, just two weeks before NATO launched its air war in Kosovo. Polish forces participated in peacekeeping operations in Kosovo and Bosnia, and Polish officials were convinced that a strong NATO commitment to the defense of Europe was fundamental to their own country's security. However, the war in Kosovo persuaded EU members that they needed their own defense capability. When Britain and France pressed for creation of an EU rapid reaction force, Poland irritated many EU members by opposing the idea on the grounds that it might weaken NATO. Poland later revised its position and became a supporter of the European Security and Defense Policy.[17]

However, French officials continued to voice concern that Poland's close ties with the United States made its loyalty to Europe questionable. When a Polish diplomat expressed support for a U.S.-British air attack on Iraq, French Foreign Minister Hubert Vedrine complained that Poland and Canada were the only countries in the world that favored the attack. The Polish government spokesman replied that Poland's foreign policy was "conducted by Poland's foreign ministry, not France's." Like the British, Polish leaders took the position that there was no conflict between their ties with the United States and the EU.[18]

## Poles Serving in a United Europe

When Poland enters the EU in 2004, one of the government's most urgent tasks will be filling some twenty-five hundred positions reserved for Polish citizens in EU institutions, including a thousand jobs in the Commission. Poland will also nominate its first commissioner and elect fifty new members of the European Parliament. One might think that a former communist nation would be overstocked with bureaucrats, but according to Poland's European Affairs Minister Dunata Hubner, it would be a major challenge to find people with the necessary skills, including languages and a knowledge of how the EU operates. She also noted a shortage of people qualified to work on EU issues in government ministries in Warsaw and in the sixteen regional governments around the country. Badly needed EU aid funds often went untapped by these offices because of the difficult paperwork required in order to apply for them.[19]

Several academic programs were created to attract and train people with the necessary skills. For instance, the College of Europe in Natolin, a Warsaw suburb, organized an interdisciplinary program in European studies. This elite college had close ties to a similar institution in Bruges, Belgium. Since it drew people from all over Europe, Poles made up only about a fifth of the student body. Larger numbers of Polish students entered the twenty-month public administration course at the National School of Public Administration.

Another very popular and selective program for would-be administrators of EU programs was run by Poland's ruling political party, the Democratic Left Alliance. The program was organized in 1998, and four years later it enrolled three hundred students, who were chosen from a nationwide pool of three thousand applicants. They met on weekends all through the year, converging on Warsaw each Saturday morning for lectures by academics, ambassadors, and senior administrators. Most of the students in this program were in their twenties and thirties, and many had already launched promising careers in business or government.

All of the students in the latter program had higher degrees from good universities and certificates in English. Most of them spoke at least one other EU language, and many had lived and worked in EU countries. Although they could make much more money in the private sector, their goal was to represent their country's interests in embassies, EU bodies and other international organizations, or to work in EU affairs in Poland. As the first generation to serve their country in a united Europe, they could look forward to unlimited opportunities.

## NOTES

1. Andrew H. Dawson, "Poland," in *The Central and East European Handbook*, ed. Patrick Heenan and Monique Lamontagne (Chicago: Fitzroy Dearborn Publishers, 1999), pp. 3–11. See also "Europe After Communism," *The Economist* (November 6, 1999): pp. 21–23.

2. Heather Grabbe, *Profiting from EU Enlargement* (London: Centre for European Reform, 2001), pp. 30–33.

3. Haig Simonian, "Berlin, Warsaw United on Early EU Entry," *Financial Times* (June 19, 2001).

4. Michael J. Baun, *A Wider Europe* (Lanhan, Md.: Rowman & Littlefield, 2000), pp. 4–20. Baun notes (p. 214) that in a 1999 *Eurobarometer* survey sponsored by the EU Commission, only 43 percent of EU citizens favored EU membership for Poland. See also Christopher Preston, *Enlargement and Integration in the European Union* (London and New York: Routledge, 1997), pp. 195–209.

5. John Reed, "Polish EU Negotiator Prefers the Long Game," *Financial Times* (July 3, 2001).

6. John Reed, "Poland Approves Plan to Revive Economic Growth," *Financial Times* (January 30, 2002); and John Reed, "Polish Government Sees Popularity Slide," *Financial Times* (January 25, 2002). John Reed, "Aftershocks as Warsaw Finance Minister Quits," *Financial Times* (July 4, 2002).

7. EU Commission, *Making a Success of Enlargement, Annex I: Conclusions of the Regular Reports,* Brussels, November 2001, pp. 51–54.

8. John Reed, "Protecting Poland," *Financial Times* (April 24, 2002).

9. Christopher Preston, "Poland and EU Membership: Current Issues and Future Prospects," in *Enlarging the European Union: The Way Forward,* ed. Jackie Gower and John Redmond (Burlington, Vt.: Ashgate, 2000), pp. 58–59.

10. John Reed, "Worried in Warsaw," *Financial Times* (January 10, 2002).

11. Judy Dempsey, "Poles Juggle the Hard and Soft Approach to Border Patrol," *Financial Times* (April 16, 2001).

12. Andrew H. Dawson, "Poland," pp. 4–5.

13. When the European Commission conducted a poll of fifteen thousand EU citizens in November 2002, just before the Copenhagen summit, two-thirds supported the eastern enlargement and believed it would bring practical benefits, according to the Commission's *Enlargement: Weekly Newsletter,* December 17, 2002, pp. 5–6.

14. John Reed, "Polish President Sets Out Vision for 'Europe of Fatherlands,'" *Financial Times* (February 19, 2002).

15. Ibid. As a former prime minister of Poland, Mr. Cimoszewicz's views carried considerable weight.

16. Colleen Barry, "NATO Links Itself with Russia," *Washington Post* (May 15, 2002): p. A19.

17. John Reed, "Poland's U.S. Ties May Leave It Out of Step with New Partners," *Financial Times* (March 15, 2001).

18. Ibid. See also the comments of Foreign Minister Cimoszewicz, "The Political Aspects of Poland's Accession to the EU," in *Poland's Way to the European Union,* ed. Wladyslaw Czaplinski (Warsaw: Scholar Publishing House, 2002), pp. 150–75.

19. John Reed, "From Communism to Unionism," *Financial Times* (March 26, 2002).

# CHAPTER 5

# Economic Leaders: Hungary, Czech Republic, Slovakia, and Slovenia

Because they are smaller than Poland but share many of its advantages as EU candidates, the four central European countries considered in this chapter encountered fewer economic problems in preparing for EU membership. In fact, they have the strongest and most competitive economies of the ten eastern European applicants. Hungary, the Czech Republic, Slovakia, and Slovenia were all part of the Austrian empire until the end of the First World War. Today, they are closely linked economically to Germany, and like Poland, they have also established stable democratic institutions.

At times, however, relations between these four central European countries have been strained because of the presence of ethnic minorities within their borders. Under pressure from the EU, many of these issues have been dealt with, but some have cropped up again in the final stages of the accession process.

This chapter begins by examining some of the economic and social aspects that are common to all or most of these countries, then looks at each of them individually and the transition they have gone through to prepare for EU membership. Finally, we try to predict what sort of role these countries will play in a united Europe.

## VISEGRAD GROUP AND CENTRAL EUROPEAN FREE-TRADE AREA

In 1990, Hungary's newly elected noncommunist prime minister, Josef Antall, invited the leaders of Poland and Czechoslovakia to the town of Visegrad in northern Hungary to discuss common problems. Symbolically,

**Figure 5.1**
**Central Europe**

they met near the palace where Hungary's great renaissance king, Matthias
Corvinus, once met with the rulers of central Europe. The modern-day
leaders and their countries became known as the Visegrad group. They
repudiated their military ties with the Soviet Union, and Czechoslovak
President Vaclav Havel announced the final dissolution of the Warsaw Pact

in Prague in 1991. In 1993, the Czech and Slovak republics severed their federal ties, and the Visegrad Three became the Visegrad Four. They formed a Central European Free Trade Area, which Slovenia joined in 1996.

## Negotiations with the EU

The EU signed association agreements (called "Europe agreements") with the newly independent countries and provided aid under its PHARE (Poland-Hungary: Actions for Economic Reconstruction) program. However, western European leaders were reluctant to invite these countries to join the EU, especially at a time when they were intent on deepening their economic and political Union. In April 1993, the Visegrad leaders took the initiative and issued a statement declaring their desire for full membership in the EU. By pointing out the gap between EU leaders' professed support for the new democracies and their failure to open the door to membership, they forced the heads of EU governments to respond.

At their Copenhagen summit in June 1993, EU leaders spelled out the criteria that a country must meet in order to become a viable candidate for Union membership: stable democratic institutions; the rule of law; protection of all human rights (including the rights of minorities); a market economy capable of competing within the EU; and support for EU laws and policies including the goals of political, economic, and monetary union. In 1997, Poland, Hungary, the Czech Republic, and Slovenia were invited to begin accession negotiations along with Cyprus and Estonia.[1]

Because of the undemocratic behavior of Slovak Prime Minister Vladimir Meciar, Slovakia had to wait until 2000 to begin negotiations, along with Latvia, Lithuania, Romania, Bulgaria, and Malta. However, all of these countries except Romania managed essentially to catch up with the first group by 2002. The Commission encouraged each of the central and eastern European states to complete their negotiations as rapidly as they could, and the EU promised that none of them would be held back by the slowest ones. Thus, despite some initial coordination of their negotiating positions, each of the candidates tended to operate very much on their own and often in competition with each other. For example, they each negotiated separate deals with the EU on the issue of allowing foreigners to buy farmland in their countries.[2]

As table 5.1 shows, the five central European countries had the strongest economies of all the candidates for EU membership, although Poland's per capita GDP was only slightly higher than that of the Baltic states. Economic growth slowed in most of the candidate countries in 2001, partly because of the global economic downturn, but also because reform programs faltered in some candidate countries. However, the outlook for economic growth improved in 2002 as growth picked up in the EU and as newly elected governments in several candidate countries

**Table 5.1**

**Central and Eastern European Countries: 2001 Economic Data**

|                  | Population (millions) | GDP per Capita | EU average (%) | Exports to EU (%) | Average GNP growth 1995-2000 (%) |
|------------------|-----------------------|----------------|----------------|-------------------|----------------------------------|
| Central Europe   |                       |                |                |                   |                                  |
| Poland           | 38.6                  | 8,700          | 39             | 69.9              | 5.4                              |
| Hungary          | 10.0                  | 11,700         | 52             | 75.1              | 4.0                              |
| Czech Republic   | 10.3                  | 13,500         | 60             | 68.6              | 0.6                              |
| Slovakia         | 5.4                   | 10,800         | 48             | 59.1              | 4.2                              |
| Slovenia         | 2.0                   | 16,100         | 72             | 63.8              | 4.0                              |
|                  |                       |                |                |                   |                                  |
| Baltic States    |                       |                |                |                   |                                  |
| Estonia          | 1.4                   | 8,500          | 38             | 76.5              | 4.3                              |
| Latvia           | 2.4                   | 6,600          | 29             | 64.6              | 3.7                              |
| Lithuania        | 3.7                   | 6,600          | 29             | 47.9              | 2.7                              |
|                  |                       |                |                |                   |                                  |
| Eastern Balkans  |                       |                |                |                   |                                  |
| Bulgaria         | 8.2                   | 5,400          | 24             | 51.2              | -1.7                             |
| Romania          | 22.4                  | 6,000          | 27             | 63.8              | -2.2                             |
| Turkey           | 65.3                  | 6,400          | 29             | 52.3              |                                  |
|                  |                       |                |                |                   |                                  |
| EU Average       | -                     | 20,650         | -              | -                 | 4.0                              |

*Source:* European Commission

revived the momentum of their economic reforms. The candidates had reoriented their trade toward the EU, and half of them were growing as fast or faster than the Union average.

As table 5.2 suggests, the eastern European states had greater instability than the EU, which was reflected in higher rates of inflation. Unemployment rates also varied considerably among the candidates. Agriculture provided a higher percentage of GDP in the central and eastern European states than in the EU (and it employed a much higher percentage of the workforce in the candidate countries).

## Foreign Investment

An important reason for the successful economic transition of most of the candidate states was that they attracted substantial foreign investment, which made up for a severe shortage of domestic savings. The experience of previous enlargements indicates that the eastern Europeans could expect a very substantial increase in foreign investment in the first

**Table 5.2**
**Inflation, Unemployment, Agricultural Employment, and Foreign Direct Investment in 2000**

| Central Europe | Inflation (%) | Unemployment (%) | Agriculture (% of GDP) | FDI (% of GDP) |
|---|---|---|---|---|
| Hungary | 10.0 | 6.4 | 6 | 2.9 |
| Czech Republic | 3.9 | 8.8 | 6 | 9.0 |
| Slovakia | 12.1 | 18.6 | 5 | 10.8 |
| Slovenia | 8.9 | 7.0 | n/a | 1.0 |
| Poland | 10.1 | 16.1 | n/a | 5.3 |
| | | | | |
| Baltic States | | | | |
| Estonia | 3.9 | 13.7 | 5 | 8.0 |
| Latvia | 2.6 | 14.6 | 7 | 5.7 |
| Lithuania | 0.9 | 16.0 | 14 | 3.4 |
| | | | | |
| Eastern Balkans | | | | |
| Bulgaria | 10.3 | 16.4 | 23 | 7.1 |
| Romania | 45.7 | 7.1 | 15 | 2.8 |
| Turkey | 54.9 | 6.6 | 15 | 0.5 |
| | | | | |
| EU Average | 2.5 | 9.0 | 2 | 10.0 |

*Note:* Figures for agriculture as a percentage of GDP are for 1998 and were taken from *The Economist, Pocket Europe in Figures* (London: Profile Books, 2000), 50. The figures cited above as "EU Averages" were calculated by the author on the basis of data in the same volume.
*Source*: European Commission

eight years or so after joining the EU because of increased investor confidence.[3]

In fact, in some of the candidate countries, foreign investment had already increased sharply by 2002 in anticipation of enlargement. For example, Poland and the Czech Republic were each expected to receive about $7 billion from foreign investors in 2002. Although wages were still much lower in the candidate countries than in western Europe, major corporations realized that they would catch up with western wages in five to ten years, and this was no longer the main reason why they were investing in the region. While the availability of skilled workers was an important factor, what really attracted manufacturers to the region were factors like the convenience of being near companies that produced components for their products and also the fact that they could market their products locally.[4]

## Varying Approaches

All of the candidate states recognized the importance of foreign investment, but some of them had become more selective about the kinds of
investment they wanted to attract. During the 1990s, the Slovenian government was the most cautious of the ten candidates about allowing its
successful companies to be bought by foreigners, but in 2002, they
launched a major privatization program. The Czechs and Slovaks were
among the most eager to attract foreign investors. The Polish government
elected in September 2001 indicated that it was not very happy about the
policies of foreign-owned banks in Poland, and they also considered con-
solidating some of Poland's remaining state enterprises, such as steelworks, and keeping them as state companies.[5]

## Increasing Nationalism

The Hungarian government of Viktor Orban had somewhat similar
ideas about developing the state sector of the economy. Although Orban
lost the April 2002 election (by a narrow margin) in Hungary, his nationalistic rhetoric was echoed by a number of other political leaders in central
and eastern European countries. In 1999 and 2000, *Eurobarometer* polls
sponsored by the Commission showed declining public support for EU
membership in many of the candidate countries, which was mirrored by
declining support for the eastern enlargement in EU countries.[6]

More than likely, people in the candidate countries were beginning to
realize that EU membership meant losing some of their hard-won sovereignty. They were also finding that the financial costs of membership
tended to be front-loaded, while the benefits were spread over a longer
period. In many of the eastern European countries, allowing foreigners
(i.e., citizens of other EU countries) to buy their precious farmland was a
deeply emotional issue. Another expression of nationalism—prejudice
against ethnic minorities—was exploited by extremist politicians, and
even by a few supposedly mainstream politicians such as Viktor Orban in
Hungary.[7]

## The Roma Minority

Discrimination against the Roma (as Gypsies prefer to be called) is a
social issue common to Hungary, the Czech Republic, Slovakia, Poland,
Romania, and Bulgaria. The Roma, who are estimated to number between
five and ten million worldwide, live in every part of Europe, but the
largest numbers are found in countries of central and eastern Europe, the
Balkans, and former Soviet republics. Romania and Hungary are each
home to approximately half a million Roma. An estimated one hundred

thousand live in the Czech and Slovak republics, mainly concentrated in Slovakia, and there are much smaller numbers of Roma in Slovenia.[8]

Most of the Roma living in Europe have given up their traditional lifestyle of traveling about in caravans, but they have generally met with active discrimination wherever they have tried to settle. At least half a million Roma were murdered by the Nazis during World War II. Their economic condition may have gone from bad to worse since the collapse of communism, because they tended to have at least marginal jobs under communism, while now very large numbers are unable to find any work at all.

While they are determined to maintain their ethnic identity, the Roma in central Europe have been largely unsuccessful in uniting to advance their political and economic interests. However, that may be changing. In May 2002, representatives of thirty Romany organizations met in the Polish city of Lodz to try to unify their efforts to improve their condition. Lodz was selected as the site for the meeting because during World War II, the Nazis gathered two hundred thousand Jews and five thousand Roma in a ghetto at Lodz, and nearly all died there or were sent to death camps.[9]

Fearing a wave of Roma immigration after the candidates join the Union, EU member states have urged the eastern countries to adopt laws banning ethnic discrimination and to implement programs to improve the education, housing, and job opportunities for Roma. Hungary and the Czech Republic have made the most progress in this regard. In Hungary, for example, the first Roma radio station in central Europe began broadcasting in 2002.[10] With fewer resources, Slovakia, Romania, and Bulgaria have outlawed ethnic discrimination, but they have only begun to implement social programs to aid the Roma. It is generally recognized that it will require a sustained effort over many years to deal effectively with their plight in all of these countries.

## HUNGARY: A KEY PLAYER IN CENTRAL EUROPE

To understand Hungary's current relations with its neighbors, it is essential to know something of its history. The Magyar (Hungarian) people migrated from Asia eleven centuries ago and have survived numerous invasions. The Turks occupied most of Hungary from 1526 to 1686 before being driven out by the Austrians, who then dominated Hungary for the next two centuries. In 1867, Hungary reached a compromise with Austria that made Hungary a power in its own right within the vast Austro-Hungarian Empire. Budapest became one of Europe's most opulent cities, but Hungarians created deep resentment by trying to impose their culture on ethnic minorities such as the Serbs, Croats, Romanians, and Slovaks.

Hungary was on the losing side in World War I, and was forced to sign the Treaty of Trianon in 1920, ceding control of a third of its population and two-thirds of its territory to neighboring countries. Eighty years later, the presence of large Hungarian minorities in Romania and Slovakia was still a major issue in its relations with those countries and to a lesser degree with Serbia.

In World War II, Hungary's authoritarian ruler, Admiral Horthy, sided with Hitler in order to regain the lost territory. Heavy casualties suffered by Hungarian troops on the eastern front and forced labor at home caused Horthy to try to declare Hungary neutral in 1944. To prevent this, the Nazis invaded and set up the fascist Arrow Cross Party, which carried out a reign of terror against the large Jewish and Roma minorities. Soviet "liberating" forces fought a long battle with the Nazis that left Budapest in ruins.

### Soviet Period

Soviet occupation forces installed a Hungarian communist regime that was brutally Stalinist. This led to the 1956 uprising by Hungarian students and workers, which was crushed by Soviet tanks. However, under the communist regime of Janos Kadar, who ruled Hungary for the next three decades, Hungarians were allowed some leeway to engage in private enterprise, although the economy was basically state controlled. By 1989, the Hungarian Communist Party was weakened by internal conflict, and quickly yielded its monopoly on political power when noncommunist political groups demanded the right to take part in public life.

Foreign Minister Gyula Horn opened Hungary's western border in September 1989 and allowed sixty thousand East Germans (who had come to Hungary as tourists) to cross into Austria. This event helped precipitate the final collapse of communism throughout central and eastern Europe. After Hungary's first free elections in 1990, a center-right government took office, but it failed to cope with a severe economic crisis, including massive inflation and public debt, plus the collapse of eastern markets for Hungary's exports.

The reformed communist party won the 1994 election and Gyula Horn, who was foreign minister in 1989, became prime minister. After a faltering start, this government imposed a tough economic reform program. They raised taxes, cut welfare spending, reduced the public debt and inflation, and privatized many state companies. These liberal policies were vital to long-term economic recovery and growth, but initially they led to a 9 percent drop in household incomes. Living standards began to recover in 1996, and economic growth averaged 4 percent a year for the next five years. Prime minister Horn's government also began to resolve outstanding differences with Hungary's neighbors, including the status of Hungarian minorities living in those countries.

As a result of these achievements, in 1997 Hungary was invited to join NATO, and in the following year it began negotiations to join the European Union. However, the Horn government lost the 1998 elections because its austerity measures were highly unpopular. The new center-right government led by Viktor Orban's Fidesz Party continued most of Horn's liberal economic reform policies, which were essential to qualify for EU membership, but the EU criticized the government for its efforts to control the media and for using a state-controlled bank to privatize state companies without revealing the terms of the deals. Orban also hinted at a willingness to ally his party with the far-right Justice and Life Party, which was anti-EU and anti-Semitic.

### Hungary's Status Law

The most controversial aspect of Orban's leadership was his provocative nationalism. He kept neighboring governments on edge by hinting that, after they all joined the borderless EU, Hungary would effectively control the areas of their countries peopled by ethnic Hungarians.[11] In June 2001, he enacted the so-called Status Law, making ethnic Hungarians in neighboring countries eligible for social benefits funded by Hungary. The law also provided these people with Hungarian identity documents and allowed them to work three months of the year in Hungary. However, because it applied only to ethnic Hungarians, it violated an EU law against discrimination and had to be amended so that it did not apply to the seventy thousand ethnic Hungarians living in Austria, Hungary's only EU neighbor. Once Hungary's other neighbors enter the EU, it will presumably no longer be legal to discriminate in favor of ethnic Hungarians in those countries either.

The Commission told Hungary that some of the provisions of the law "apparently conflict with the prevailing European standard of minority protection." Therefore, Hungary was directed to reach agreement with its neighbors on the matter and bring its law into conformity with EU law and standards of minority protection before joining the Union.[12]

### Socialist-Free Democratic Government

The Socialist Party won the April 2002 election and formed a coalition with the Free Democrats, the same partners with whom they had instituted most of Hungary's free-market reforms. Peter Medgyessy, the new prime minister, had served as finance minister in the earlier coalition. Although the Socialists had voted for the Status Law, they took a much more conciliatory line than Viktor Orban had toward Hungary's neighbors, and Medgyessy's victory was greeted with relief in those countries. Coming seven months after a similar center-left coalition won election in Poland, it also contrasted with the trend toward center-right electoral victories in many of the countries of western Europe.

## Accession Negotiations

Among the issues that Hungary had to deal with in the final stages of the accession negotiations were fiscal stability and corruption. During its last weeks in office, the Orban government signed agreements to finance large amounts of highway construction and a new Budapest metro line. The Socialist Party criticized the way these contracts were awarded, and it planned to investigate corruption under the previous government, but its own election program promised increased social benefits and public-sector wages, as well as tax cuts.[13]

The new government would undoubtedly also add some of its own people to the boards controlling state-owned public service broadcasters. The Commission had criticized the previous government for appointing only members of Orban's Fidesz Party to these boards. Finally, the Medgyessy government had to get the best terms possible on the last negotiating chapters on agriculture and regional aid, or they could expect strong criticism from Euroskeptic parties. The government coalition had a majority of only twenty votes in the Hungarian parliament.

## THE CZECH AND SLOVAK REPUBLICS

The Czech Republic includes the old provinces of Bohemia, Moravia, and Czech Silesia, which are often called the Czech Lands. Prague, the capital, became the seat of the Holy Roman Empire in 1355, and in the 1700s, the Czech Lands became part of the vast Austrian empire, which lasted until Austria's defeat in World War I.

In 1920, the victorious Allies created the Republic of Czechoslovakia, made up of the Czech Lands and Slovakia. Prague was the capital, and the Czechs dominated the country politically and economically. Czechoslovakia offered a rare example of democracy in central Europe between the two world wars, but the Slovaks came to resent Czech domination, as did the Sudetan German minority in Bohemia. When Hitler's Nazi armies invaded Czechoslovakia in 1938, they annexed the German-inhabited areas and occupied the rest of the Czech Lands, but the Nazis allowed right-wing nationalists to run Slovakia until almost the end of the war, when the Slovak people rebelled.

## Expulsion of Sudetan Germans

After Soviet armies liberated Slovakia and the Czech Lands, the Republic of Czechoslovakia was restored. Under what became known as the "Benes decrees," 3.5 million Sudetan Germans were expelled to Germany and Austria. After being ignored for decades, their cause was taken up in 2002 by some German and Austrian politicians, who demanded that the

Benes decrees be scrapped as a condition for the Czech Republic's admission to the EU.[14]

The Czech government refused to make any such gesture "under pressure," and the situation was inflamed by Czech Prime Minister Milos Zeman, who described the expellees (many of whom were children) as traitors to Czechoslovakia and Hitler's fifth column. However, Zeman did not seek reelection in June 2002, and Commissioner Verheugen helped to move the issue out of the limelight after the German and Austrian elections later in the year.[15]

## Communist Period

With Soviet support, Czech and Slovak communists ruled Czechoslovakia from 1948 to 1989. Communism brought a major transformation of the Slovakian economy, with a large percentage of the workforce moving from agriculture to jobs in the new industrial sector that specialized in manufacturing arms. However, the Czech Lands, which began the postwar period with well-established industries, failed to keep pace with western technological advances. The communist regime isolated Czechoslovakia from the West and focused on the production of low-quality goods for Soviet bloc consumption. Economic growth slowed and finally stagnated in the 1980s.[16]

During the spring of 1968, Prime Minister Alexander Dubcek called for a more humane brand of socialism, but the "Prague spring," as his movement was called, was soon crushed by Soviet bloc military forces. In November 1989, the spirit of rebellion that brought down the communist regimes in Poland, Hungary, and East Germany reached Czechoslovakia. Mass demonstrations were touched off in Prague by acts of police brutality, and two brief general strikes caused the regime to panic and allow the election of a federal assembly. In December 1989, this body chose Vaclav Havel, a charismatic playwright and political dissident, as president.

In June 1990, the first free national elections were won by Civic Forum, an umbrella organization that included most of the anticommunist groups. Vaclav Klaus, the conservative finance minister, subjected the country to three years of "shock treatment" economic reform. The cost of imports increased sharply, wages were controlled by the government, and living standards fell. Nevertheless, Klaus emerged as leader of the Czech Lands after the 1992 election, and the extreme nationalist Vladimir Meciar won in Slovakia. They were unable to agree on any common program for the Czechoslovak federation except to dissolve it, so on January 1, 1993, the Czech Lands became the Czech Republic with its capital at Prague, while Slovakia gained its independence with Bratislava as its capital.

Vaclav Klaus continued as prime minister of the Czech Republic from 1993 to 1997, and his program of privatizing state enterprises brought mixed results. In some cases, strong western corporations bought Czech firms like Skoda and invested enough capital to make them profitable, but the managers of some state enterprises stole their most valuable assets, a practice known as "tunneling." Prime Minister Klaus's party was linked to these scandals, and he resigned in 1997. His successor, Social Democrat Milos Zeman, was a member of the opposing party and could only govern because Klaus's party agreed not to unseat him. This arrangement was unpopular with Czech voters.[17] Nevertheless, Vaclav Klaus was elected by the Czech Parliament to succeed Vaclav Havel as president in 2003.

## SLOVAKIA EMERGES AS AN INDEPENDENT STATE

Although the Slovak people have enjoyed only brief periods of political independence, they are united by devotion to their national culture. World War I, which ended centuries of Hungarian domination, was a major turning point in Slovakia's history. The Hungarian overlords who ruled Slovakia in the Austro-Hungarian Empire generally treated their subjects with disdain, and relations between the two peoples have only gradually improved in recent years.

Slovak cultural nationalism took hold in the nineteenth century under L'udovit Stur and other great writers. Slovak nationalism also flourished among the large numbers of Slovak immigrants to the United States, who, along with Czech immigrants, petitioned President Woodrow Wilson during World War II to support their countries' independence and partly as a result, Czechoslovakia was created in 1920 with its capital at Prague and with Slovakia playing a secondary role in the new republic.

During World War II, Nazi Germany dismembered Czechoslovakia and allowed the Slovaks to form a fascist state run by the clergy, but an anti-Nazi resistance movement aided Soviet forces that liberated the country. As a reward, Slovakia's status was increased when Czechoslovakia was reconstituted after the war, but the Czech Lands were still dominant. Under communist rule, Slovakia was transformed from a farming country into a major producer of armaments, and Slovak living standards began to approach parity with the more urbanized Czech people. One result of the "Prague spring" liberalization in 1968 was that Slovakia gained equal status with the Czech Lands in a federal arrangement.

### Slovakia Since 1989

In the first free elections after the collapse of communism, Vladimir Meciar became prime minister of Slovakia in 1992, and the country severed its ties with the Czech Republic in 1993. Meciar dominated Slovakia's political scene for the next six years. During this time, he was a major obstacle to political and economic reform, and he encouraged intolerance of ethnic minorities in the country. He was criticized, at home and abroad, for his abuse of political opponents and frequent resort to undemocratic tactics. For example, he was believed to have ordered the bizarre kidnapping of the son of his main political rival, President Kovacs. As a result, the EU refused to consider Slovakia's application for membership until he left office.[18]

In 1998, Meciar was defeated by a broad coalition of parties led by Mikulus Dzurinda, a marathon runner who announced his aim of catching up as quickly as possible with Slovakia's neighbors in the race to join the European Union. Dzurinda instituted far-reaching political and economic reforms and improved Slovakia's relations with its neighbors, including Hungary. In December 1999, EU leaders invited Slovakia to begin accession negotiations, and by November 2001, Commissioner Verheugen was able to report that Slovakia was rapidly creating the necessary administrative capacity and an independent judiciary. Twelve hundred new civil servants were recruited and trained in 2002 to work on European integration matters.[19] These were very impressive achievements for a small country with such a limited history of self-rule.

The main cloud on the horizon, as far as Slovakia was concerned, was the September 2002 election. Polls in the first half of the year indicated that Vladimir Meciar might regain power as prime minister. Although in 2002 Meciar claimed to be a strong supporter of democratic values and European integration, NATO and EU officials had threatened to block Slovakia from joining both organizations if he returned to power.[20] However, the parties opposed to Meciar won enough seats to form a coalition government, which was again led by Mikulus Dzurinda.

## SLOVENIA: THE FIRST BALKAN STATE TO JOIN THE EU

With two million people, the Alpine nation of Slovenia is the smallest of the former communist candidates except for Estonia, and it is also the richest. The Slovenes are a Slavic people, mainly Roman Catholic, with a strong western heritage. An EU official recently described Slovenia as "a small, uncomplicated country for the EU to absorb," but while polls show that the people are eager to join the EU, they do not like the idea of being "absorbed."[21]

Slovenia has known only a few years of full independence. For nearly six hundred years, the country was part of the Austrian empire. When the map of Europe was redrawn after World War I, Slovenia was included in what came to be known as Yugoslavia. After World War II, Yugoslavia was reconstituted as a communist federation under Marshal Josip Broz Tito, but Slovenia's communist regime was more liberal than those of other

Yugoslav republics. A wide range of quality products from skis to kitchen appliances were manufactured in Slovenia mostly for the western European market.

In July 1991, Slovenia gained its independence after a brief battle with the Serb-led Yugoslav army. For most of the 1990s, former communist leader Milan Kucan served as president of Slovenia, and Janez Drnovsek was prime minister. Just before the Copenhagen EU summit in December 2002, Drnovsek was elected president, having led Slovenia to membership in the EU and NATO.

### Foreign Investment

Although Slovenia has received less foreign investment per capita than any of the other eastern European candidates, the economy has grown at an annual rate of about 4 percent. This reflects the country's relatively high rate of domestic savings, and the fact that Slovenia was less in need of tech transfer than the other candidates because it has been producing all along for the western market. The people of Slovenia have been worried about becoming a "colony" if foreign corporations are allowed to buy up their assets indiscriminately.

Nevertheless, in 2001, the government launched a major privatization program in which it planned to sell shares in the two largest banks, the main insurance company, the telecom utility, and a string of industrial assets, including the national steelworks. According to the finance minister, because the country's fiscal base was sound, its main objective was to improve the competitiveness of these establishments.[22]

### Slovenia's Balkan Presence

While maintaining control over its own economy, Slovenia has been a major investor in neighboring Bosnia. The appearance of the red and white logo of Mercator supermarkets in Sarajevo and other cities showed that Bosnia was on the mend after years of ethnic warfare. Slovenia was also training treasury officials from several Balkan nations and helping to set up a new stock market in Sarajevo. Slovenia sent a mechanized army company to serve with the NATO peacekeeping forces in Bosnia, and Slovenia's de-mining operation was one of the largest in former Yugoslavia.

## WHAT SORT OF EU MEMBERS WILL THEY BE?

Like Poland, the four smaller central European candidates will support closer European integration, but they will also want to preserve their national identities. Thus, they are likely to side with countries like Britain,

Austria, and Denmark that prefer the intergovernmental approach to decision making. Nevertheless, they look forward to the financial stability that is likely to result from adopting the euro currency, and they will be more than willing to play their part in programs to protect the security of Europe.

### Allied with the Commission

During the long accession process, these central European countries have worked closely with Enlargement Commissioner Gunter Verheugen and his staff. They have come to regard the Commission as their ally in the accession process, because the Commission has supported enlargement more consistently than many of the member states. Also, the Commission has traditionally been seen as the protector of small states' interests, especially when the large ones seek to form a directorate to run the EU.

The Visegrad states are taking part in the debate over Europe's future constitution, but they have not caucused as a group, and their powers to influence the process will be limited until they become full members. They will be net recipients of EU funds for at least a few years after joining the Union, but some of them will become net contributors before very long. They are likely to ally themselves with Germany on most issues that come before the Council of Ministers because their ties with Germany are extensive.

In foreign affairs, Hungary, the Czech Republic, Slovakia, and Slovenia will favor eventual EU membership for the countries of former Yugoslavia and Albania. As of 2002, they saw NATO as indispensable to Europe's security. They also supported the EU's security and defense policy, but only if it did not conflict with NATO's mission. If the EU continues to take over the Balkan peacekeeping role from NATO, this may cause the Visegrad states to rethink the relative importance of the EU and NATO for European security.

### NOTES

1. The Commission opinions on the ten applications were issued in Brussels on July 17, 1997. Instead of assessing the applicants' current qualifications, they attempted to predict whether they would be ready to join the EU by 2002.

2. Judy Dempsey, "Hungary Unlocks Progress in Talks on Enlarging EU," *Financial Times* (June 13, 2001).

3. Heather Grabbe, *Profiting from EU Enlargement* (London: Centre for European Reform, 2001), pp. 25–33.

4. Peter Marsh, "Czech Republic Switches on to the Right Mix of Foreign Investors," *Financial Times* (May 21, 2002).

5. Robert Anderson, "Poland's Steelworks to Break the Mould," *Financial Times* (April 26, 2002).

6. Michael J. Baun, *A Wider Europe* (Lanham, Md.: Rowman & Littlefield, 2000), pp. 212–17.

7. Charlemagne, "Viktor Orban: An Assertive Hungarian," *The Economist* (March 2, 2002): p. 52.

8. Patrick Heenan and Monique Lamontagne (eds.), *The Central and East European Handbook* (Chicago: Fitzroy Dearborn, 1999), pp. 42, 51, 203. See also *The Economist, Pocket Europe in Figures,* 4th ed. (London: Profile Books, 2000), pp. 38–39.

9. Peter Green, "Roma Seeking Sense of Unity to Combat Racial Bias," *New York Times* (May 10, 2002).

10. Ibid.

11. Robert Wright, "Neighbors Bridle at Hungarian Welfare Handouts," *Financial Times* (August 27, 2001).

12. EU Commission, *Making a Success of Enlargement,* Strategy Paper, November 2001, pp. 43–44.

13. Robert Wright, "No Political Honeymoon for Hungary's New Coalition," *Financial Times* (April 24, 2002).

14. Peter Finn, "Debate Is Rekindled over WW II Expellees," *New York Times* (February 11, 2002).

15. Commissioner Verheugen, a German, was trusted by all the parties concerned with the issue.

16. Heenan and Lamontagne (eds.), *The Central and East European Handbook,* pp. 40–42.

17. Charlemagne, "Vaclav Klaus: An Unusually Combative Czech," *The Economist* (February 3, 2001): p. 58.

18. Charlemagne, "The Menace of Vladimir Meciar," *The Economist* (January 26, 2002): p. 50.

19. EU Commission, *Making a Success of Enlargement: Strategy Paper,* November 2001, pp. 57–60.

20. Charlemagne, "The Menace of Vladimir Meciar," *The Economist* (January 26, 2002): p. 50.

21. In a Commission-sponsored *Eurobarometer* poll taken in the fall of 2001, Slovenians who said they would vote in a referendum on joining the EU favored accession by a margin of 72 percent to 28 percent.

22. Stefan Wagstyl, "Sell-Off Route to Competitiveness," *Financial Times* (July 9, 2001): p. 12.

# CHAPTER 6

# Estonia, Latvia, and Lithuania

Because of their countries' location and long history of Russian domination, the leaders of Estonia, Latvia, and Lithuania sought the security of EU and NATO membership and a chance to help shape Union policy toward Russia in the years ahead. At the end of 2002, they were invited to join both the EU and NATO, and Russia did not actively oppose this historic development.

During the cold war years, the three Baltic states were completely integrated into the Soviet economy and political system unlike the other central and eastern European candidates for EU membership. When they declared their independence in 1990, Moscow used military force and economic pressures to try to stop them. President Yeltsin supported their independence, but he ranted against their treatment of Russian minorities. After President Putin's election, he and EU leaders began to cautiously feel their way toward a much broader EU-Russian relationship, one in which the Baltic states and Kaliningrad might have a special role to play.

The distinct national identities of the Baltic states were formed over centuries in which there was little contact between them. In the Middle Ages, Estonia and Latvia were conquered and Christianized by the German Livonian Knights. To avoid being overrun by that military and religious order, the Lithuanians formed a strong, unified state, which became the largest country in medieval Europe, stretching southward all the way to the Black Sea. However, in the 1700s, Tzar Peter the Great conquered the Baltic states, and despite frequent attempts, they did not succeed in gaining their independence until 1918.

**Figure 6.1**
**Baltic States**

Of the three nations, Estonia had the smallest population (1.43 million). Its highly successful economic transition and preparations for EU membership made it a model for the other candidates. The Estonians had close ethnic and linguistic ties with Finland, and their relationship with Russia was improving after a tense decade in the 1990s. The change was symbolized by the recent restoration of commercial shipping on Lake Peipus, which lies between Estonia and Russia.

Latvia's population (2.42 million) was larger than Estonia's, and Sweden was its strongest EU supporter. The German merchants and nobles who dominated Latvia for centuries influenced its ethnic mix and left their mark on the elegant architecture of Riga, the capital. Of the three Baltic states, Latvia had the largest community of ethnic Russians who were settled there when Moscow tried to Russify the Baltic states.

Lithuania had almost as many people (3.69 million) as Latvia and Estonia combined. It had a long history of close ties to Poland, and its strongest EU supporter was Denmark. Until the Nazis occupied it in World War II, Vilnius (the capital) was the foremost center of Judaism in Europe. Its Russian minority was the smallest in the Baltic states, which helped make its recent relations with Moscow less antagonistic than Estonia's. Because of its location next door to Kaliningrad, Lithuania will play a key role in EU relations with that Russian enclave.

## THE BALTIC STATES IN THE TWENTIETH CENTURY

At the end of the nineteenth century, a spirit of nationalism flourished in each of the Baltic states, and Russian efforts to counter it by imposing the Russian language and culture only strengthened these national movements. The Baltic peoples supported the unsuccessful Russian revolution in 1905 and suffered bloody reprisals by the tzarist regime, but Russia's weakness after World War I allowed them finally to assert their independence.

In all three countries, political inexperience led to a series of unstable coalition governments in the 1920s, followed by the imposition of authoritarian rule in the 1930s. Soviet forces invaded the Baltic states in 1940 and seized control by murdering or deporting large numbers of people—sixty thousand in Estonia alone. The Nazis occupied all three countries from 1941 to 1944 and murdered most of the Jewish inhabitants. In 1944, the Soviets returned and reestablished control by once again killing or deporting large numbers of people.

During the 1950s, most of the Baltic states' industries were nationalized and agriculture was collectivized. Thousands of Russians, including retired military officers and their families, were settled in the Baltic states, and Russian became the official language for government and education in all three countries. However, the people never accepted Russian rule, and the international community never officially recognized the USSR's incorporation of the Baltic states. When Moscow's grip on eastern Europe began to weaken in the 1980s, noncommunist political groups in the Baltic states (and reform-minded communists) began to speak out.

In March 1990, the people of Lithuania and Estonia each declared their independence from the Soviet Union. The Latvians followed in May, but

Russian military and Communist Party officials were firmly opposed to independence for any Soviet republics and particularly the Baltic states, which were seen as crucial to Russian security. President Mikhail Gorbachev therefore rejected the Baltic states' aspirations and ordered Soviet troops to use force against people who were demonstrating against Russian rule.

Boris Yeltsin, head of the Russian Supreme Soviet, had emerged as Gorbachev's rival, and he supported the Baltic states' independence. On January 12, 1991, he flew to Tallinn and signed an interim agreement on relations with the leaders of Estonia. Although he appealed to Soviet forces not to fire on civilian demonstrators, he himself barely escaped being kidnapped in Tallinn by angry Soviet troops who considered him a traitor. The next day, fifteen civilians were killed in Lithuania by Soviet interior ministry troops, and they shot six more civilian demonstrators in Latvia a few days later. Nevertheless, despite these and other Soviet efforts to intimidate them, the Baltic states were determined to break free.

In August 1991, Yeltsin persuaded Gorbachev to sign a new union treaty. This and the prospect of independence for the Baltic states caused hard-line party and military leaders to mount a coup in Moscow, which failed because of Yeltsin's intervention. In September 1991, Moscow finally recognized the independence of the Baltic states, and three months later the USSR itself was dissolved, but tension remained high between Russia and its three small neighbors.

## RUSSIAN MINORITIES IN THE BALTIC STATES

Russia insisted that the Baltic states grant citizenship to all of the ethnic Russians who were living in those countries in 1991 and wanted to be citizens. Lithuania was able to comply because Russians constituted only about 8 percent of the population, but 28 percent of Estonia's population and 30 percent of Latvia's were Russian, and both countries had Belarusian and Ukrainian residents as well. Estonia and Latvia each wanted to ensure the survival of their own national language and culture, so they enacted laws that granted citizenship automatically to people who were born there before 1940 and their descendants. All other non-nationals would have to pass an examination in the local language and show that they could answer questions about the constitution in order to become citizens.[1]

The new laws were bitterly attacked by the Russian government as a violation of the Russian residents' human rights. Relatively few ethnic Russians living in Latvia or Estonia in 1991 could speak the local languages, which were difficult and unrelated to their own. Not many older Russian residents who had settled in the Baltic states after 1940 were willing to make the effort to learn the local languages. However, their children wanted to become citizens of the Baltic states and were much more interested in learning the languages. Very few members of either generation were eager to move to a Russia they hardly knew, but from Moscow's perspective, they were part of the enormous diaspora of twenty-five million ethnic Russians living in former Soviet republics for whom the Russian government considered itself the protector.[2]

President Yeltsin, who had risked his life to support the Baltic states' independence, was incensed when the Estonians renounced the agreement they had signed with him in 1991 promising to grant citizenship to any Russians living in Estonia. When they passed their new citizenship law in 1993, Yeltsin warned them that they "seemed to have forgotten about some geopolitical and demographic realities," but Russia "had the ability to remind them." Moscow doubled the import duties on Estonian goods, and later it reinforced its troops in the Pskov region bordering Estonia and Latvia. Reducing oil exports was another means used to punish Latvia.[3]

## EU Position

The European Union made it clear to Estonia and Latvia that if they wanted to join, they would have to modify their citizenship laws and try to integrate the Russian minorities into their societies. In the late 1990s, both countries responded to this pressure and changed their laws, enabling more Russian residents to meet the citizenship requirements. In 2001, Estonia removed the language requirement for candidates for election to parliament, and Latvia did the same the following year.[4]

In 2002, according to Estonian government figures, 80 percent of the total population was Estonian, and 7 percent was ethnically Russian but had acquired Estonian citizenship by birth or by taking the examination. (Most of those who took the exam passed it because a high degree of fluency was not required, and examinees were allowed to answer questions about the constitution while looking at a text.) The rest of the ethnically Russian residents (about 170,000 people) were not Estonian citizens. In its November 2001 Strategy Paper assessing progress toward enlargement, the Commission indicated that it was generally satisfied with Estonia's policies for dealing with the subject. However, the Commission said that Estonia should ensure that the "implementation of language legislation respects the principles of justified public interest and proportionality" as well as Estonia's international obligations and its original "Europe agreement" with the EU.[5]

The Commission took a similar position regarding Latvia. By 1998, about 40 percent of the ethnic Russians living there had become Latvian citizens either by birth or by naturalization. In that year, the law was further liberalized, and 15,183 ethnic Russians applied to take the examination for citizenship in 1999. The following year, the number applying dropped to 10,692, but the number of Russians who were actually naturalized increased each year.[6]

## PREPARATIONS FOR EU MEMBERSHIP

### Estonia

In his 2001 assessment, Commissioner Verheugen commended Estonia for its progress in preparing to implement EU laws and policies. Further work was needed to execute the Common Agricultural Policy and to administer EU structural funds, and large investments were also still required to comply with EU environmental standards. Estonia sought a long transition period to close out the practice of burning oil shale in its industrial plants and to deal with the disposal of nuclear waste from its nuclear-powered plant.

### Latvia

Although it started negotiating two years after Estonia, Latvia had closed the same number of chapters by May 2002. The country's chapter on Justice and Home Affairs was still open, reflecting its weaker record on dealing with corruption and instituting border controls. According to the Commission, Latvia still had much work to do in developing the necessary administrative bodies to implement EU laws and policies.

Recruiting and training the significant number of administrators needed for this purpose posed a great challenge for such a small country, largely because so many able people had been murdered or exiled during the long period of Soviet domination. A number of talented people, including President Vaira Vike-Freiberga, returned from abroad to serve their country, but Latvians who had lived in North America were often unfamiliar with the EU and its programs.

### Lithuania

Like Latvia, Lithuania began its accession negotiations in 2000, but quickly caught up with the other candidates. The Commission commended Lithuania for making a good start at creating an administration capable of administering EU laws and policies, but much work remained to be done. Closing the nuclear power plant at Ignalina because its design was considered unsafe was the most difficult and costly requirement that Lithuania faced. Denmark provided some funds for this purpose, but the cost would run into billions of euros, most of which would be borne by the European Union.[7]

Figure 6.2   President Vaira Vike-Freiberga of
Latvia supported changes in her country's laws
to make it easier for the Russian minority to
obtain Latvian citizenship. *Credit:* Office of the
President of Latvia.

## Reorienting Baltic States' Trade toward the EU

All three Baltic states are heavily dependent on foreign trade, and in
preparing to join the European Union they reoriented much of their trade
away from the former Soviet republics and toward the EU. This was partly
the result of political pressures, including the doubling of Russian tariffs
on Estonian products and the reduction of Soviet oil exports through Latvian ports. By 1998, 56.6 percent of Latvia's trade was with the EU, as was
55.1 percent of Estonia's and 38 percent of Lithuania's. The Russian financial crisis in 1998 caused a brief recession in the Baltic states, and all three
of them speeded up the process of reorienting their trade. By 1999, Estonia
sent 72.7 percent of its exports to the EU, Latvia sent 62.5 percent, and
Lithuania 50.1 percent.

In the long run, the Baltic states would gain many direct and indirect benefits from closer trade ties with the EU. For example, the more their economies converged with those of western Europe, the more they were likely to benefit from their eventual membership in the eurozone, but first they had to make some difficult adjustments. For instance, a U.S. company was building a large plant in Estonia to produce galvanized steel, and it wanted to use Russian steel in the process, but steel imports from Russia would become subject to EU quotas (although this problem would ease somewhat when Russia joined the World Trade Organization).

The Baltic states also imported large quantities of fish products from Russia, which would become subject to EU tariffs, and some of the Baltic states' exports to Ukraine would also be less competitive under existing Union trade rules. However, in addition to gaining greater access to EU markets, the Baltic states would also have a chance to help shape future EU trade policy toward the former Soviet republics. EU membership, therefore, might benefit their trade ties with the East as well as the West.

## Agricultural Subsidies and Rural Development

In all three Baltic states, a large percentage of the population was made up of farmers and people living in rural areas who tended to be left behind by an economic transition process that mainly benefited young, well-educated people living in cities.[8] The total farm population of the Baltic states was about the same as Hungary's, a number that would not greatly strain the EU budget. However, like all of the candidates, the Baltic states were concerned that their farmers were unlikely to receive anything close to the subsidies enjoyed by other EU farmers, and they claimed this would place them at a competitive disadvantage. Structural aid to the candidates would also be less than what was provided to EU members in the past, so the new member states would have to rely much more on their own resources than western European countries did when they joined the Union.

## Economic Prospects

As table 6.1 shows, economic growth slowed somewhat in 2002 from the rapid pace in 2000–2001. The slowdown was mainly due to weakness in the Baltic states' export markets, which it was partly compensated by strong domestic demand. Estonia felt the effects of weakness in the information technology sector in Finland and Sweden. Lithuania's exports held up better because they were directed more toward emerging markets, including Poland, Russia, and Ukraine. The outlook was for increased economic growth in all three Baltic states in 2003 because foreign investment was likely to increase in anticipation of their membership in the EU and NATO.

Table 6.1
Actual and Projected GDP Growth in the Baltic States (2000–2003)

|           | 2000 (%) | 2001 (%) | 2002 (%) | 2003 (%) |
|-----------|----------|----------|----------|----------|
| Estonia   | 6.9      | 5.0      | 3.7      | 5.5      |
| Latvia    | 6.6      | 7.0      | 4.5      | 6.0      |
| Lithuania | 3.9      | 4.5      | 4.0      | 4.8      |

*Source:* International Monetary Fund, Washington, D.C., *World Economic Outlook* (April 2002): 40. The figures for 2002 and 2003 are projections.

## Treaty Ratification

Latvia and Estonia planned to hold referenda in 2003 as part of the process of ratifying their accession treaties, and Lithuania would probably do so as well. As in most other European countries, farmers and people living in rural areas of the Baltic states tended to be more Euroskeptic than other citizens, although their views varied depending on the size of their landholdings and what they produced. In addition to the issue of subsidies, many farmers were unhappy that their governments had agreed to allow non-nationals to buy farmland in their countries, even though the EU had accepted relatively long transition periods before this would take effect. In spite of these concerns, an October 2001 *Eurobarometer* poll showed that a majority of people in each of the Baltic states who said they would vote in a referendum would support EU membership. The numbers were: Estonia, 59 percent for joining the EU and 41 percent against; Latvia the same; and Lithuania 71 percent for, with 29 percent against.

## THE RUSSIAN ENCLAVE OF KALININGRAD

Lithuania and Poland form the land borders of Kaliningrad, a Russian enclave about the size of Rhode Island that serves as headquarters for the Baltic Sea Fleet. However, the fleet is rusting away for lack of maintenance, and if Kaliningrad has a future, it is probably as a center for trade between Russia and the EU. The port includes an oil terminal, and a natural gas pipeline that runs through Lithuania is being upgraded to supply a large gas-fired electricity generating plant. Russia reportedly plans to develop Kaliningrad as a major center for exporting oil, natural gas, and surplus electricity to EU countries.[9]

The Kaliningrad oblast (region), which had a population of 404,000 people according to the 1990 census, can be reached by sea from St. Petersburg, but when Poland and Lithuania join the EU, they will surround Kaliningrad, and the only land access from Russia will be through Union territory. The most direct rail route from Moscow to Kaliningrad runs through Lithuania.[10] Russian President Putin demanded that the EU allow Kaliningrad residents to travel in and out of the enclave without visas after Poland and Lithuania join the Union. After lengthy negotiations, Russia and the EU agreed that Russian citizens would be required to obtain (free or at very low cost) something called a "Facilitated Transit Document," which appeared to be a euphemism for a visa.[11]

## When Kaliningrad Was Konigsberg

The city of Konigsberg, as it used to be called, was founded in 1255 as a fortress for the Teutonic Knights. It became an elegant German city and the capital of East Prussia, but it was almost completely destroyed by heavy fighting during World War II before being occupied by Soviet forces. Stalin renamed it for one of his cronies and deported the German population to Siberia, but some forty thousand of them returned in the 1990s and sought asylum in Germany. Today, Kaliningrad has the highest incidence of AIDS and tuberculosis in Europe and serious problems of crime, corruption, unemployment, and alcoholism.[12] Yet surprisingly, it attracts busloads of German tourists who come to visit the grave of philosopher Immanuel Kant and other landmarks of the past such as the partially restored cathedral.

After the 1998 devaluation of the ruble, living standards fell in Kaliningrad for the first time in five years. According to Russian data, real incomes in the region fell by 22.4 percent, leaving more than 40 percent of Kaliningrad residents with incomes below the subsistence level. In 1999, overall inflation reached 44.7 percent, but food prices more than doubled as agricultural production in the region fell. The number of unemployed people rose to 66,800, probably a major reason why the crime rate also increased (by 14 percent according to Russian figures).[13]

Since the Russian economy registered stronger growth in 2000 and 2001, some benefits probably reached Kaliningrad. In 2002, Moscow approved funding for construction of a second 900 megawatt gas-fired power plant in Kaliningrad, which would presumably help to ease the unemployment problem in the region, and Lithuania was well positioned to help supply Kaliningrad with food. The Russian oil company, Lukoil, the gas monopoly, Gazprom, and UES, the giant electricity utility, were all involved in plans to develop Kaliningrad.[14]

## Energy Cooperation around the Baltic

As of 2002, Estonia, Latvia, and Lithuania were still linked to the Russian electricity grid, and they remained dependent on Russia for imports of oil, natural gas, and coal. These imports made up about a third of domestic demand in Estonia, 60 percent in Lithuania, and nearly three-quarters of Latvia's needs. Latvia also imported electricity from Estonia and Lithuania. Russia's natural gas pipeline ran through Lithuania to Kaliningrad, and Russia also exported oil and natural gas through Latvia to western Europe. In preparation for eventual connection to the Nordic and EU electricity grids, Estonia, Latvia, and Lithuania joined Baltrel, an association of electricity companies owned by Baltic countries.[15]

## THE BALTIC STATES AND THE EU'S "NORTHERN DIMENSION"

After joining the EU in 1995, Finland took the lead in promoting a "Northern Dimension" in EU foreign policy, which basically means broadening the Union's relationship with Russia. The Baltic states have been included in a number of EU–Russian meetings on this subject, and since Vladimir Putin was elected president of Russia in 2000, the tone of relations between Russia and the Baltic states has improved markedly. As part of his effort to broaden relations with the West, President Putin relaxed his government's objections to the Baltic states joining NATO. Russia and the individual EU member states have tended to deal with each other bilaterally rather than by negotiations between Russia and the EU as a community, but the Commission negotiates on behalf of the member states on trade issues.

In August 2002, Denmark hosted a ministerial meeting in Greenland to choose a new series of priorities for the Northern Dimension. All ten central and eastern European candidate countries were invited to the meeting because the focus was on the new situation after the eastern enlargement. Kaliningrad was one of the main priorities chosen because of its need for economic development, and this was followed later in the year by the EU–Russia agreement on travel to and from Kaliningrad.

## NOTES

1. Patrick Heenan and Monique Lamontagne (eds.), *The Central and East European Handbook* (Chicago: Fitzroy Dearborn, 1999), pp. 27–30.

2. Ibid. Article 61 of the Russian Constitution gives Russia the right to intervene on behalf of its "compatriots."

3. The Baltic states were disappointed when the United States approved an amendment to the Treaty on Conventional Forces in Europe, allowing Russia to strengthen its military units on its northern and southern flanks.

4. "Latvia Moves to Ease NATO Entry," *Financial Times* (May 10, 2002).

5. EU Commission, *Making a Success of Enlargement,* Strategy Paper, Brussels, November 2001, p. 39.

6. Rafael Behr, "Integration Process Moves at a Slow Pace," *Financial Times* (June 15, 2002): p. 13.

7. *Washington Post* (June 8, 2002): p. A15.

8. In Estonia, 7.4 percent of the population was employed in the agricultural sector. In Latvia, the number was 13.5 percent, and in Lithuania it was 19.6 percent, according to EU Commission figures.

9. Rafael Behr, "Dispute Hots Up over the Cold War City on the EU's Doorstep," *Financial Times* (May 28, 2002).

10. According to Heenan and Lamontagne (eds.), *Central and East European Handbook,* p. 33, Russia and Lithuania reached an informal agreement in 1991 to allow Russian troops to cross Lithuania by rail, with a maximum of 180 soldiers on any one train and their weapons in a separate car. Lithuanian soldiers had the right to inspect the rail transports to ensure that these rules were being followed.

11. European Commission, "EU–Russia Summit, November 11, 2002: Joint Statement on Transit between the Kaliningrad Region and the Rest of the Russian Federation." On a visit to Moscow in June 2002, Polish President Kwasniewski rejected President Putin's request to allow Russians to travel across Poland to Kaliningrad without visas. Robert Cottrell, "Poland Rejects Kaliningrad Corridor Hopes," *Financial Times* (June 7, 2002).

12. A former governor of Kaliningrad, Yurii Matochkin, published an article entitled "The Kaliningrad Region—2000" in the *Lithuanian Foreign Policy Review* (2000): pp. 143–60, Foreign Policy Research Center (VAGA Publishers, Gedimino Avenue, 50, LT-2600, Vilnius, Lithuania). The article cites economic and social statistics compiled by the Russian government and the Regional Statistic Committee of Kaliningrad. Its tone is highly critical of the administration of Governor L. Gorbenko, and Matochkin noted that he was running against Gorbenko in the October 2000 gubernatorial election—they both lost to Admiral Vladimir Yegorov.

13. Ibid., pp. 144–47. One local industry that seemed to be thriving, according to Matochkin, was vodka distilling, which increased more than 80 percent in 1959.

14. Andrew Jack, "Status of Baltic Enclave Overshadows Summit," *Financial Times* (May 30, 2002).

15. Heenan and Lamontagne (eds.), *Central and East European Handbook,* p. 131.

# CHAPTER 7

# Romania and Bulgaria: Seeking to Stabilize Southeastern Europe

By the end of the 1990s, Romania and Bulgaria began to make headway with their economic reforms, and the EU invited them to begin accession negotiations in 2000. These talks progressed reasonably well, and the two countries were expected to join the union by 2007. They actively promoted security cooperation with their Balkan neighbors and were invited to join NATO in November, 2002.

However, Romania and Bulgaria were left with some of the worst economic and social problems in Europe after four decades of communist rule, and resolving differences with their Balkan neighbors was no easy task. This chapter begins by noting the historical background of some of these regional relationships. Then Bulgaria and Romania's reform efforts are assessed along with their progress in negotiations to join the EU. Finally, the countries' ambitious efforts to stabilize their region and contribute to the strategic goals of NATO and the Union are examined.

## THE CONTEXT OF SOUTHEAST EUROPEAN REGIONALISM

In terms of their history, location, and culture, Romania and Bulgaria appear to have much in common. They share access to two great commercial routes, the Danube River and the Black Sea. Orthodox Christianity survived as the major religion in both countries, despite centuries of Turkish domination in which their national traditions were kept alive in remote rural villages and monasteries. In the twentieth century, brutally repressive communist regimes moved millions of people off the land into crowded industrial slums.

**Figure 7.1**
**Southeastern Europe**

In spite of their commonalities, only recently have ties between Bulgaria and Romania begun to assume much importance. Bulgaria was more involved with countries on the Balkan Peninsula, while Romania was oriented more toward central Europe. In the Middle Ages, Bulgarian empires rivaled the Byzantine Empire. In the tenth century, Tzar Simeon's rule extended from the Black Sea to the Adriatic and included all of Macedonia. A second golden age of artistic and commercial achievement occurred in the thirteenth century. By contrast, Romania's three large provinces were seldom united under a Romanian ruler, with the exception of Prince Michael the Brave's brief reign at the end of the sixteenth century, which has become the subject of one of the country's great national legends. Freed from Turkish rule in the late nineteenth century, neither Romania nor Bulgaria enjoyed much stability before communist rule was imposed after World War II.

## The Communist Period, 1945–1989

The long-serving communist rulers of Romania and Bulgaria were each fond of grandiose social and economic schemes that seldom achieved any positive results. Nicolae Ceausescu, who dominated Romania from 1965 to 1989, forced millions of people to move from their rural villages into overcrowded industrial slums where food was scarce and basic amenities like heat and indoor plumbing were often lacking. Ceausescu was obsessed with raising the country's low birthrate, and women were coerced into having more children than they could care for. Because of the extreme poverty and crowded living conditions of working-class families, many children were placed in huge government orphanages or ended up as street children.[1]

### Bulgaria, the Willing Soviet Ally

Todor Zhivkov, who ran Bulgaria from 1954 to 1989, was so subservient to Moscow he once offered to make Bulgaria a Soviet republic, but the offer was declined.[2] Zhivkov transformed Bulgaria's agrarian economy into one based on manufacturing low-quality goods for export to Russia, so the economic collapse of the USSR in 1991 was a major disaster for Bulgaria. Creating new industries to trade with the West was especially difficult for Bulgaria, which had few attributes to attract international investors.

### Foreign Relations

Todor Zhivkov and Nicolae Ceausescu got along well together and usually met at least twice a year, despite the fact that Zhivkov followed Moscow's foreign policy line, while Ceausescu sided with China in opposing Russia's claim to lead the communist movement. Zhivkov supported the Warsaw Pact intervention in Czechoslovakia in 1968 to suppress Dubcek's Prague Spring reform movement. Ceausescu denounced the intervention and welcomed Presidents Nixon and de Gaulle to Bucharest during the Brezhnev era. However, later in the 1980s, Zhivkov and Ceausescu both rejected Gorbachev's call for liberalization. Their resistance to change led to their downfall—Zhivkov's colleagues politely asked Moscow's permission before dismissing him, while Nicolae Ceausescu and his wife were executed by the Romanian army.

## Major Ethnic Groups and Relationships

### Romania

With a population of 22.5 million, Romania is one of the larger countries in Europe. About 90 percent of the people are Romanians, an ethnic group descended from soldiers and colonists who settled in Dacia, the eastern-most province of the Roman Empire in the early Christian era. Between one and a half and two million Hungarians live in the Romanian province of Transylvania, which was ruled for centuries by Hungarian nobles. Other ethnic groups in Romania include: Roma (Gypsies), Germans, Bulgarians, Russians, Turks, and Jews.[3]

### Bulgaria

At 8.3 million, Bulgaria's total population is only a little over a third the size of Romania's. Most of the people (85 percent) are Bulgarians, an ethnic group composed mainly of the Bulgars and the Slavs, whose main migrations into the region were only about a hundred years apart. By the end of the ninth century, they shared a common Slavic language and Orthodox Christian religion. The largest minority groups are the Turks (between six and seven hundred thousand) and the Roma (about six hundred thousand). Other smaller groups include Greeks, Armenians, Jews, and Macedonians.[4]

### Turkish Rule in the Balkans

In 1453, the Ottoman Turks captured the Byzantine capital of Constantinople, and invaded the Balkan Peninsula. Turkish rule was direct and oppressive in Bulgaria and lasted longer than in Romania, where it was mainly exercised through intermediaries. A considerable number of Bulgarians were converted to Islam, but the Romanians were allowed to practice Christianity. After reaching its zenith in the 1600s, Turkish influence was slowly driven out of Europe over the next two centuries.

### Bulgaria's Turkish Minority

When Ottoman rule finally ended in Bulgaria, Turks constituted about 20 percent of the population, but many were forced to leave, and by 1990 they comprised less than 10 percent. In 1984–85, Todor Zhivkov mounted a particularly ruthless campaign to assimilate the Turks, denying them all cultural freedom and forcing them to adopt Bulgarian names, which they regarded as sacrilegious. In 1989, more than three hundred thousand fled to Turkey to escape further persecution.[5]

During the 1990s, despite resistance from Bulgarian nationalist groups, the Bulgarian government finally recognized its obligation to allow the remaining Turks full religious and cultural freedom. This produced a rapprochement between the two governments, even though Bulgarian leaders were very slow to implement their promises because they were afraid of going against strong nationalist and anti-Turk sentiment in the country. By setting a high standard for the treatment of minority groups, the EU played a significant role in reinforcing the democratic instincts of mainstream political groups in Bulgaria (and other candidate countries), helping them to overcome the resistance of extreme nationalists.[6]

## Hungarian Rule in Transylvania

Transylvania was controlled by Magyar (Hungarian) nobles from about 1000 A.D. to the end of World War I, when the Austro-Hungarian Empire was broken up by the victorious Allies, and Transylvania was returned to Romania. However, the status of between one and two million ethnic Hungarians living in the province remained a key issue in Romania's relations with Hungary through the end of the 1990s.

In 2001, Hungary adopted a so-called Status Law that provided social benefits to ethnic Hungarians living in neighboring countries, a move that was seen by some people as an effort to extend Hungary's cultural boundaries. The EU took the position that the law must be brought into conformity with those of the Union; that it must not discriminate against any group of EU citizens; and that before Hungary could join the EU, it must reach agreement with its neighbors on how the law was to be applied. Hungary and Romania signed an agreement on the matter in November 2001.[7]

## Bulgarian Relations with Macedonia

Throughout the twentieth century, Bulgaria and Macedonia conducted a classic Balkan feud in which each accused the other of having designs on their territory. A key issue was the ethnic status of a quarter of a million inhabitants of the Pirin region in Bulgaria—Macedonia said they were Macedonian and Bulgaria claimed they were Bulgarian. Highly imaginative histories of Macedonia were invented, and census figures were deliberately distorted. Officials on both sides abused their powers, but fortunately there was no mass violence of the kind that took place in Bosnia and Kosovo.[8]

Reason began to prevail after the collapse of communism in Bulgaria and Yugoslavia (to which Macedonia had belonged). Bulgaria conceded

that about ten thousand inhabitants of the Pirin region considered themselves ethnically Macedonian. Both governments had much more urgent
problems to deal with, so they reined in their most extreme nationalists. In
1999, Bulgaria and Macedonia formally agreed that they harbored no ter-
ritorial claims on each other, and the declaration was signed in the official
languages of both countries, symbolizing the end of the linguistic-ethnic
conflict. The two countries also signed agreements on trade, investment,
and a framework for military cooperation. Both expressed strong support
for the aims of the EU's Stability Pact for Southeastern Europe, which was
launched in 1999 with efforts to promote increased economic cooperation
between countries in the region.

## POLITICAL AND ECONOMIC TRANSITION

Because they had little past experience with democracy and free enterprise, reform came more slowly in Romania and Bulgaria than in the central European states. The former communist parties of Bulgaria and
Romania called themselves "Socialist" with little change of leadership or
policy, but they were better organized than their noncommunist opponents. For most of the decade, they blocked political or economic reforms
that threatened the careers of old communist colleagues who still held
many positions of power. In both countries, the former communists were
politically astute enough to institute land reform policies to gain the support of the large rural populations. However, the parcels of land were
very small and the titles were insecure, so those who acquired land had
little incentive to invest and make the land more productive.

In Bulgaria, noncommunist political groups formed a coalition called
the Union of Democratic Forces (UDF) that failed to cooperate with the
Turkish minority's party and was easily outmaneuvered by the former
communists. As a result, Bulgaria stumbled along through most of the
1990s with sharply declining living standards and increasingly angry public demonstrations against the corrupt and incompetent politicians.

In Romania, the 1996 elections brought the center-right Democratic
Convention of Romania to power in coalition with the party of the Hungarian minority. The new government began to initiate reforms, including
selling off some state-owned companies to foreign investors. Price controls were reduced, as was the overvalued exchange rate, but after two
years, the reform process lost momentum. The EU's annual reports noted
that some progress had been made, but much more needed to be done.[9]

### Bulgaria Catches Up

Bulgaria's 1997 election brought Ivan Kostov to power as head of a
coalition led by the center-right UDF. Kostov instituted an even more

ambitious reform program than the one put in place in Romania. Nevertheless, 1997 was a disappointing year for Bulgaria because its application for NATO membership was not accepted, even though it had hosted a meeting of the Balkan countries' defense ministers and made plans to create a Southeastern Europe Brigade with troop contributions from countries in the region. A second major disappointment came when the European Commission did not include Bulgaria in the group of applicants that were invited to begin accession negotiations in 1998. Although taking note of the new government's reform plans, the Commission opinion on Bulgaria's application was largely negative:

Bulgaria would not be able to cope with competitive pressure and market forces within the Union in the medium term. If the authorities can translate their renewed commitment to economic transition into successful and sustained action, a rapid turnaround in Bulgaria's prospects is possible. However, the country has been set back by six largely wasted years. Incomplete reform has hampered the emergence of a modern agricultural sector. Slow privatization and economic instability has weakened state enterprises and delayed the development of a dynamic private sector.[10]

Despite this discouraging assessment, Prime Minister Kostov and his government persevered. By the year 2000, Bulgaria's economy was growing at a rate of 5.8 percent, and it achieved 4.5 percent growth in 2001, in spite of the general economic slowdown in Europe. Inflation fell to 7.5 percent in 2001, and the International Monetary Fund (IMF) projected a further decline to 4.5 percent in 2002. Foreign investment, which had been very low all through the 1990s, reached 7.1 percent of GDP in 2000.[11] However, the Bulgarian people did not experience much immediate improvement in their living standards, and Kostov's government was linked to a series of corruption scandals. Thus, he lost the 2001 election to Simeon Saxe-Coburg Gotha, Bulgaria's former king, who returned from Spain where he had been living since he was exiled in 1946.

The former king took the title of prime minister and promised to clean up corruption and raise living standards within eight hundred days. He also pledged to seek early membership in NATO and the EU and to use his business contacts to gain more foreign investment in Bulgaria. The former king appointed two young Bulgarians who had worked in London as emerging market analysts to serve as his economic and finance ministers. The Socialist and Turkish parties supported the new government.[12]

## THE ACCESSION PROCESS

With the main parties agreed on seeking EU and NATO membership, Bulgaria began to catch up with the other candidate countries in the accession process. By October 2001, it had opened twenty-three chapters and closed twelve, and by June 2002, it had opened all thirty chapters and closed twenty. (This put it close to the other candidates that had closed from twenty-four to twenty-eight chapters. However, Romania had closed only eleven.) Bulgarian officials complained privately that it was unfair of the EU, which claimed to want each country to move as quickly as it could, to make Bulgaria wait to join the Union when Romania was ready to do so.

## Romania Presses Reform

However, things were also starting to move in Romania. A reform branch of the Socialist Party led by Adrian Nastase won the 2000 election after the center-right government's reform program ran out of steam. Nastase proved to be an energetic leader who took the bold step of privatizing the huge Sidex steel complex, Romania's largest employer, after the foreign buyer promised to keep all twenty-seven thousand workers on the payroll for five years.[13] Nastase also appointed a new chief negotiator for the accession negotiations, and by June 2002, Romania was negotiating on thirteen chapters that had recently been opened and had tabled position papers on the remaining six chapters.

In a 2001 speech in Washington shortly after the September 11 terrorist attack, Prime Minister Nastase noted that all of the NATO candidates had opened their air and land facilities to U.S. and allied traffic, shared intelligence, frozen financial assets linked to terrorist groups, and pledged military forces. He reminded his audience that Romania and Bulgaria had provided peacekeeping forces in Bosnia and Kosovo. Turning to the subject of economic development, Nastase noted that 70 percent of his country's economic growth was coming from the private sector, and that GDP growth was the best in years—led by strong increases in industrial output and exports, it reached 5.3 percent in 2001. A particular bright spot was the growth of Romania's information technology sector.

In March 2002, Nastase hosted a summit meeting of the heads of governments seeking NATO membership. Leaders of Greece, Turkey, Hungary, and the Czech Republic supported the candidacies of Romania, Bulgaria, and other NATO candidates. President Bush sent an encouraging message to the summit in Bucharest, where he was represented by Deputy Secretary of State Richard Armitage, who made warmly supportive comments about the candidacies of Romania and Bulgaria.[14]

## Romanian Orphans

For years, EU officials urged the Romanian government to address the problem of large numbers of Romanian children living in the streets or in badly run state orphanages. By promoting international adoptions, how-

Figure 7.2    Prime Minister Adrian Nastase of Romania pressed
for major reforms to support the rights of minorities and
improved conditions in orphanages. *Credit:* Romanian Embassy,
Washington, D.C.

ever, the orphanages were a major source of revenue for the government.
In May 2001, the European Parliament's specialist on Romania recommended suspending accession negotiations until the situation was resolved.
Five months later, Prime Minister Nastase announced that ten thousand
children would be deinstitutionalized by the end of 2001, and forty child
welfare institutions would be restructured by the end of 2002. The EU and
the United States were helping to fund these reforms.[15]

The Romanian government instituted a ban on international adoptions
and began replacing its large dormitory-style orphanages with apart-

Figure 7.3   Simeon Saxe-Coburg Gotha, former king of Bulgaria, was elected prime minister in 2001, after promising faster economic
growth and early EU membership. *Credit:*
Government of Bulgaria, www.government.bg

ments where small groups of orphans lived with a few adults. The government also began reuniting some of the abandoned children with their
families and providing small amounts of aid to help the families support
them.[16]

### Status of the Roma

The exact size of Romania's Roma (Gypsy) minority is not known, but
estimates range from a quarter of a million to as many as two million.[17] In
2001, the government adopted a four-year action plan for improving the

situation of the Roma, and the EU was providing funds to implement it. A Roma citizen was appointed to head the National Office for Roma and to advise the president on issues affecting the Roma. The EU Commission's October 2001 assessment of the enlargement noted these developments, but said that Romania still needed to concentrate on eliminating discrimination and improve the living conditions of the Roma.

### Combating Anti-Semitism

In an October 2001 speech at the Johns Hopkins School of Advanced International Studies in Washington, Prime Minister Nastase announced measures that had been or would be taken to deal with discrimination against the country's Jewish population, which was estimated at twenty to twenty-five thousand. The measures included protecting thirty-three synagogues as historical and architectural monuments and making an inventory of 786 Jewish cemeteries. The government also planned to introduce a course on the Holocaust in the National Defense College and to add Holocaust issues to the curriculum in colleges and elementary schools. In March 2002, the Romanian government passed a law banning fascist symbols.

### Economic Prospects

As table 7.1 shows, the economies of Romania and Bulgaria grew in 2000 and 2001, and the International Monetary Fund predicted these trends would continue through the end of 2003. The IMF recommended that Bulgaria continue to follow a cautious budgetary policy in order to attract badly needed foreign investment. According to the IMF, Romania's economic policies were "broadly on track," but further structural reforms were needed, particularly in the energy sector.[18]

## REGIONAL COOPERATION IN SOUTHEAST EUROPE

NATO's air war in Kosovo, which closed the Danube River to commercial traffic, caused severe economic losses to Romania and Bulgaria, but leaders of both countries supported NATO peacekeeping efforts in the Balkans. They saw these operations as important to their own security, and were eager to qualify for membership in NATO. Now that the EU seeks to assume responsibility for stabilizing the Balkans, Romanian and Bulgarian efforts in this regard may help them achieve their goal of EU membership. As noted earlier, Bulgaria has resolved its differences with Macedonia, and Romania now has good relations with Hungary. Romania and Bulgaria are now mutually supportive; in international meetings, their foreign ministers often speak on behalf of both countries. They have

Table 7.1
Romania and Bulgaria: Actual and Projected GDP Growth, 2000–2003

|           | 2000  | 2001  | 2002  | 2003  |
|-----------|-------|-------|-------|-------|
| Romania   | 1.8%  | 5.3%  | 4.5%  | 5.0%  |
| Bulgaria  | 5.8%  | 4.5%  | 4.0%  | 5.0%  |

Source: International Monetary Fund, World Economic Outlook, Washington, D.C., (April 2002): 40.

also improved their relations with Greece and Turkey and are trying to help those traditional rivals resolve their dispute over Cyprus. Greece and Turkey supported the NATO applications of Bulgaria and Romania, which were accepted in November 2002.

### Bridging the Danube

After years of delay, Romania and Bulgaria finally agreed in 2000 to link their countries with a second bridge across the Danube, which forms their common border. By opening a new line of north–south communication, this could aid the development of depressed areas on both sides of the river. Leaders of both countries support the EU's initiatives in the region and have urged the Union to speed up its plans for major capital investment.

### Visa Requirement

Citizens of most eastern European countries were no longer required to have visas to enter the EU when their countries' accession to the Union became imminent in 1999. However, Bulgarians and Romanians were still required to have visas after that date because the EU was concerned about the large number of illegal immigrants from outside Europe who were entering the Union through those two Balkan countries. Naturally, citizens of Bulgaria and Romania felt discriminated against, and their leaders repeatedly asked the EU to repeal the visa requirement, which was finally done in 2001. In its October 2001 assessment, the Commission noted that Bulgaria had made "some progress" in the area of border control and Romania had made "significant progress," but both countries still had considerable work to do in controlling the movement of people through their territory.[19]

## Southeast Europe Cooperative Initiative (SECI)

To address this problem, a Regional Center for combating transborder crime was launched in Bucharest in 1996 with Romania, Bulgaria, Greece, Turkey, Albania, and the former Yugoslav republics as members. This initiative was a serious and badly needed effort to deal with the main forms of organized crime in southeastern Europe, but it was clearly also intended to advance the members' political goal of joining NATO and the EU. In October 2001, Prime Minister Nastase announced that during the year, Romania had arrested 106 persons involved in human trafficking. The Regional Center claimed credit for breaking up a network responsible for most of the trafficking of women toward Macedonia from Ukraine, Moldova, and Romania. After the September 11 terrorist attacks in the United States, the center added counterterrorism to its mission.[20]

## NATO and EU Aspirations

Joining NATO became a top priority of the Romanian and Bulgarian governments after they were passed over in 1997. In March 2002, Romanian Prime Minister Nastase hosted a meeting in Bucharest of the heads of governments that hoped to be invited to join NATO later in the year. This meeting helped focus the U.S. administration's attention on the importance of strengthening NATO's southeastern flank and the possibility of using bases in Romania and Bulgaria as a springboard for attacking the regime of Saddam Hussein in Iraq.[21]

Romania and Bulgaria were invited to join NATO in November 2002, and in December of the same year, EU leaders reaffirmed that "the objective is to welcome Bulgaria and Romania as members of the European Union in 2007." The EU emphasized the importance of judicial and administrative reform in both Romania and Bulgaria and promised to ensure that the pace of accession negotiations on all remaining chapters, including those with financial implications, would be maintained and would match the efforts of the two candidates. The EU also approved a significant increase in pre-accession aid for the two countries and urged that the additional funds be used in key areas such as Justice and Home Affairs.[22] The fact that Romania and Bulgaria both supported U.S. policy on Iraq drew criticism from some EU leaders, but it seemed unlikely that this would derail their prospects for membership in the union.

## NOTES

1. Patrick Heenan and Monique Lamontagne (eds.), *The Central and East European Handbook* (Chicago: Fitzroy Dearborn, 1999), pp. 68–79. See also Ronald D. Bachman (ed.), *Romania: A Country Study* (Washington, D.C.: Library of Congress,

Federal Research Division, 1991), pp. 72–75. Ceausescu's resettlement program, known as "systematization," is described on pp. 78–79.

2. John D. Bell (ed.), *Bulgaria in Transition* (Boulder, Colo.: Westview, 1998), p. 305.

3. Bachman, *Romania: A Country Study*, pp. 80–81.

4. Glen E. Curtis (ed.), *Bulgaria: A Country Study* (Washington, D.C.: Library of Congress, Federal Research Division, 1993), pp. 76–87.

5. Antonina Zhelyazkova, "Bulgaria's Muslim Minorities," in *Bulgaria in Transition*, ed. John D. Bell (Boulder, Colo.: Westview, 1998), pp. 165–70.

6. Zhelyazkova, "Bulgaria's Muslim Minorities," pp. 174–84.

7. European Commission, *Making a Success of Enlargement*, Strategy Paper and Report on the Progress towards Accession by Each of the Candidate Countries, October, 2001, pp. 43–44. Romanian coalition governments began in 1996 to include the party that represents ethnic Hungarians, and Romania has made considerable effort to accommodate the interests of its large Hungarian minority.

8. John D. Bell, "The 'Ilindentsi'—Does Bulgaria Have a Macedonian Minority?" in *Bulgaria in Transition*, ed. John D. Bell, pp. 189–206.

9. European Commission, *Making a Success of Enlargement*, October 2001, pp. 54–57.

10. Commission Opinion on Bulgaria's Application for Membership of the European Union, July 15, 1997.

11. European Commission, *Making a Success of Enlargement*, October 2001, p. 67; and International Monetary Fund, Washington, D.C., *World Economic Outlook* (April 2002): p. 40.

12. Ivan Kostov, the former prime minister, became leader of the opposition, but he and the UDF continued to support the goal of EU and NATO membership.

13. The huge steel complex, which was sold for just $82 million, was reportedly losing a million dollars a day at the time of the sale. Phelim McAleer, "Bringing a Hard Line to Romania's Steel Sector," *Financial Times* (June 7, 2002).

14. By March 2002, the Bush administration was issuing broad hints that it supported all or most of the seven candidates to join NATO, but the decision was not announced formally until November 2002. Peter Finn, "War Boosts NATO Hopes of 2 Nations, Romania, Bulgaria Gain New Relevance," *Washington Post* (March, 26, 2002).

15. European Commission, *Making a Success of Enlargement*, October 2001, p. 54.

16. However, the U.S. government took the unusual step of publicly warning Romania and the EU that the ban on international adoptions might cause the U.S. Congress to reject Romania's application to join NATO. Phelim McAleer and Brendan Hightower, "Romania's Unwanted Babies Threaten Its Bid to Join NATO," *Financial Times* (April 6, 2002).

17. Bachman, *Romania: A Country Study*, pp. 80–81.

18. International Monetary Fund, Washington, D.C., *World Economic Outlook* (April 2002): pp. 39–40.

19. European Commission, *Making a Success of Enlargement*, October 2001, pp. 32–33, 56.

20. In his October 2001 speech at Johns Hopkins School of Advanced International Studies in Washington, D.C., Prime Minister Nastase described the center and its recent accomplishments.

21. "War Boosts NATO Hopes of 2 Nations," *Washington Post* (March 26, 2002): p. A15.

22. *Presidency Conclusions*, Copenhagen, December 12–13, 2002, pp. 4–5.

# CHAPTER 8

# Reforming Agricultural and Regional Policy

In July 2002, Agriculture Commissioner Franz Fischler unveiled a revolutionary plan for reforming the Common Agricultural Policy (CAP), This was the EU's oldest common policy that provided about 40 billion euros (roughly $40 billion) a year to EU farmers, mainly for production subsidies—meaning the more the farmers produced, the more aid they received. The twin purposes of Fischler's proposal were to move the CAP away from production subsidies and to avoid a huge increase in support payments to eastern European farmers after their countries joined the EU.

## No More Production Subsidies

The most radical element of Fischler's proposal (in the eyes of farm lobbies) was to eliminate production subsidies. Instead, he would give farmers direct payments based on an average of what they had received in recent years. These payments would then be reduced by 3 percent a year over six or seven years, with the money saved going to rural development. Payments to farmers would also be linked more closely to food safety and environmental standards. An increased emphasis on rural development was seen as a step toward returning control of agricultural policy to the member states because they would be responsible for paying part of the cost.[1]

## CAP Reform Linked to Enlargement

The issues of CAP reform and enlargement were clearly linked because most of the candidate countries had large and underdeveloped

Figure 8.1  Agriculture Commissioner Franz Fischler
favored reform of the Common Agricultural Policy to
phase out production subsidies and increase rural aid.
*Credit:* European Commission Audiovisual Library.

farm sectors. Under existing CAP rules, these countries would be eligible for huge subsidies after they joined the Union. EU members that
were the largest net contributors to the Union budget, including Germany and Britain, were determined to reduce their contributions. Therefore, they wanted a commitment to CAP reform that would reduce
CAP's share of the budget before deciding how much aid the candidate
countries would receive after joining the Union.[2] Table 8.1 shows which
EU members were net contributors to the Union budget and which ones
were net recipients.

### Budget Battles

Germany was becoming much more reluctant to pay such a disproportionate share of the EU budget because of the high cost of unification

**Table 8.1**
**Net Contributors to the EU Budget and Net Recipients (1998)**

| Net Contributors | (billion Euros) | Net Recipients | (billion Euros) |
|---|---|---|---|
| Germany | 11.46 | Spain | 5.54 |
| France | 1.76 | Greece | 4.31 |
| Netherlands | 1.22 | Ireland | 2.80 |
| Sweden | 1.20 | Portugal | 2.68 |
| Austria | .87 | Belgium | 1.71 |
| Britain | .66 | Luxembourg | .72 |
| Italy | .56 | Denmark | .09 |
|  |  | Finland | .001 |

The EU's 5 Main Recipients of Farm Subsidies

| Recipient | % of Total |
|---|---|
| France | 23.8 |
| Germany | 14.6 |
| Spain | 13.2 |
| Italy | 11.8 |
| Britain | 9.9 |

*Source:* European Commission

and other competing domestic needs. Therefore, the initial reaction of German leaders to Fischler's reform program was at least partly negative, since it did not reduce their overall budget contribution. France received much of what it contributed back in the form of agricultural or regional aid, so their per capita contribution to the EU budget was much smaller. The French government responded to the Commission's plan by refusing even to discuss CAP reform until 2006, when the current budget cycle ends.

Britain was generally in favor of CAP reform, but some of its farms were very large, so it opposed the provision in Fischler's plan that would limit the payment to any one farmer to 300,000 euros per year. Spain, the largest of the relatively poor EU states, was a major recipient of CAP support and regional aid, and it could be counted on to fight against any reduction of this assistance.[3]

In spite of these initial reactions, Fischler and his staff believed public opinion was beginning to favor CAP reform because of recent food scares over mad cow disease and foot and mouth disease, which were linked to the large-scale, factory farming methods CAP had spawned. Europeans were also getting tired of seeing their tax money used to prop up food prices, so Fischler deliberately sought to reorient CAP away from subsidies and toward objectives that European citizens as a whole supported, such as food safety, rural development, environmental protection, and animal welfare. As a bonus, the shift from subsidies to direct payments to farmers would also bring the EU into compliance with World Trade Organization rules.[4]

### Partial CAP Aid for New Members

Originally, the EU's budget for 2000–2006 did not specify any CAP subsidies for the new member states. However, early in 2002, Commissioner Fischler suggested that the EU member states offer the candidates 25 percent of the existing subsidy package at the time they join the Union, with incremental increases over the next few years. Britain and other net contributors to the budget objected to this because it sounded like prolonging the subsidy regime rather than ending it. The candidates also complained that their farmers were being asked to compete against much more heavily subsidized farmers in the EU.[5]

### THE COMMON AGRICULTURAL POLICY: EUROPE'S SACRED COW?

The Common Agricultural Policy is the EU's oldest and most expensive common program. Many of the changes that have taken place over the years were for the purpose of accommodating new members, so the program is essentially a grand political bargain in which each country has some vested interests. Federalists are inclined to fear that the whole process of economic and political integration might start to unravel if this major program were renationalized (i.e., given back to the member states to finance and run). Nevertheless, the program has become more expensive with each enlargement, and it constantly threatens to swamp the EU budget, leaving little revenue for other priorities.

The CAP was conceived in the late 1950s when European agriculture consisted of millions of small, mostly unmechanized farms. Drastic food shortages during and after World War II were still fresh in peoples' minds. The original aims of the CAP, spelled out in the 1957 Treaty of Rome, were to raise agricultural productivity, ensure that farmers made a decent living, stabilize markets for farm produce, guarantee adequate food supplies, and ensure that the prices consumers paid for food were reasonable. All of these objectives were met except the last one.[6]

In the late 1950s, French leaders insisted on the CAP as a condition for joining the single market in manufactured goods, because they were uneasy about exposing France's weak industrial sector to free-market competition. Through the CAP, they transferred the cost of modernizing French agriculture to their European Community partners, and French leaders (particularly conservatives, who are supported by the farmers' unions) have generally opposed CAP reform.

## CAP and the Eastern Enlargement

After the central and eastern European countries regained their independence from Russia, the EU provided aid to them and signed "Europe agreements," which essentially gave them associate membership status. However, these agreements did not allow duty-free entry into the EU of textiles, steel, coal, or agricultural products, and during the 1990s, the balance of agricultural trade between western and eastern Europe favored the EU countries.[7]

East Germany joined the EU (by becoming part of the German Federal Republic) in 1990. Subsidizing East German agriculture added considerably to the Union farm budget and prompted the first major reform of CAP in the EU's history. In 1992, the EU began gradually to reduce the level of price supports for major commodities like wheat and beef, and in some cases, the EU replaced price supports with direct income payments to farmers. Through these kinds of reforms, the large-scale overproduction of commodities was reduced, and the share of CAP in the EU budget declined from 64 percent in 1988 to 50.5 percent in 1996.[8]

However, the eastern enlargement would increase the EU's farmland by half and double its farm labor force, so unless the rules for allocating CAP funds were changed, most of the EU budget would again be taken up by the CAP. As table 8.2 shows, in central and eastern Europe, a large percentage of the workforce is engaged in farming, and their productivity is often lower than in the EU countries.

## Agenda 2000

In July 1997, the Commission issued its Agenda 2000, in which it proposed that the EU budget for the period 2000–2006 should total 684 billion euros. Of this sum, 21.84 billion euros would be used to help the

**Table 8.2**
**Agricultural Productivity in Eastern and Western Europe, 1995–97**

|                | Farmland (thousands of hectares) | Percentage of Workers in Farming | Tons of Wheat per Hectare | Tons of Milk per Cow |
| -------------- | -------------------------------- | -------------------------------- | ------------------------- | -------------------- |
| Bulgaria       | 4,402                            | 22                               | 2.7                       | 3.1                  |
| Czech Republic | 3,334                            | 6                                | 4.6                       | 4.4                  |
| Estonia        | 1,143                            | 7                                | 2.1                       | 3.8                  |
| Hungary        | 5,036                            | 8                                | 3.9                       | 5.3                  |
| Latvia         | 1,726                            | 18                               | 2.3                       | 3.1                  |
| Lithuania      | 3,007                            | 24                               | 3.0                       | 3.0                  |
| Poland         | 14,452                           | 27                               | 3.5                       | 3.3                  |
| Romania        | 9,882                            | 34                               | 2.6                       | 2.7                  |
| Slovakia       | 1,608                            | 8                                | 4.4                       | 3.3                  |
| Slovenia       | 285                              | 7                                | 4.1                       | 2.8                  |
| France         | 19,461                           | 4                                | 6.8                       | 5.4                  |
| Germany        | 12,064                           | 3                                | 7.2                       | 5.5                  |
| Italy          | 10,768                           | 6                                | 3.1                       | 5.1                  |
| Spain          | 20,129                           | 9                                | 2.3                       | 4.7                  |
| Sweden         | 2,812                            | 4                                | 6.1                       | 6.9                  |
| United Kingdom | 6,133                            | 2                                | 7.8                       | 5.1                  |

*Source:* European Commission, *Agenda 2000: Commission Opinions on Applications for Membership of the EU,* Brussels, 1998. UN Food and Agriculture Organization, *FAO Yearbook: Production 1997,* Rome, 1998.

central and eastern European countries prepare to join the Union. The report also recommended substantial reforms in the Common Agricultural Policy and regional aid programs, and it assumed that the member states' economic growth would generate enough added revenue to finance the budget.[9]

### Berlin Summit

At their 1999 summit in Berlin, EU leaders reduced the seven-year budget to 640 billion euros, but they approved the 21.84 billion that the Commission had proposed for the candidate countries. President Chirac (who had once served as French agriculture minister) resisted pressure from other EU leaders for major reforms of CAP because he

**Table 8.3**
**EU Budget for 2000–2006 (millions of euros)**

|                                                                          | 2000   | 2003    | 2006    |
|--------------------------------------------------------------------------|--------|---------|---------|
| CAP (price supports and rural development)                               | 40,920 | 43,770  | 41,660  |
| Structural funds (includes regional aid and cohesion fund)               | 32,045 | 30,285  | 29,170  |
| Internal EU Policies (research, energy, transport, industry, and environment) | 5,930  | 6,260   | 6,600   |
| External EU programs (except aid to East Europe)                         | 4,550  | 4,580   | 4,610   |
| Pre-accession aid to Eastern Europe                                      | 3,120  | 3,120   | 3,120   |
| Administration                                                           | 4,560  | 4,800   | 5,100   |
| Reserves                                                                 | 900    | 400     | 400     |
| Total                                                                    | 89,600 | 101,590 | 103,840 |

*Source:* European Commission, *Europe's Agenda 2000: Strengthening and Widening the European Union,* Brussels, 1999, p. 17.

relied heavily on the support of farmers and their unions. The Berlin summit achieved some incremental reforms of CAP, plus a commitment to review the subject in 2002 after the French elections. EU leaders also approved a program known as SAPARD (Special Assistance Programme for Agriculture and Rural Development), the first major EU aid program specifically for the farm sector of the candidate countries.[10]

Table 8.3 shows the Agenda 2000 budget for the years 2000, 2003 (the highest spending year), and 2006 (the lowest spending year). The category "regional aid" is designed to help the poorest regions of EU countries catch up with the richer ones. The "cohesion fund" was created in the 1980s to help the poorest member states (Greece, Spain, Portugal, and Ireland).

## Food Safety

In addition to the eastern enlargement, food safety issues also provided an important incentive for CAP reform. In the 1990s, cases of mad cow disease (bovine spongiform encaphalopathy, or BSE) were reported on some British farms. In March 1996, the British government acknowledged a possible link between BSE and Creutzfeldt-Jakob disease in humans. The European Commission banned exports of live cattle, beef, veal, or products of bovine origin from the United Kingdom to other EU or non-EU countries.[11]

Mad cow disease spread to herds on the continent, and this was followed by an EU-wide problem of foot and mouth disease, which also originated in the United Kingdom. The CAP was partly to blame, because it had transformed European agriculture into a system of large-scale, intensive farming in which livestock were often transported over long distances before slaughter. Diseases could also be spread by including infected animal parts in commercial feeds, which were not well controlled. In 1996, Agriculture Commissioner Franz Fischler proposed creating an EU Food and Drugs Agency similar to the U.S. Food and Drug Administration, but it was not until December 2002 that a decision was made to locate the new European Food Safety Authority in Brussels.[12]

## AGRICULTURE ISSUES BETWEEN THE EU AND ACCESSION CANDIDATES

### Zero-Zero Farm Trade Agreements

By September 2000, each of the ten central and eastern European countries had signed agreements with the EU that would allow duty-free trade of most farm products within a specified period of time. These were called "zero-zero" agreements because tariffs would eventually be reduced to zero on westbound and eastbound trade. Of the ten eastern applicants, Poland drove the hardest bargain and gained the most comprehensive agreement with the EU.[13]

### Eastern European Farmland

Another very sensitive agricultural issue concerned the right of EU citizens to buy farmland in the eastern European states. Poland, Hungary, and several other applicants requested long transition periods before non-nationals could buy farmland in their countries, where land was from five to twenty times cheaper than in western Europe. The eastern Europeans were afraid that land speculators would drive up land prices and distort their economies. In Poland, farmers were particularly worried that Germans would flock to buy up the farmland in parts of Poland than had once belonged to Germany.

In May 2001, the EU member states agreed to a common position on land purchases, despite the French government's desire to wait and settle that question as part of an overall agreement on farm issues in the accession negotiations. Once the EU member states decided on their common position on land purchases, the Czech government broke ranks with Poland and Hungary and accepted the EU's seven-year transition period. Poland wanted an eighteen-year transition period, but it finally accepted a twelve-year transition for lands that had once belonged to Germany.[14]

## REGIONAL AND SOCIAL POLICY

As the EU has steadily expanded to include more and more countries of Europe, reducing the gap between richer and poorer regions has become one of the Union's fundamental aims. The original six member states were all located in western Europe, and they were roughly equal in wealth, although southern Italy and some overseas French territories were much poorer than the rest of the European Community. The enlargements in the 1970s and 1980s added four poor countries: Ireland, Greece, Spain, and Portugal. Britain, which joined in 1974, also had some pockets of poverty and high unemployment in old industrial regions, as did France and Germany.

In the 1980s, the Commission realized that creation of the Common Market was actually increasing the gap between rich and poor regions, because the rich areas were usually much better able to take advantage of new opportunities to increase their production and expand their markets. Led by Commission President Jacques Delors, the EU responded with a series of programs designed to promote social cohesion—meaning a reduction in the gap between rich and poor people. This policy was inspired by idealistic as well as practical motives.

Creating more equal opportunities for people throughout the community was seen as a positive good in itself, but it was also expected to lead to faster and more uniform economic growth and reduce political friction between rich and poor countries. These were not minor considerations, because slow growth and political gridlock were among the most frustrating problems that EU countries faced. One of Commission President Delors's main achievements was to persuade the initially skeptical heads of rich member states that it was in their interest to transfer large sums of money to their poorer partners to help them catch up.[15]

**Table 8.4**
**Regional and Social Aid Budgeted for 2000–2006 (billions of euros)**

|  | Objective 1 | Objective 2 | Objective 3 |
| --- | --- | --- | --- |
|  | Regions Lagging Behind in Development | Regions in Structural Crisis | Regions Needing Support for Training/Jobs |
| EU funds available (Billions of Euros) | 135.9 | 22.50 | 24.05 |
| EU funds used | ERDF, ESF, EAGGF, FIFG | ERDF, ESF | ESF |
| Percent of population covered | 22.2 | 18 | (not relevant) |

*Note:* ERDF = European Regional Development Fund; ESF = European Social Fund; EAGGF = European Agricultural Guidance and Guarantee Fund; and FIFG = Financial Instrument for Fisheries Guidance.

*Source:* European Commission

## Structural Funds

Several programs, known collectively as "structural funds" were created to help the poor countries and regions. The largest of these programs is the European Regional Development Fund (ERDF), which was proposed by French President Georges Pompidou and set up in 1975 to help Prime Minister Edward Heath build support for European Community membership in Britain. The United Kingdom has continued to receive a significant share of ERDF money.

The European Social Fund (ESF) was created to combat long-term unemployment and to provide young people in particular with vocational training. Other structural funds include the so-called guidance section of the European Agricultural Guidance and Guarantee Fund (EAGGF). Table 8.4 shows the amounts budgeted for regional and social aid in the Agenda 2000 budget that was approved in March 1999.

To qualify for EU aid, a region of a member state must have per capita income that is below 75 percent of the EU average. In 2001, ten of Spain's seventeen regions qualified for regional aid, but after the eastern enlargement reduces the average per capita income in the EU by 16 percent, only two Spanish provinces (Extremadura and Andalusia) will qualify.

"Why should the poorest regions in Spain pay for the costs of enlargement?" asked Prime Minister Jose Maria Aznar. He threatened to block a common EU position on the free movement of labor from eastern Europe unless Spanish claims to regional aid were protected, but the leaders of Germany and other EU states that were net contributors to the EU budget refused to agree to his demands. They insisted that the Union had treated Spain generously, and now it was the eastern Europeans' turn. Consequently, Spain was forced to agree to the EU's common position on the free movement of labor.

### Commission Plan

The Commission suggested the possibility of limiting regional aid to the accession countries by invoking an existing EU rule that no country can receive regional aid that is more than 4 percent of its gross domestic product. The rationale for the limit was that any more aid could probably not be absorbed. Given the small size of the accession countries' economies, this would leave most of the regional aid budget to be divided among the current member states. The Commission estimated that by 2006 the new member states would be receiving regional aid worth 137 euros per person, compared with 231 euros per person for Spain, Portugal, Greece, and Ireland.[16]

## AGREEMENT ON FINANCIAL AND BUDGETARY ISSUES

At the Copenhagen summit in December 2002, the EU agreed to provide about 40.8 billion euros to the ten accession states between 2004 and 2006. This figure was arrived at after intense, last-minute bargaining between Poland (representing the candidate countries) and Germany, as the largest contributor to the EU budget. Poland managed to gain an extra 1 billion euros cash for its government budget in 2004–2006, which was taken from its allocation for regional aid. The other nine candidates received a total of 300 million euros up front rather than as regional aid.

The advantage of having the money in advance was that it would have greater political impact in the candidate countries and might ensure that they all approved the accession treaty in their national referendums. Regional aid money tends to go to projects like road building that may take years to finish, or the money may be lost to the candidate countries when they find such projects difficult to administer.

The money provided at Copenhagen for agricultural aid followed a Franco–German plan that was agreed two months earlier at Brussels. The candidates would receive 25 percent of the full EU rate in 2004, and the amount would increase in annual increments. However, the candidates were allowed to top up these subsidies, at first by using funds provided by the EU for rural development until 2006, and later out of their national budgets.[17]

## NOTES

1. Steven Erlanger, "European Union to Tackle Overhaul of Farm Subsidies," *New York Times* (July 11, 2002): p. A8.

2. Ibid.

3. Michael Mann, "Fischler Faces a Battle to Convince Colleagues of Farms Plan," *Financial Times* (July 10, 2002): p. 4.

4. Ibid. Bringing the EU's farm subsidies regime into compliance with World Trade Organization (WTO) rules would greatly improve the EU's bargaining position in the Doha Development Round of world trade negotiations. In February 2003, French President Chirac conceded that EU export subsidies hurt developing countries, but it was not clear that he was prepared to make meaningful reform.

5. Judy Dempsey and Stefan Wagstyl, "Divisions Widen over EU Expansion," *Financial Times* (June 12, 2002). See also "To Get Them In, Cut the Costs," *The Economist* (February 2, 2002): p. 48.

6. Desmond Dinan, *Ever Closer Union* (Boulder, Colo.: Lynne Rienner, 1999), pp. 334–38.

7. Andras Inotai, "The CEEC's: From Association Agreements to Full Membership," in *The Expanding European Union: Past, Present, Future,* ed. John Redmond and Glenda Rosenthal (Boulder, Colo.: Lynne Rienner, 1998), pp. 165–66.

8. Dinan, *Ever Closer Union,* pp. 338–44.

9. Dick Leonard, *Guide to the European Union,* 7th ed. (London: The Economist/Profile Books, 2000), pp. 93–94. Leonard gives the annual breakdown of the EU's pre-accession aid during the years 2000–2006: Agriculture = 529 million euros; Structural aid = 1,058 million euros; and PHARE aid = 1,587 million euros.

10. Ibid., pp. 140–46.

11. Dinan, *Ever Closer Union,* pp. 344–45; Leonard, *Guide to the European Union,* pp. 207–8.

12. Renate Kunast, a member of the Green Party in Germany, was appointed minister of agriculture, and she proposed increasing support for organic farming and much tighter rules for food safety.

13. "Poland's Tough Farm Stance Pays Off," *Financial Times* (September 28, 2000).

14. "EU Enlargement Boosted by Czech 'Land Buy,'" *Financial Times* (June 2, 2001). Hungary accepted the EU's offer of a seven-year transition period.

15. Leonard, *Guide to the European Union,* pp. 156–64.

16. "To Get Them In, Cut the Costs," *The Economist* (February 2, 2002): p. 48.

17. European Council, *Presidency Conclusions,* Copenhagen, December 12–13, 2002. European Commission, "Enlargement: Weekly Newsletter," December 17,

2002. The *Financial Times* noted that, after taking into account the money the ten accession countries will pay into the EU, the net transfers from the Union to the ten countries will be about 12 billion euros. Furthermore, the actual transfers may be no more than 9 billion euros because some new members will have difficulty implementing EU-financed projects. Stefan Wagstyl, "EU Entry Deal Secures Poland's Date with Destiny," *Financial Times* (December 14, 2002).

# CHAPTER 9

# Treaty of Nice: Essential Reforms

EU leaders decided in 1996 that certain institutional reforms must be adopted to clear the way for the eastern enlargement. Unless they changed such things as the voting system in the Council of Ministers, there might be gridlock after new states joined the Union.

In December 2000, the reforms were finally incorporated in the Treaty of Nice, which had to be ratified by each member state before they agreed on terms of accession with the candidate countries. In May 2001, Irish voters created a crisis by rejecting the Treaty of Nice in a May 2001 referendum, partly because they feared it would violate Ireland's neutrality.[1] However, in October 2002, after EU leaders issued a statement saying the treaty did not compromise Ireland's neutral status, the Irish finally ratified it in a second referendum.

## REFORM AND ENLARGEMENT

The idea of linking institutional reform to enlargement was not new. The Commission had urged reform each time a few member states had been added, but the heads of government usually managed to avoid this task because it was likely to mean giving up some cherished national prerogatives. Nevertheless, they all agreed that adding ten or more new members made it obvious that reforms were necessary. An organization designed for six countries could not function smoothly with twenty-five or more members.[2]

The first thing they had to decide was whether to attempt a major overhaul of EU institutions or limit the exercise to the most necessary reforms.

Federalists hoped for a major overhaul because they feared that enlargement would make further integration all but impossible. However, most EU leaders favored the intergovernmental approach to decision making, and they opted for a very limited menu of reforms:

- First, they wanted the number of weighted votes assigned to each member state in the Council of Ministers to correspond more closely to the country's population. This reform benefited the larger member states because the existing allocation of weighted votes strongly favored the small countries.

- Second, EU leaders wanted more issues to be decided by majority vote, thus reducing the range of issues where any member state could exercise the right to veto decisions. Federalists favored this reform because it was likely to open the way to more common policies on a greater range of subjects.

- Third, EU leaders saw a need to change the existing system of choosing commissioners, whereby large states could choose two and small states could choose one. The big countries wanted to avoid having too many commissioners, but small states were determined to keep the right to name one.

### Amsterdam Treaty

The intergovernmental conference (IGC) that was convened in 1996 to prepare for the Treaty of Amsterdam was supposed to lay the groundwork for these reforms, but because the EU leaders had other priorities, the treaty failed to address even the short list of reforms they had agreed were needed, When they arrived in Amsterdam in June 1997 to complete the treaty, they faced a typically overcrowded EU summit agenda, chose to focus on Justice and Home Affairs, and failed to reach a consensus on institutional reform.[3]

Leaders of the central and eastern European countries were alarmed by the EU's failure to address the reforms that the EU itself had declared essential. Polish and Hungarian leaders were the most outspoken, and they began publicly to question the EU's sincerity and its commitment to enlargement, even after the Union agreed to begin accession negotiations with them in 1998.[4] EU officials complained that Polish negotiators behaved as if the EU wanted to join Poland rather than the other way around.[5]

After much further discussion among the EU member states, another intergovernmental conference was convened in January 2000 with instructions to prepare for the Treaty of Nice, which would finally embody the reforms needed to prepare for enlargement. EU leaders were at last beginning to warm to the subject. Joschka Fischer's speech in Berlin in March 2000 (excerpts of which appear in the appendix) launched a public debate in which many of the EU heads of state or government laid out their ideas about how an enlarged union should be run. However, polls in the first half of 2000 showed support for enlargement declining in the EU and also in many of the candidate countries.[6]

## FRENCH PRESIDENCY PRODUCES TREATY OF NICE

In July 2000, it was France's turn to assume the six-month rotating presidency of the EU, but for President Chirac and Prime Minister Jospin, who were gearing up to compete in the next French presidential election, neither the eastern enlargement nor EU institutional reform offered any political rewards. Polls showed that support for enlargement was lower in France than in any other EU country. French voters were worried about unemployment, crime, and other social problems that were easily (if unfairly) blamed on foreigners. Moreover, the French people disliked the fact that the role of leading player in the EU was passing from France to Germany.

Under these circumstances, it took courage for Chirac to announce at the start of his EU presidency, that he would give top priority to achieving the most necessary institutional reforms so the enlargement could move ahead. No doubt he wanted to thwart efforts by federalists to propose more far-reaching reforms, but he clearly also wanted to show that France was still capable of championing important causes for the good of Europe.

However, a special October summit in Biarritz, which was meant to reach preliminary agreement on the main reforms, got sidetracked by the fact that President Milosevic of Yugoslavia had just been overthrown. His moderate successor, Kostunica, was invited to the summit in Biarritz and lionized by EU leaders, who were glad to have a chance to claim some credit for the fact that political stability was returning to the Balkans.

During his presidency of the EU, Chirac was expected to preside over meetings in a fair and neutral manner, but instead he antagonized his colleagues by trying to advance French interests. The summit at Nice in December lasted four days and nights, twice as long as the usual EU summit, and by the end of it tempers were short from lack of sleep. Much of the time was spent haggling over how many weighted votes to give each member state for voting in the Council of Ministers. Under the existing system, a small country like Luxembourg had far more weighted votes in relation to its population than a large country like Germany. The imbalance was partially corrected at Nice, but Chirac irritated the Germans in particular by insisting that France have exactly the same number of weighted votes as Germany, despite its much smaller population.[7]

Table 9.1 shows the number of weighted votes currently allotted to each member state at the time of the Nice summit and the number they would be assigned in 2005. The most obvious anomaly was the fact that Germany had one weighted vote for every 2.8 million people, while

Table 9.1
Weighted Votes Assigned to Member States

|  | Weighted Votes | | Population |
|  | Current | 2005 | (millions) |
|---|---|---|---|
| Germany | 10 | 29 | 82.0 |
| Britain | 10 | 29 | 59.2 |
| France | 10 | 29 | 59.0 |
| Italy | 10 | 29 | 57.6 |
| Spain | 8 | 27 | 39.4 |
| Netherlands | 5 | 13 | 15.8 |
| Greece | 5 | 12 | 10.5 |
| Belgium | 5 | 12 | 10.2 |
| Portugal | 5 | 12 | 10.0 |
| Sweden | 4 | 10 | 8.9 |
| Austria | 4 | 10 | 8.1 |
| Denmark | 3 | 7 | 5.3 |
| Finland | 3 | 7 | 5.2 |
| Ireland | 3 | 7 | 3.7 |
| Luxembourg | 2 | 4 | 0.4 |
| TOTAL | 87 | 237 | 375.3 |
| Qualified majority | 62 | 169 |  |
| Blocking minority | 26 | 69 |  |

*Source:* European Commission

Luxembourg had one weighted vote for every hundred thousand people.

### Candidates' Aims at Nice

The candidate countries were also allotted a quota of weighted votes to use when they became members of the EU, as shown in table 9.2. They were anxious to have as many weighted votes assigned to them as EU states with the same population. Poland received twenty-seven votes, the

**Table 9.2**
**Weighted Votes Assigned to Candidate Countries**

|                | Weighted Votes | | Population |
|                | Current | 2005 | (millions) |
|----------------|---------|------|------------|
| Candidates     |         |      |            |
| Poland         | 8       | 27   | 38.7       |
| Romania        | 6       | 14   | 22.5       |
| Czech Republic | 5       | 12   | 10.3       |
| Hungary        | 5       | 12   | 10.1       |
| Bulgaria       | 4       | 10   | 8.2        |
| Slovakia       | 3       | 7    | 5.4        |
| Lithuania      | 3       | 7    | 3.7        |
| Latvia         | 3       | 4    | 2.4        |
| Slovenia       | 3       | 4    | 2.0        |
| Estonia        | 3       | 4    | 1.4        |
| Cyprus         | 2       | 4    | 0.8        |
| Malta          | 2       | 3    | 0.4        |
|                |         |      |            |
| Total          |         |      |            |
| 12 Candidates  | 47      | 108  | 105.9      |
| 15 EU States   | 87      | 237  | 375.3      |
| Grand Total    | 134     | 345  | 481.2      |

*Note:* With twenty-seven member states, a qualified majority = 258, and a blocking minority = 91, out of a total 345 votes.

*Source: The Economist* (December 16, 2000) and *Financial Times* (December 24, 2000).


same number as Spain, and Lithuania received seven votes, the same as Ireland. However, Romania was allotted only fourteen, just one more than the Netherlands, which had a much smaller population.

Since the candidate countries were not invited to participate directly in the summit at Nice, they had to obtain the support of EU members for their objectives. For example, during one all-night negotiating session, Lithuanian leaders managed to contact the German chancellor's foreign policy advisor by phone, and he made sure they got the same number of votes as Ireland.

Countries like Romania that had less support from the large member states did not fare as well. The French government sometimes supports

Romania's interests, but French leaders were so busy at Nice that this task fell to the Belgian prime minister, Guy Verhofstadt. Although his efforts were not always successful, Verhofstadt earned the gratitude of the Romanians, as well as some of the smaller candidate countries.[8]

### Small States vs. Large States

Many of the issues negotiated at Nice pitted small member states against large ones (e.g., over the allocation of weighted votes). As previously noted, small states like Luxembourg were overrepresented with the existing allocation of votes, and they did their best to maintain their advantage. While Germany clearly failed to improve its position, other large states made slight gains, and Germany partially made up for this initial failure by gaining a much bigger allotment of seats in the European Parliament.

In general, big states like France and Britain that favored an intergovernmental approach won most of the battles at Nice. Leaders like Belgian Prime Minister Verhofstadt, who favored the interests of small states and a more federal approach to decision making, lost more often than they won. They failed to get a significant increase in the number of issues that could be decided by majority vote. Even though this was supposed to be one of the main reforms in the treaty, it seems to have been crowded out of the agenda at Nice. Certain kinds of trade issues were declared subjects for qualified majority vote, but British leaders made certain that taxation and social security would still be subject to the national veto.

Prime Minister Verhofstadt also tried to reduce the number of votes needed for a "qualified majority" under the new weighted voting system. However, analysts discovered afterward that the opposite result was achieved, probably because the overstressed leaders at the summit made a mathematical error.[9]

### Complications Added

The Treaty of Nice added a new requirement that a qualified majority must include more than half of the member states with at least 62 percent of the EU's total population. This convoluted formula was probably meant to prevent the voting process from being dominated by either a small coalition of big states or a large coalition of small states. However, when all the candidates have been admitted, a coalition of the fourteen poorest countries will be able to achieve a qualified majority, and a coalition of the richest countries (net contributors to the EU budget) will be able to achieve a blocking minority. So on budgetary matters, the Treaty of Nice may have increased the possibility of gridlock, exactly the opposite of what it was supposed to do.[10]

## System for Choosing Commissioners

In addition to revising the voting system in the Council and adding subjects that could be decided by majority vote, the treaty was also supposed to provide a new formula for choosing commissioners. Under the existing system, large states could choose two commissioners, while small states had the right to choose one. (The European Parliament was also involved in approving the nominees, but this aspect was not under review at the Nice summit.) Small states wanted to lock in their right to nominate one commissioner, and large states wanted to keep the College of Commissioners, as it is called, from becoming too large and unwieldy.

Since neither side was willing to give much ground at Nice, all they could agree on was that a solution reconciling these conflicting aims must be found before the number of member states reached twenty-seven. The next Commission would be chosen in time to take office on January 1, 2005. According to the treaty, each member state (including those who enter the Union before that date) will be allowed to choose one commissioner. When the Union consists of twenty-seven member states, the number of commissioners will be kept lower than the number of member states. The Council, acting unanimously, will adopt a system for choosing commissioners "according to a rotation system based on the principle of equality."[11]

## Allocating Seats in Parliament

The Nice summit achieved a clearer result in setting the number of seats each member state (including new members) would be able to elect to the European Parliament in the 2004 election. Table 9.3 shows the number of seats the current fifteen member states will be able to elect. Because new states would probably join the Union in time to take part in the election, the total number of seats allotted to the fifteen current member states had to be reduced to make room for the new member states. As table 9.3 shows, Germany managed to keep the ninety-nine seats it had in the 1998 election, while all the other members except Luxembourg gave up some seats.

## Seats Reserved for Candidate Countries

As table 9.4 shows, the Treaty of Nice also specified the number of European Parliament members the candidates could elect if they joined the Union before the 2004 parliamentary election. Here again, the great concern of the candidates was that they should get the same allocation of seats as member states with the same population. On the whole, the allocation was done on that basis.

Table 9.3
Seats Allocated to EU Members in the European Parliament

|  | 1998 * Seats | 2004 Seats | 1998 Population (millions) |
|---|---|---|---|
| Germany | 99 | 99 | 82.13 |
| France | 87 | 72 | 58.68 |
| Britain | 87 | 72 | 58.65 |
| Italy | 87 | 72 | 57.37 |
| Spain | 64 | 50 | 39.63 |
| Netherlands | 31 | 25 | 15.68 |
| Greece | 25 | 22 | 10.60 |
| Belgium | 25 | 22 | 10.14 |
| Portugal | 25 | 22 | 9.87 |
| Sweden | 22 | 18 | 8.88 |
| Austria | 21 | 17 | 8.14 |
| Denmark | 16 | 13 | 5.27 |
| Finland | 16 | 13 | 5.15 |
| Ireland | 15 | 12 | 3.68 |
| Luxembourg | 6 | 6 | 0.42 |

Table 9.4
Seats Allocated to Candidate Countries in the 2004 European Parliament

|  | 2004 Seats | Population (millions) |
|---|---|---|
| Poland | 50 | 38.72 |
| Romania | 33 | 22.47 |
| Czech Republic | 20 | 10.28 |
| Hungary | 20 | 10.12 |
| Bulgaria | 17 | 8.34 |
| Slovakia | 13 | 5.38 |
| Lithuania | 12 | 3.69 |
| Latvia | 8 | 2.42 |
| Slovenia | 7 | 1.99 |
| Estonia | 6 | 1.43 |
| Cyprus | 6 | 0.77 |
| Malta | 5 | 0.38 |

Source: European Commission

## Nonenlargement Issues

The Treaty of Nice runs to eighty-seven pages in the *Official Journal of the European Communities*, and covers a number of issues that are not directly related to institutional reforms in preparation for enlargement. For example, the treaty includes an elaborate formula for dealing with a situation where a member state commits what its partners consider a "breach of EU principles." Such a situation arose earlier in 2000 when an Austrian government was formed that included the extreme nationalist Freedom Party.[12] The Treaty of Nice provision seeks to balance support for EU principles with respect for the rights of EU citizens to elect leaders of their own choosing.

In regard to Common Foreign and Security Policy, the treaty creates the Political Security Committee to deal with peacekeeping and crisis management situations. It also provides procedures by which two or more member states can engage in "enhanced cooperation" on security issues and in other policy areas.

The treaty also lays down guidelines for the Court of First Instance, which is supposed to take some of the burden off the European Court of Justice. This is, in fact, related to enlargement because the addition of ten new member states will probably add substantially to the caseload of the Court of Justice.

## Timetable for Enlargement

The Treaty of Nice pleased no one, except perhaps some Euroskeptics, who were glad that it contained so little of what the federalists wanted. Nevertheless, it fulfilled an important legal requirement by achieving the minimum reforms that EU leaders had agreed were necessary for enlargement to proceed. The leaders declared at Nice that a convention should be organized to consider more far-reaching reforms, but this should not delay the eastern enlargement.

Before ending their summit at Nice, the EU leaders endorsed the timetable for completing enlargement that had been proposed by the Commission and seconded by the European Parliament. Negotiations with the most advanced candidates were to be finished by the end of 2002, so that accession treaties with these countries could be ratified during 2003, and the new states could join the Union in time to take part in the 2004 elections for the European Parliament. However, the Treaty of Nice would have to be ratified by all fifteen member states before the accession treaties.

## The Irish Referendum

In May 2001, the Irish government submitted the Treaty of Nice to a referendum, as required by their constitution. Irish voters shocked EU officials by rejecting the treaty in a referendum with a low turnout. Opponents of the treaty had claimed it would violate Ireland's neutrality. It was the first EU treaty Irish voters had ever rejected, and it showed that Irish leaders and ordinary citizens had begun to question some aspects of European integration, in spite of having received enormous economic benefits from their EU membership. Analysts noted that Prime Minister Ahern, who supported the treaty, might have succeeded in getting it approved if he had held the second referendum the same day as the national election, which would have produced a larger turnout.[13] In any case, the treaty was approved in a second referendum in 2002.

### Constitutional Convention

Meanwhile, at their December 2001 summit in Laeken, Belgium, EU leaders agreed to hold a Convention on the Future of Europe, beginning in February 2002, to take a closer look at needed reforms and make recommendations that might lead to drafting a constitution to replace the existing treaties. (According to a *Eurobarometer* poll taken in the fall of 2001, two-thirds of EU citizens favored a constitution.) Representatives of the candidate countries were allowed to take part in the convention. Valery Giscard d'Estaing, former president of France, was chosen to be chairman, while Giuliano Amato and Jean-Luc Dehaene, former prime ministers of Italy and Belgium, were named vice chairmen.[14]

The convention brought together 105 representatives of the member state and candidate governments and their national parliaments. There were also representatives of the Commission, members of the European Parliament, and observers from the Economic and Social Committee, the Committee on Regions, and the Ombudsman. A forum of civil-society representatives—public interest groups, research institutes, and the like—could also channel ideas into the convention.[15]

The convention met for at least two half-day sessions a month during the year ending March 1, 2003. Its conclusions and recommendations would be presented to an intergovernmental conference that might produce a draft constitutional treaty. A longtime observer of the EU described the role of the accession states in the convention:

Attempts to caucus are going on at every level: there are regular meetings of each political "family"—social democrats, conservatives, liberals and the like; each set of institutional representatives is trying to co-ordinate its line...and each country has meetings of its own nationals as well. The 13 accession candidates, including Turkey, are the only ones that seem to be trying not to look like a caucus.[16]

### Who Will Lead the EU?

Prime Minister Tony Blair of Britain and Commission President Romano Prodi offered diametrically opposed plans for how the EU should be run.

**Table 9.5**
**Council of Ministers Rotating Presidency**

| | |
|---|---|
| Denmark | January-June 1993 |
| Belgium | July-December 1993 |
| Greece | January-June 1994 |
| Germany | July-December 1994 |
| France | January-June 1995 |
| Spain | July-December 1995 |
| Italy | January-June 1996 |
| Ireland | July-December 1996 |
| Netherlands | January-June 1997 |
| Luxembourg | July-December 1997 |
| Britain | January-June 1998 |
| Austria | July-December 1998 |
| Germany | January-June 1999 |
| Finland | July-December 1999 |
| Portugal | January-June 2000 |
| France | July-December 2000 |
| Sweden | January-June 2001 |
| Belgium | July-December 2001 |
| Spain | January-June 2002 |
| Denmark | July-December 2002 |
| Greece | January-June 2003 |
| Italy | July-December 2003 |

Blair's plan, which was supported by some of the larger states, was for the heads of member states to choose a president, who would serve for a term of five years.[17] It was generally agreed that the current rotating presidency of the Council that puts a new country in charge every six months provides inadequate leadership for a Union of fifteen countries and was even more unsuited for a Union of twenty-five. Table 9.5 shows the rotation of the Council presidency.[18]

Commission President Prodi's plan would make the Commission the dominant force in the EU by putting it in charge of the Common Foreign and Security Policy, Justice and Home Affairs, and Economic and Monetary Union. The Commission president would become the EU's chief

Figure 9.1   Commission President Romano Prodi
favored a strong role for the Commission and also
said ratifying the Treaty of Nice was essential for
enlargement. *Credit:* European Commission Audiovisual Library.

executive, while the Council would be reduced to the role of acting on legislation proposed by the Commission.[19]

Giscard d'Estaing, the chairman of the convention, gave the impression
in press interviews that he opposed Prodi's proposal. "Europeans don't
want a strong central political power. They want certain things done in
common," he said, meaning "things done in common" by the member
states rather than by the Commission. Federalists like Andrew Duff, a liberal member of the European Parliament, expressed dismay at his atti-
tude. "Giscard seems to feel the Commission has completed its work and
can now just service the Council," Duff said. "He treats the Commission
with contempt, and that's a big mistake."[20]

Figure 9.2    Valery Giscard d'Estaing, former president of France, presided over the Convention on Europe's Future, the first meeting of its kind. *Credit:* Peter Schrank (artist).

Giuliano Amato, vice chairman of the convention, offered a plan that would combine some elements of Blair's and Prodi's proposals. He agreed with both gentlemen that the EU needed a strong president, who would serve for a renewable term of perhaps two and a half years. In Amato's plan, the EU president would not be the Commission president; he or she would be chosen by the heads of member state governments and might well be from one of the smaller states (it would be easier for EU leaders to agree on someone from a smaller country). However, Amato would also strengthen the Commission's role by having a commissioner chair the meetings of member state ministers when they were discussing policy rather than deciding on legislation.[21]

The debate was far from over, but important decisions about the EU's future were likely to be made by the time the central and eastern European countries joined the Union in 2004 or soon thereafter. They had participated actively in the convention and clearly felt they had an important stake in the Union's future.[22]

## NOTES

1. "Ahearn Warns on Nice Treaty Vote," *Financial Times* (June 13, 2002). The Irish constitution required that treaties be submitted to a national referendum, but this was the first EU treaty that Irish voters rejected. Although they had gained enormous economic benefits from Union membership, by the turn of the century they were beginning to show some signs of Euroskepticism.

2. In 2000, a public debate by EU leaders about needed reforms was launched by Joschka Fischer's speech, portions of which appear in the appendix. Many of the proposed reforms went well beyond the agreed "short list" of changes needed to make enlargement possible, but Fischer and other EU leaders generally maintained the distinction between reforms that must be included in the Treaty of Nice and those that should not delay the enlargement process.

3. Desmond Dinan, *Ever Closer Union,* 2d ed. (Boulder, Colo.: Lynne Rienner, 1999), pp. 170–78.

4. Michael Baun, *A Wider Europe: The Politics of European Union Enlargement* (Boston, Mass.: Rowman & Littlefield, 2000), pp. 199–212.

5. Dinan, *Ever Closer Union,* p. 199.

6. "Balancing Act for Enlargement Broker," *Financial Times* (October 24, 2000).

7. *The Economist* (December 16, 2000) and the *Financial Times* (December 24, 2000) each included special sections on the Nice summit that provided detailed coverage of the interplay between EU leaders.

8. Ibid., and interviews with EU and accession country diplomats.

9. "Europe Got Its Sums Wrong," *Financial Times* (December 23, 2000).

10. "Europe's Guaranteed Gridlock," *Financial Times* (July 9, 2001).

11. *Official Journal of the European Communities* (2001/C 80/01), Treaty of Nice, March 10, 2001, pp. 51–52.

12. Ibid., p. 6.

13. "Ahern Shows His Hand in Battle for Nice Treaty," *Financial Times* (June 25, 2002).

14. Giscard d'Estaing was a strong defender of the principle that the nation states were the building blocks of EU legitimacy, and he emphasized that he hoped the convention would produce a constitutional treaty that defined and limited the powers of Union institutions, particularly the Commission. "Call for EU Treaty to Be Written in Clear Language," *Financial Times* (June 24, 2002).

15. Eric Philippart, "The 'European Convention': Anatomy of the New Approach to Constitution-Making in the EU," European Union Studies Association, *EUSA Review* 15, no. 2 (spring 2002): pp. 5–7. Philippart notes that the convention established many new precedents, not least being the inclusion of the accession candidates.

16. Quentin Peel, "A Merry Dance around Europe," *Financial Times* (June 10, 2002): p. 13.

17. "Proposals to Boost EU Presidency under Attack," *Financial Times* (June 10, 2002): p. 2.

18. Denmark held the EU presidency both in 1993, when Union leaders decided that European countries meeting the "Copenhagen criteria" could apply to join the Union, and again in the second half of 2002, when the accession process was due to end at the Copenhagen summit in December. Thus, Denmark adopted

the slogan, "From Copenhagen to Copenhagen," signifying its determination to complete the difficult final negotiations.

19. "Prodi Tries to Enlarge His Powers," *Financial Times* (June 19, 2002).

20. Charlemagne, "Valery Giscard d'Estaing, Europe's Conductor," *The Economist* (June 22, 2002): p. 50.

21. "Amato Calls for Strong President to Lead EU," *Financial Times* (July 8, 2002).

22. Eric Philippart, "The 'European Convention,'" p. 6. According to Philippart, the accession countries tried to have one of their parliamentary representatives chosen to serve on the convention presidium. The Poles were particularly upset when this effort failed, but the presidium invited a representative of the candidate countries to join them as an observer.

# CHAPTER 10

# Enlargement and the Euro

The eastern enlargement and monetary union—two of the most ambitious feats ever tried in Europe—could not be kept on separate tracks forever; they were always destined to become entangled. Throughout the decade of the nineties, preparing a new currency for 300 million people was an absorbing task for EU leaders, and they stuck to it with grim determination. As the eastern European states struggled to change from Soviet-style government to democratic and free-market standards, some EU leaders tried to slow enlargement for fear it might upset their timetable for launching the euro.

The eastern states wanted to enter the "eurozone" as soon as possible to enjoy the increased stability and foreign investment that this would bring, but they will have to meet much higher standards of economic and financial management before they will be allowed to join. In addition, the monetary union was still very much a work in progress, with important problems still unsolved. When the new countries enter the eurozone, the increased diversity of the membership will make it even harder to adopt a monetary policy that suits all or most of the member states.

This chapter begins by describing how the monetary union was put in place and how it worked during its first four years in operation. Next, we examine what obstacles the central and eastern European states must overcome before they can join it. Then, we look ahead and try to predict what benefits and risks they can expect from membership—and how the currency union will be affected by enlargement.

## LAUNCHING THE EURO

On New Year's Day 2002, the euro became legal tender, and people were enjoying the winter holidays in the twelve eurozone countries from Finland to Greece. Although banks and most stores were closed, ATMs (automatic teller machines) had been filled with euros, cafes and restaurants were open, and people could make small purchases at convenience stores, newspaper kiosks, and some food shops. The press reported that people seemed pleased with the new currency, which was obviously a powerful symbol of European integration.[1] The new coins all had the same markings on one side and a design chosen by a member state on the other side (like the American quarters that have a state design on one side).

Relatively few problems were reported with price gouging or businesses that were unable to make change in euros. The new currency had already been in existence since January 1999 as an electronic currency, used by banks, governments, and large corporations for major transactions. Prices in stores had been listed in euros as well as the local currency, but only the latter had been accepted as legal tender. According to media reports, most people felt they had been adequately prepared for the changeover, and their initial resistance to the idea (in the early and mid-1990s) changed to support when they learned more about it.[2]

In each of the eurozone countries, the changeover was completed within two months, and the national currency was then withdrawn from circulation, but for an extended period people could still exchange their old money for euros at banks. The smooth logistical operation was the result of years of careful planning, including a public information campaign by the Commission and member states. The latest security devices were embedded in the new bills to protect them from being counterfeited.

However, before the new money could be minted, the member states had to muster the political will to surrender control over one of their most cherished sovereign rights and then they had to bring their economies into line with each other, a difficult process that is still far from complete. Figure 10.1 illustrates some of the main milestones on the road to economic and monetary union.

As late as the 1980s, the economies of member states—including their growth rates, inflation, budget deficits, and business cycles—were way out of alignment with each other. Throughout the 1990s, most EU governments struggled to converge their economies with the criteria for euro membership that were set by the Treaty of European Union. Despite considerable success, there is still enough difference in the way their economies perform to make it very difficult to design one monetary policy to fit all their needs.

**Figure 10.1**
**The Long March to a Common Currency**

---

1969    The Hague summit calls for enlargement of the community and monetary union. Werner Plan foresees monetary union by 1980.

1979    European Monetary System and Exchange Rate Mechanism created as first step toward monetary union.

1986    Single European Act sets goal of completing common market by 1992 to lay basis for common currency.

1989    Delors Report says monetary union requires centralized control over national fiscal policies.

1992    Treaty of European Union binds EU members to take the necessary steps to create monetary union by 2000.

1992    Exchange Rate Mechanism attacked by speculators, forcing devaluation of British and Italian currencies.

1995    Madrid summit adopts timetable for move to common currency, which is named the "euro."

1996    Dublin summit agrees on Stability and Growth Pact to impose discipline on member states after launch of euro.

1998    Brussels summit chooses first group of eleven countries to participate in common currency; Wim Duisenberg named president of the European Central Bank (ECB), which is located in Frankfurt.

1999    Euro currency is launched as an electronic currency.

1999–2001    Euro's exchange rate relative to the U.S. dollar declines (because it was set too high). ECB adopts very cautious anti-inflationary policy.

2002    On January 1, euro coins and bills circulate as legal tender throughout the eurozone. Germany and France each argue for more flexibility in the Stability and Growth Pact.

2003    Britain, Sweden, and Denmark may hold referendums on joining the common currency. Wim Duisenberg retires as ECB president in July.

---

As figure 10.1 shows, the 1992 Treaty of European Union was a decisive turning point because it set the criteria for joining the common currency and made it legally binding on all member states to meet the criteria within a specific time frame. Only the United Kingdom and Denmark were allowed to opt out. Meeting the criteria meant that governments could not increase expenditures during a recession to help revive their economies, so when unemployment rose, the rules that prevented governments from trying to stimulate their economies became very unpopular. However, government leaders persevered with their plans for establishing the euro because the Union's credibility was at stake and because they believed the common currency would lead to major economic gains.

### Stability and Growth Pact

German leaders worried that their EU partners would lapse back into their free-spending habits after meeting the criteria and being allowed to join the common currency. Therefore, at Germany's insistence, a Stability and Growth Pact was concluded in 1996 that required all member states to maintain strict limits on budget deficits after joining the euro. Nevertheless, the final decision about which countries would be allowed to join the eurozone was a political one made by EU heads of government, which overlooked the failure of some countries to comply with the European Union Treaty criteria.

As table 10.1 shows, Belgium and Italy were the least successful in bringing government debts within the required limit of 60 percent of GDP; however, they were given credit for moving toward compliance. Italian leaders, desperate to ensure that Italy entered the eurozone in the first wave, made politically courageous efforts to reduce the country's annual budget deficits during the 1990s, but they only managed to squeeze under the 3 percent limit by passing a special tax that they refunded to taxpayers the following year. France also brought its budget in balance on a one-time basis by selling some of its gold reserves. Even Germany had to do some creative accounting to meet the criteria. Britain and Denmark met the criteria but opted not to join; Sweden avoided meeting the criteria in order not to join; and Greece failed to meet the criteria in time to join in 1999, but did manage to qualify by 2001.

### European Central Bank

At the German government's insistence, the European Central Bank (ECB) was located in Frankfurt, the home of Germany's central bank, to reassure the German public that it would continue the Bundesbank's anti-inflation policy. The ECB's first president was Wim Duisenberg, former president of the Netherlands' central bank, where his main task had been to keep in close step with the interest rate policy of the Bundesbank. President Chirac of France had lobbied to have Jean-Claude Trichet, head of the French central bank, named president of the ECB. In 2002, Duisenberg announced that he would retire the following year, and Trichet or another French candidate appeared likely to succeed him.[3]

**Table 10.1**
**EU Member States and Criteria for Joining Euro**

|  | Budget Deficit Under 3% of GDP (%) | Public Debt Under 60% of GDP (%) |
|---|---|---|
| Belgium | 2.1 | 122.2 |
| Denmark | 0.7 surplus | 64.1 |
| Germany | 2.7 | 61.3 |
| Greece | 4.0 | 108.7 |
| Spain | 2.6 | 68.3 |
| France | 3.0 | 58.0 |
| Ireland | 0.9 surplus | 67.0 |
| Italy | 2.7 | 121.6 |
| Luxembourg | 1.7 | 6.7 |
| Netherlands | 1.4 | 72.1 |
| Austria | 2.5 | 66.1 |
| Portugal | 2.5 | 62.0 |
| Finland | 0.9 | 55.8 |
| Sweden | 0.4 | 76.6 |
| Britain | 1.9 | 53.4 |

*Note:* Denmark, Ireland, and Luxembourg had budget surpluses rather than deficits.
*Source:* Agence Europe, February 28, 1998.

## REACTIONS OF EU MEMBER STATES OUTSIDE THE EUROZONE

The successful introduction of euro notes and coins led to increased public support for joining the common currency in the United Kingdom, Denmark, and Sweden, the three EU member states that were outside the eurozone. In Britain, however, polls showed that the increase lasted only a few weeks, suggesting that the British people were waiting to see what sort of case their government would make for joining the common currency. For most of the last decade, roughly two-thirds of the British people have told pollsters they opposed the euro, but almost the same number have said they expected the United Kingdom would be in the eurozone "ten years from now."[4]

In Sweden, weakness of the local currency (the krona) was cited as another reason for the sharp increase in support to 51 percent from 31 percent a year earlier. The same poll showed opposition to joining the euro falling from 64 percent to 44 percent. Prime Minister Goran Persson planned to hold a referendum in September 2003, although Swedish public opinion appeared to be turning against the common currency in 2002. The economic case for Sweden joining the eurozone would be strengthened if Britain and Denmark joined first because they were two of Sweden's main trading partners, but the Swedish government seemed likely to be the first to hold a referendum.[5]

The Danes rejected euro membership in a September 2000 referendum, but the result probably was skewed by the Danish peoples' opposition to an EU effort to punish Austria for including the extremist Freedom Party in its government. In January 2002, opinion polls showed Danish support for joining the euro running as high as 57 percent, the highest rating in two years. Seventy-five percent of businesses in Denmark said they were willing to carry out transactions in euros, and shoppers in Copenhagen found stores willing to accept the new currency even though Denmark had not adopted it. Although the government was eager to join, Prime Minister Anders Fogh Rasmussen discouraged talk of an early referendum because he clearly wanted to be more confident of public support before scheduling a vote.[6]

## STRENGTHS AND WEAKNESSES OF MONETARY UNION

Analysts agree that the euro's original exchange rate against the U.S. dollar was set too high, and that this was a major reason why it declined by about 25 percent against the dollar during 1999, the first year in which the euro functioned as an electronic currency. Although the 2001 recession was milder in Europe than in the United States, the euro remained about 25 percent lower than the dollar until 2002, when the dollar's sharp decline in value brought the two currencies close to parity in June 2002. However, since the EU and the United States were both very large, wealthy, and self-contained economies with less than 10 percent of their GNP derived from exports, their exchange rates were not generally of great concern to U.S. or EU officials.[7]

The economic benefits that analysts expected from the EU's adoption of the euro included reduced transaction costs and much easier cross-border trade and investment operations. The main drawback was the extreme difficulty of adopting a monetary policy that suited the needs of all or most of the member states. Price differentials between EU countries for the same product were also likely to disappear over time because of the existence of a common currency, but this did not happen very quickly. *The Economist* magazine issued occasional reports on its "Big Mac Index," the varying prices in McDonald's restaurants across Europe.[8]

## Revising the Stability and Growth Pact

Historically, monetary unions have seldom lasted very long without the backing of a sovereign state with control over fiscal policy. In the EU as presently constituted, the member states retain control over fiscal policy within rules set by the Stability and Growth Pact. During the 1990s, these rules were remarkably effective in goading EU governments to reduce their budget deficits and public debt because most of them were extremely eager to be included in the monetary union.

By 2002, however, many analysts and member states believed the five-year-old pact needed revising. The German government, which originally insisted that the pact was needed to discipline the free-spending habits of countries like Italy, found itself in the embarrassing position of arguing for a looser interpretation of the rules as it struggled to put its economic house in order in an election year.[9]

Although eleven EU governments had nearly balanced budgets in 2002, the three largest eurozone economies—Germany, France, and Italy—did not. Center-right governments in France and Italy were cutting taxes and allowing their budget deficits to rise on the theory that more growth could be achieved over the course of a business cycle by a less rigid adherence to annually balanced budgets. Germany's slow growth was caused mainly by its overly regulated labor market. The difficult and important political task of labor market reform could probably not be achieved without allowing the government more flexibility in its fiscal policies.

In 2002, the Commission and EU finance ministers were considering allowing eurozone countries to do what France and Italy had already authorized themselves to do: apply tighter budget controls when the economy was growing and loosen the controls when it slowed down, thereby achieving an average budget deficit of no more than 3 percent over the course of a business cycle.

This would still leave a limit on government borrowing that was not equally appropriate for countries with very high debt levels like Italy and very low debt levels like Britain, which also needed to invest heavily in rebuilding its public health and transportation services. One way of revising this debt restriction would be to allow government borrowing only for the purpose of investment, a rule that was already being followed by Germany and Britain.[10]

### ECB Management Problems

The ECB was criticized for having only one policy goal—keeping inflation below 2 percent in the eurozone—whereas other major central banks generally had a policy for promoting economic growth. ECB President Duisenberg was said to lack the breadth of vision needed to run monetary policy for all of Europe, and was also criticized for revealing more about his plans than central bankers normally do. For example, he once implied in a press interview that he would not intervene any further to support the falling euro, causing it to drop to a new low the next day.[11]

However, the president of the ECB was not alone in making policy, but was assisted by an executive board appointed by those member states that were participating in the common currency. The European System of Central Banks provided a forum for the heads of national central banks. Economic Commissioner Solbes and the finance ministers and prime ministers of member states often commented on monetary policy. Consequently, one of the main problems of the ECB was that too many senior officials were sending conflicting signals to the financial markets.

## THE CENTRAL AND EASTERN EUROPEAN STATES AND THE EUROZONE

In March 1998, the EU and the central and eastern European states adopted Accession Partnerships, which laid out precisely what the candidate countries must do to prepare to join the Union. Under these agreements, the candidates were required to adopt the complete single-market *acquis.* Their central banks had to be independent of political control, committed to a low inflation policy, and legally prohibited from financing public-sector projects. The candidate countries had to adopt policies "which aim to achieve real convergence in accordance with the Union's objectives of economic and social cohesion."

After joining the EU, the eastern European states will not be allowed by their Union partners to "opt out" of participating in the monetary union, as were Britain and Denmark. First they will have to meet all the convergence criteria listed in the Treaty on European Union, so they will have to join the Exchange Rate Mechanism and keep their currency stable for two years.[12] Most of the eastern European states have been deliberately aiming to join the eurozone as soon as possible, and their budget deficits and public debt levels have been close to the European Union Treaty criteria. However, as windfall profits from selling state enterprises decline, it may become harder for some of the candidate countries to meet these targets.

They will find they have very little flexibility in fiscal or monetary policy, and because most of the eastern European economies are growing rapidly, it will be hard for them to meet the treaty criteria for inflation and reduce their interest rates to the level in the eurozone. There is also a danger of trying to meet the treaty criteria too soon, because joining the monetary union will greatly limit their ability to deal with an economic slowdown or recession.[13]

Joining the eurozone too early would expose their least viable industries and sectors to competition when they could no longer benefit from depreciated exchange rates. Moreover, EU restrictions on the free move-

Figure 10.2    Economic Commissioner Pedro
Solbes Mira strongly supported the Stability and
Growth Pact, which limits EU members' debts and
budget deficits. *Credit:* European Commission.

ment of labor within the Union will not help countries like Poland that
may have to cope with high unemployment while applying tight fiscal
policies.

Although eastern European leaders realize the road to monetary union
will not be easy for them, they are actively preparing to join the eurozone
for the same reasons the southern EU countries were willing to make large
sacrifices in order to qualify by 1999. They know the process leading up to
their entry into the eurozone will make their finances much more stable,
and this will attract more foreign investment, which is essential to their
continued economic growth.[14] Table 10.2 shows how the central and eastern European countries have reoriented their trade toward the EU, and
the varying amounts of foreign investment they are receiving.

**Table 10.2**
**Candidates' Economic Ties with EU, 2000**

|  | Imports to EU (%) | Exports to EU (%) | Main Trading Partners | Net Inflow of FDI as % of GDP |
|---|---|---|---|---|
| Bulgaria | 44 | 57 | Italy (13%) Germany (11%) | 7.1 |
| Czech Rep. | 62 | 69 | Germany (39%) Slovakia (11%) | 9.0 |
| Estonia | 63 | 77 | Finland (19%) Sweden (17%) | 8.0 |
| Hungary | 58 | 75 | Germany (36%) Austria (11%) | 2.9 |
| Latvia | 52 | 65 | UK (30%) Germany (16%) | 5.7 |
| Lithuania | 43 | 48 | Russia (17%) Germany (13%) | 3.4 |
| Poland | 61 | 70 | Germany (20%) Italy (6%) | 5.3 |
| Romania | 57 | 64 | Italy (22%) Germany (20%) | 2.8 |
| Slovakia | 49 | 59 | Germany (29%) Czech Republic (20%) | 10.8 |
| Slovenia | 68 | 64 | Germany (28%) Italy (14%) | 1.0 |

*Source: The Economist, Pocket Europe in Figures* (London: Profile Books, 2000), 70–71, 82. Trade figures are 1998.

## Will the Eastern Europeans Benefit from Joining the Eurozone?

If a country has strong trade ties with the members of a currency union, this is one indication that it may benefit from joining the monetary union. By 2002, all of the eastern European states had substantially reoriented their trade toward the EU. Lithuania and Bulgaria still sent about half of their exports to non-EU countries, but they were steadily increasing their trade with the Union. Moreover, trade counted for a high percentage of GDP for all of the central and eastern European countries, which is another indication that they would be likely to benefit from joining the eurozone.[15]

## Economic Structure

A third test of possible success in a currency union is the degree to which a candidate country's economy is structured like those of the other members of the union. If it is, then centralized decisions about monetary and fiscal policy are more likely to fit the new country's needs. In all of the candidate countries, the size of the agricultural workforce and the contribution of agriculture to GDP is larger than the EU average.[16] This could be a disadvantage for countries like Lithuania, which are likely to want to join the eurozone as soon as they can.

## Labor Mobility

A country is also likely to benefit from membership in a currency union if its workforce is highly mobile, because worker mobility is an important means of adjusting to a recession. However, some of the EU member states will not allow free movement of workers from eastern Europe for a period of up to seven years after they join the Union. Some of the structural rigidities found in western European labor markets also apply in eastern Europe. In addition to these obstacles, language and cultural differences will continue to limit the movement of workers between EU member states. Therefore, none of the new member states will have much labor mobility to help them adapt to life in the eurozone.

EU and eurozone membership will generate increased foreign investment to eastern European states, which will bring technology transfer and improved management practices, in many cases including higher ethical standards and greater respect for the environment. In spite of the progress the eastern Europeans have made, these are areas in which the Commission's annual assessments have noted they are still deficient.[17]

## Benefits of Waiting

Although the eastern states were eager to join the eurozone as soon as possible, the Commission advised them to concentrate on catching up with the western countries first, rather than trying to meet the criteria for eurozone membership sooner than necessary, because they would have plenty of time to meet the convergence criteria after they entered the EU.[18] Once they join the EU (probably in 2004), the eastern Europeans will have to spend at least two years in the Exchange Rate Mechanism (ERM), so 2006 is the earliest any of the new Union members are likely to enter the eurozone. Hungary hopes to do just that, while Poland, Latvia, and Slovenia have indicated they want to join the currency union by 2007. Some countries may need to spend longer than two years in the Exchange Rate Mechanism, which would give them the freedom to adjust their exchange rates as they try to speed economic growth to catch up with the western EU members.

## Will the Eurozone Benefit from an Eastern Enlargement?

During the decade of the 1990s, economic relations between the older EU members and the accession states were mutually beneficial because of the high degree of complementarity between the eastern and western halves of Europe. However, the EU restricted imports of coal, steel, textiles, and farm products from the eastern European states (products in which they had a comparative advantage), so the western European countries benefited more than the eastern Europeans from their trade ties. The return on capital invested by the EU countries in eastern Europe was high. Companies like Fiat increased their profit margins by moving manufacturing operations eastward, and the fastest-growing countries in the EU, including the Netherlands and Ireland, benefited by importing skilled workers from eastern Europe. After the new countries join the EU and the eurozone, this complementarity should continue to strengthen the eurozone economy.[19]

The eastern European countries will be invited to join the eurozone only when they have stabilized their finances, so they will be even better partners for the older member states than they were during their economic transition. Although they have sold many of their state enterprises that were most attractive to foreign investors, there is an enormous amount of pent-up demand for foreign goods in central and eastern Europe and a large pool of skilled and low-wage workers, which will almost certainly attract a new wave of investment after the eastern Europeans join the EU and the eurozone.

## NOTES

1. "Small Change, Giant Leap," *Financial Times* (January 2, 2002). See also "Euro Clears Its First Big Hurdle with Ease," *Financial Times* (January 3, 2002).

2. European Commission, *Eurobarometer* 56 (fall 2001). In the twelve euro countries, 68 percent of the people polled expressed support for the euro. The highest levels of support were in Belgium, the Netherlands, Luxembourg, Italy, Greece, and Ireland.

3. Tony Barber, "Life after Duisenberg," *Financial Times* (February 8, 2002).

4. "Many See Euro as Inevitable," *Financial Times* (April 20, 2002).

5. Christopher Brown-Humes, "Swedes Face Second Poll if They Reject Euro," *Financial Times* (December 24, 2002); and Christopher Brown-Humes, "Fears of Being Frozen Out Fuel Nordic Concerns about Role in Europe," *Financial Times* (December 18, 2002).

6. "Uncertainty Tempers Surge in Danish Enthusiasm for Euro," *Financial Times* (January 14, 2002).

7. Martin Wolf, "A Catalyst for Further Change," *Financial Times* (January 2, 2002).

8. See "Burgonomics," *The Economist, Pocket Europe in Figures*, 4th ed. (London: Profile Books, 2000), p. 82.

9. "Berlin Attacked over Stance on Deficit," *Financial Times* (February 13, 2002).

10. "Rewriting the Pact," *Financial Times* (July 11, 2002).

11. Ed Crooks, "The Wrong Man for an Impossible Mission," *Financial Times* (February 8, 2002).

12. Heather Grabbe, *Profiting from EU Enlargement* (London: Centre for European Reform, 2001), pp. 37–49.

13. European Commission, "Unity, Solidarity, Diversity for Europe, Its People and Its Territory," Second Report on Economic and Social Cohesion, Brussels, January 2001.

14. In 1998, foreign direct investment (FDI) accounted for more than 22 percent of the total investment in the ten candidate countries, compared to 12 percent worldwide, according to the UN *World Investment Report, 2000.* The candidate countries needed such high levels of FDI because of their limited domestic savings.

15. Estonia's exports plus imports equaled 66 percent of GDP in 1998, the second highest rate in Europe (after Ireland). Trade accounted for 25 to 60 percent of GDP in all the other candidate countries, with most of them at the upper end of the scale.

16. On average, agriculture contributes just 2 percent of GDP in the fifteen EU countries, while it contributes 23 percent in Bulgaria, 15 percent in Romania, and 14 percent in Lithuania. In the other candidate countries, agriculture's contribution to GDP ranges from 5 to 7 percent. Table 8.2 in Chapter 8 shows the size of the agricultural workforce in the candidate countries.

17. European Commission, *Making a Success of Enlargement*, October 2001. The need to improve ethical and environmental standards is emphasized in the individual country reports appended to the overall Commission assessment.

18. European Commission, *Towards the Enlarged Union*, October 2002 COM (2002) 700 final, pp. 14–15, 27.

19. Heather Grabbe, *Profiting from EU Enlargement*, pp. 21–33.

# CHAPTER 11

# Immigration and Enlargement

When Europeans talk about the eastern enlargement, they almost always link it to the highly controversial topic of immigration. Those with strong doubts about the enlargement fear that it will bring an unwelcome surge of immigration into the present EU states, while optimists argue that it will enlist the accession countries in the task of controlling illegal immigration from the poor countries of Asia, Africa, and the Middle East. Those who are aware of western Europe's aging and shrinking workforce hope that European migrants from the accession states will be able to make up the deficit.

Each of the viewpoints described above are missing important parts of the picture. The EU's eastern border will soon move farther east, but it is not meant to be a new iron curtain. Europe had a hard time coming to grips with the fact that it needed more immigration to expand its workforce, and has just begun to address the complex and politically sensitive subject of designing an immigration policy aimed at meeting its substantial and growing need for foreign-born workers. The new member states could make up only part of the shortfall because their demographic trends were similar to those in western Europe.

## INFLUX OF IMMIGRANTS

During the decade of the 1990s, Europe was flooded with millions of refugees from former Yugoslavia, along with millions of illegal immigrants from Asia, Africa, and the Middle East. The Yugoslav refugees began returning to their homes as soon as the Balkans became more stable, but large numbers of illegal immigrants remained in the EU. They undoubtedly contributed to some serious problems, including crime, overcrowded schools, and overburdened welfare programs; however, they also helped the European economy grow by working at low-paying, menial jobs that no one else wanted.

Because of pressure from labor unions, countries of the European Community had virtually closed the door to legal immigration from Third World countries in the 1970s. The main exceptions were for people who came to join family members living in Europe, often brides imported for arranged marriages. However, the annual number of illegal immigrants arriving in Europe rose sharply from an estimated fifty thousand in 1993 to half a million in 1999.[1]

The collapse of the Soviet Empire made it relatively easy for the immigrants to enter the EU via eastern Europe, and a multibillion-dollar people-smuggling racket sprang up to exploit their needs. No one knows how many people drowned at sea or suffocated in the backs of trucks while trying to reach Europe.

### Asylum Seekers

After World War II, many European countries adopted generous asylum policies out of remorse for failing to help the Jews escape the Nazis. In later years, thousands of people who entered Europe illegally managed to prolong their stay semi-legally by taking advantage of laws that allowed them to stay for long periods of time while their cases were being processed. Most EU countries became heavily backlogged with asylum applications, some by people actually fleeing persecution, but many by people whose primary motive for leaving home was economic. Although they were only a small percentage of all the immigrants in Europe, asylum seekers attracted a disproportionate share of attention because the programs were badly administered, and governments accused each other of encouraging asylum seekers to move on to the next country.[2]

By the year 2000, the total number of illegal aliens living in the EU was estimated to be from three to six million, while an additional fifteen million or more immigrants were legal residents or citizens of EU countries. Table 11.1 shows the estimated size of the foreign-born population in each EU country in 1999.

### Europe's Muslim Population

More than half of the immigrants living in Europe were Muslims, as shown in table 11.2. Many were legal residents or citizens of the countries where they resided, but large numbers entered the EU illegally during the 1990s, and the September 2001 attacks in the United States (which were reportedly planned in Europe) led to increased attention being focused on these communities by the media and by law enforcement agencies.

**Table 11.1**
**Foreign-Born Population of EU Countries (1999)**

|  | Total Population (millions) | Approximate Size of Foreign Population | Foreign Population as a Percent of Total |
|---|---|---|---|
| Austria | 8.14 | 724,000 | 9.0 |
| Belgium | 10.14 | 910,000 | 9.0 |
| Britain | 58.65 | 2,060,000 | 3.4 |
| Denmark | 5.27 | 223,000 | 4.2 |
| Finland | 5.15 | 69,000 | 1.3 |
| France | 58.68 | 4,000,000 | 8.0 |
| Germany | 82.13 | 7,300,000 | 9.0 |
| Italy | 57.37 | 991,000 | 1.7 |
| Luxembourg | 0.42 | 138,000 | 30.0 |
| Netherlands | 15.68 | 728,000 | 5.0 |
| Spain | 39.63 | 500,000 | 1.2 |
| Sweden | 8.88 | 532,000 | 4.4 |

*Source:* National statistics and media reports in *The Economist* and *Financial Times.*

**Table 11.2**
**Muslim Residents in EU Countries**

|  | Total Population (millions) | Main Concentrations of Muslim Residents |
|---|---|---|
| Britain | 58.65 | 2.1 |
| France | 58.68 | 4.5 |
| Germany | 82.13 | 3.2 |
| Italy | 57.37 | .7 |
| Netherlands | 15.68 | .8 |
| Spain | 39.63 | .8 |
| Scandinavian countries | .30 | .3 |
| Approximate total in EU |  | 12.4 |

*Source: The Economist* (October 20, 2001): p. 52.

Because of their religious and ethnic background, Muslims tended to be less assimilated than other immigrant groups. Those who had arrived most recently often lacked basic linguistic and other skills needed to survive independently, and their illegal status meant that only the most menial jobs were open to them. As a result, they gravitated toward ethnic ghettos and had little contact with the surrounding community. The ghettos, with high levels of crime and drug dealing, were usually no-go areas for the majority population and sometimes even for the police.[3]

The Muslim groups shown in table 11.2 came from a number of different countries. Most of those living in Germany were Kurds who came from Turkey as guest workers. Kurds also predominated in the Netherlands and Scandinavia, while most of the Muslims living in France came from the former French colonies in North Africa. The majority of Muslims in Britain came from Pakistan and Bangladesh.

### Immigration Politics and Enlargement

Radical nationalists like Jean-Marie Le Pen in France and Jorg Haidar in Austria made political gains by playing on citizens' fears that the large influx of Third World immigrants was out of control and threatening their safety and economic well-being. They offered unrealistic solutions to the immigration issue—such as sending all the immigrants home and barring the door to future arrivals.[4] The same radical nationalists were also strongly opposed to the European Union, and they warned that the eastern enlargement would bring a big increase in migrants from central and eastern Europe, competing for scarce jobs and adding to the EU's crime problem.[5]

The public's reaction to these emotionally charged messages was mixed. Polls taken at regular intervals by the Commission showed that EU citizens clearly felt that the issues of crime and unemployment deserved priority attention by their own governments and by the EU.[6] Because mainstream EU leaders were hesitant to tackle these problems, some people voted for the radical nationalists as a form of protest, even if they found the solutions they offered simplistic and their racist rhetoric embarassing.[7]

Because mainstream politicians were also slow to make a strong case for the eastern enlargement, opinion polls during the 1990s showed that EU citizens generally did not regard it as a priority for the EU. However, this did not necessarily mean they bought the extremists' warning about enlargement. People in particular EU countries tended to favor membership for some of the candidates more than others, for example, Finns wanted to see Estonia join the EU, but they might feel quite differently about Turkey.[8]

Active opposition to the eastern enlargement was strongest in areas like eastern Germany and Austria, where people were most concerned about an influx of workers from neighboring states competing for their jobs. As a result, Germany insisted that the eastern European candidate countries accept a transition period of up to seven years before their nationals could seek employment in the older EU member states.[9]

## Immigration Policy Initiatives

Building a consensus for a constructive approach to immigration was one of the most difficult challenges facing EU governments. At the national level, the British and German governments were among the few that had recently attempted to pass legislation based on the concept that immigration was needed in order to counter demographic trends and shortages of certain skills. Both governments encountered strong political resistance and had to water down their proposals. In Germany, the new immigration law was blocked by the highest court on grounds that improper voting methods were used by the governing coalition to pass it.[10]

At the EU level, the Commission and council of EU interior ministers tended to focus almost exclusively on keeping illegal immigrants out. A meeting of EU interior ministers in June 2002 agreed to some measures for this purpose, including joint surveillance operations to combat human trafficking. They also agreed to help Greece and Italy, which received the largest influx of illegal immigrants. However, adopting more positive policies for regulating immigration would probably require an extension of majority voting. Some analysts have criticized the purely negative approach to immigration as an attempt to construct a "Fortress Europe," particularly against immigrants of color.[11]

At the June 2002 EU summit in Seville, Prime Minister Blair of Britain and Prime Minister Aznar of Spain went a step further and proposed sanctions against countries that failed to stop large numbers of their citizens from leaving for the EU. Blair's own minister of overseas development criticized the proposal as a "really silly idea," and the EU heads of government removed the sanctions aspect.[12]

However, the EU countries are gradually developing common approaches to immigration issues. For example, they managed in 2002 to develop common standards for their asylum programs in an effort to prevent immigrants from shopping around to see which country offered the best deal—and to reduce the practice of one country encouraging asylum seekers to move on to the next country.[13] The development of EU policies on immigration is discussed in more detail in the chapter on Justice and Home Affairs.

## DEMOGRAPHIC CHANGE AND THE WORKFORCE

The EU faces the prospect of an aging population and a shrinking workforce. As table 11.3 shows, the fifteen countries that comprised the Union in 1998 will have 13 million fewer people in 2025, and a higher percentage of those people will be over the age of sixty-five, which is well past the age when most Europeans retire. Among other things, this points to a pressing need for pension

**Table 11.3**
**An Aging and Shrinking EU Workforce**

|            | Population (Millions) | | | Percent over age 65 | |
|------------|------|------|---|------|------|
|            | 1998 | 2025 |   | 1998 | 2020 |
| Germany    | 82.13 | 80.24 | | 16.4 | 20.8 |
| France     | 58.68 | 61.66 | | 15.9 | 19.6 |
| Britain    | 58.65 | 59.96 | | 16.0 | 19.0 |
| Italy      | 57.37 | 51.27 | | 18.2 | 23.4 |
| Spain      | 39.63 | 36.66 | | 17.0 | 20.2 |
| Netherlands | 15.68 | 15.78 | | n/a | 19.9 |
| Greece     | 10.60 | 9.86 | | 17.9 | 21.8 |
| Belgium    | 10.14 | 9.92 | | 16.7 | 20.3 |
| Portugal   | 9.87 | 9.35 | | 15.7 | 18.5 |
| Sweden     | 8.88 | 9.10 | | 17.4 | 21.8 |
| Austria    | 8.14 | 8.19 | | 14.7 | 18.5 |
| Denmark    | 5.27 | 5.24 | | 15.2 | 19.9 |
| Finland    | 5.15 | 5.25 | | 14.9 | 21.7 |
| Ireland    | 3.68 | 4.40 | | n/a | n/a |
| Luxembourg | 0.42 | 0.46 | | 14.4 | n/a |
| EU Total:  | 374.29 | 361.34 | EU average: | 16.4 | 20.4 |

*Source: The Economist, Pocket Europe in Figures* (London: Profile Books, 2000), pp. 28, 34.

reform, a difficult subject that few European countries (or other advanced countries such as the United States and Japan) have so far addressed.

An older population also requires more services, which means that a larger workforce will be needed to support a smaller population. Some of the increase may come from a larger percentage of women working outside the home and from men and women working later in their lives.[14] However, it appears likely that immigration will have to provide a growing share of the workforce in the fifteen EU countries. Polls show that western Europeans who accept this fact (and many do not) would rather allow increased immigration from eastern Europe than from Third World countries. Is this a realistic answer to western Europe's demographic problem?

**Table 11.4**
**Projected Population Change in Central and Eastern European Countries**

|  | Population (in millions) | |
|---|---|---|
|  | <u>1998</u> | <u>2025</u> |
| Poland | 38.72 | 39.07 |
| Romania | 22.47 | 19.95 |
| Czech Republic | 10.28 | 9.51 |
| Hungary | 10.12 | 8.90 |
| Bulgaria | 8.34 | 7.02 |
| Slovakia | 5.38 | 5.39 |
| Lithuania | 3.69 | 3.40 |
| Latvia | 2.42 | 1.94 |
| Slovenia | 1.99 | 1.82 |
| Estonia | <u>1.43</u> | <u>1.13</u> |
| Total | 104.84 | 98.13 |

*Source: The Economist, Pocket Europe in Figures* (London: Profile Books, 2000), p. 28.

## EASTERN EUROPE AND THE DEMOGRAPHIC GAP

As table 11.4 shows, the total population of the ten central and eastern European countries is also expected to shrink from about 105 million people in 1998 to just over 98 million in 2025. Poland and Slovakia are the only two central and eastern European countries with higher birth rates than the EU average, and their populations were projected to grow only slightly between 1998 and 2025.

Life expectancy rates are lower (by several years) in the ten eastern European countries than in the fifteen EU countries, but they are catching up as living conditions in the regions begin to converge. Thus, the demographic trends are similar (and growing more so) in eastern and western Europe. Eastern Europeans might partially meet the growing demand for workers in the fifteen older EU countries, particularly in certain skill areas such as computer programming, but the eastern European states will experience a labor shortage themselves in coming years as their people age and require more services.

Because of rapid economic growth in most of the eastern European countries, they are already attracting a net inflow of workers from abroad. The enlarged EU will have to allow immigration from other parts of the world in order to have a large enough workforce to keep its economy running. Spurred by the political gains of the radical Right, mainstream EU leaders belatedly began to address the need for a positive approach to immigration. They also began to make the case that the eastern enlargement would expand the area of freedom, security, and justice in Europe.

## NOTES

1. "Europe's Borders: A Single Market in Crime," *The Economist* (October 16, 1999): pp. 23–28.

2. Ibid., p. 28.

3. "The Muslim Diaspora," *The Economist* (October 20, 2001): p. 52.

4. "France, Race and Immigration: Who Gains?" *The Economist* (March 2, 2002): pp. 49–50.

5. Quentin Peel, "No Room for the Intolerant," *Financial Times* (May 13, 2002).

6. European Commission, *Eurobarometer* 48 (autumn 1997). Interviewees expressed support ranging from 65 to 90 percent for the EU to take action against unemployment and crime, and to implement a common foreign and defense policy as well as common rules on political asylum and immigration.

7. Philip Stephens, "Europe's Drift to the Extremes," *Financial Times* (April 26, 2002).

8. European Commission, *Eurobarometer* 51 (spring 1999).

9. Sweden brokered the common EU position on free movement of people. Since Union governments were free to adopt any transition period they chose (up to seven years), the Swedish government announced that it would allow citizens of the accession countries to seek employment in Sweden without any transition period.

10. "German Court Blocks Law for Foreigners with Skills," *New York Times* (December 19, 2002): p. A6; Alan Beattie, "Fear of Foreigners Fails to Match Reality," *Financial Times* (February 1, 2002); and Jean Eaglesham and Michael Mann, "Europe Tries to Hold Up the Traffic," *Financial Times* (June 12, 2002).

11. Ibid., and A. Geddes, *Immigration and European Integration: Towards a Fortress Europe?* (Manchester, England: Manchester University Press, 2001).

12. Philip Stephens, "A Small Wave of Immigration," *Financial Times* (May 24, 2002) provides some details from a leaked early draft of the British proposal, which was subsequently modified at the EU's Seville summit.

13. "Border Line," *Financial Times* editorial (June 14, 2002).

14. The number of working-age men and women employed outside the home varied widely from one EU country to the next. Less than half of the working-age men and women in Italy were employed outside the home, while in Denmark the figure was over 70 percent.

# CHAPTER 12

# Justice and Home Affairs

Justice and Home Affairs (JHA) is the EU's term for a wide range of internal security issues—such as crime, terrorism, and illegal immigration—plus the Union's common policies for dealing with them. These are matters that affect the daily lives of European citizens, and many people accept the idea that they can be addressed most effectively at the EU level. However, even when the member states reach agreements in the area of JHA, implementing them has been slow because national law enforcement agencies tend to be jealous of their prerogatives.

For the central and eastern European countries, meeting EU standards in the area of JHA was one of the most important tests they have faced in the accession process. Their communist-era police and justice systems were based on Stalinist models and needed drastic reform to make them compatible with EU systems, so the Union has monitored their progress very closely. Within a few years after joining the EU, the new members will be responsible for managing the Union's eastern border to prevent illegal immigration and other crimes, but it will have to be done without creating a new iron curtain dividing Europe. The accession countries were very concerned with maintaining economic ties with their eastern neighbors. Many of the new EU members also had close cultural ties with people of their own ethnic groups in neighboring countries such as Ukraine.

This chapter begins by noting how Justice and Home Affairs policy has evolved in the EU. The Amsterdam Treaty in 1997 finally brought JHA to the top of the EU agenda, and the September 2001 terrorist attacks in the United States provided new impetus. The chapter concludes with a look at how well prepared the candidates are in the area of JHA, particularly their preparations for managing the EU's eastern border.

## COOPERATION BETWEEN EU GOVERNMENTS ON JHA

Because the culture of the police and judicial systems varies considerably from one European country to the next, law enforcement officials have been reluctant to share intelligence about terrorism and other crimes for fear that their sources and methods may be compromised. Nevertheless, changes have taken place over the past thirty years, and the level of trust has increased. Judicial and law enforcement agencies have gradually begun to work together more closely.

### The Trevi Group

The first cooperation began in the mid-1970s, when senior law enforcement officials of European Community (EC) member states began to meet regularly as the "Trevi Group" to address the growing problem of terrorism in western Europe. Their activities were secret, and little information about them has been made public, but it was reported that they broadened their focus to include organized crime.[1] Figure 12.1 lists some of the most serious incidents that occurred since the early 1970s.

### The Schengen Agreement

In 1985, France, Germany, and the Benelux countries agreed to abolish their internal borders with one another and to strengthen the external border around their territory. The agreement, which was signed in the village of Schengen in Luxembourg, came into force in 1995 and was brought into the EU system by the Treaty of Amsterdam in 1997. The territory covered by the Schengen Agreement grew as new members joined the community. Some border controls were relaxed almost immediately, but the agreement could not be fully implemented until effective controls on the community's external borders were in place, a process that required years of negotiation.

The Schengen Agreement initially excluded the four southern EU members—Italy, Spain, Portugal, and Greece—because the northern members did not fully trust their law enforcement standards, and because the coastal areas of the southern states were among the favorite entry routes for illegal immigrants. Italy finally acceded to the agreement in 1990, followed by Portugal and Spain in 1991, and Greece in 1992.

The British chose not to join Schengen because they wanted to maintain tighter security arrangements to restrict the movement of non-EC nation-

**Figure 12.1**
**Thirty Years of Terrorism in Europe**

| | |
|---|---|
| 1972 | Palestinian Black September group kills eleven Israeli athletes at the Munich Olympics. |
| 1974 | IRA bomb kills twenty-one in a pub in Birmingham, England. |
| 1977 | Red Army Faction murders three public figures in Germany. |
| 1978 | Popular Front for Liberation of Palestine kills two El Al aircrew members in London. |
| 1978 | Red Brigade assassinates former Italian Prime Minister Aldo Moro. |
| 1979 | IRA bomb kills twenty-one soldiers in Northern Ireland; Lord Mountbatten assassinated in Republic of Ireland. |
| 1980 | Italian neo-fascists plant a bomb at Bologna train station, killing eighty-five people and injuring two hundred others. |
| 1984 | IRA kills five people and injures thirty in an attempt to kill British Prime Minister Thatcher at Brighton. |
| 1986 | Libyan terrorists kill three (including two U.S. servicemen) in "La Belle" nightclub, Berlin. |
| 1987 | E.T.A. (Basque separatists) kills twenty-one people in Barcelona. |
| 1988 | Libyan terrorists blow up Pan Am plane over Lockerbie, Scotland, killing 259 on board and eleven on the ground. |
| 1995 | Bomb in Paris Metro kills eight, injures more than eighty-six in first of a spate of bomb attacks in Paris. |
| 1996 | IRA car bomb kills two, injures more than one hundred in London Docklands. |
| 1998 | IRA car bomb kills twenty-nine in Omagh, Northern Ireland. |
| 2000 | Greek left-wing group kills U.K. defense attaché in Athens. |

*Source:* Press reports

als into the United Kingdom. Ireland stayed out of Schengen in order to maintain its common travel area with Britain, as did Denmark, to maintain its free movement arrangement with the other Nordic countries. However, Norway and Iceland, both non-EU members, were allowed to join Schengen, which removed the rationale for Denmark's opt-out.

## Schengen II

It took nearly five years to draw up a convention covering all the issues involved in removing internal border controls in the Schengen area. The new convention, known as Schengen II, was signed in 1990. It established guidelines for cooperation by national police and judicial systems and common policies on visas, asylum seekers, and illegal immigrants, but political issues delayed its implementation for several years. There were also difficulties in organizing the Schengen Information System, which was a computerized database on missing persons, arrest warrants, false passports, stolen vehicles, and other types of information needed by units managing the EU's external border. This system was eventually put in use with strict rules to protect the privacy of individuals and the confidentiality of the information.

## EUROPOL

Despite strong political opposition to anything resembling a European supranational police force, an agreement was reached in 1993 on creation of EUROPOL, a system for exchanging police intelligence. However, implementation of the agreement was delayed until 1996 by a dispute over whether to give the European Court of Justice responsibility for interpreting the EUROPOL convention.[2]

Meanwhile, the member states launched the EUROPOL Drugs Unit (EDU) in The Hague in 1994. The EDU did not undertake police operations of its own, but provided intelligence support to operations by the member states. While the members haggled over whether to involve the Court of Justice in EUROPOL activities, they broadened the EDU's scope to include illegal immigration, trafficking in human beings, money laundering, and stolen vehicles. In other words, the EUROPOL Drugs Unit became EUROPOL, but it lacked competence in the area of terrorism until this was added in 2001 after the September 11 terrorist attacks in the United States. EUROPOL was also given authority to help EU member states deal with other serious cross-border crimes.[3]

## The Amsterdam Treaty

By the mid-1990s, EU leaders realized that closer cooperation on JHA matters was needed and that it would help increase public support for European integration. Wars in former Yugoslavia had driven millions of refugees into the EU countries, along with Russian and Ukrainian organized crime gangs and illegal immigrants from all the poor countries of Asia and Africa. Many EU citizens were concerned that an enlargement of the Union would bring large-scale immigration from central and eastern

Europe, and they feared that the new member states would be incapable of managing the EU's eastern border.

However, within the member states there was little policy coordination in the area of JHA. Typical of the confused state of play was the failure to bring together all of the dozens of agreements between member states on border controls that had been added to the original Schengen accords. This made it impossible for the candidate countries to know exactly what laws they were supposed to adopt.

When the Dutch took over the EU presidency in the first half of 1997, they proposed moving the whole range of JHA issues into the community framework. This was an important change, because member states would no longer be able to veto initiatives. Border controls, visas, judicial cooperation on civil matters, and policies on refugees, immigration, and asylum would all become subject to community rules after a five-year transition period.

### Tampere Summit

When Finland assumed the EU presidency in the second half of 1999, it held the Union's first summit meeting that focused exclusively on JHA issues. EU leaders brought a wide range of proposals to their meeting in the town of Tampere, and they committed their governments to improving cooperation on more than two hundred JHA-related issues. This was almost as large an undertaking as preparing for the single market. Nevertheless, bureaucratic resistance remained strong, and implementation of the initiatives agreed at Tampere proceeded slowly.[4]

## IMPACT OF TERRORIST ATTACKS IN THE UNITED STATES ON EU POLICIES

The September 11, 2001, terrorist attacks in New York and Washington spurred the EU member states to much faster implementation of JHA policies. It happened that a meeting of EU justice and interior ministers had already been scheduled for September 20. At this meeting, the ministers approved about thirty measures to increase cooperation between police and intelligence services, strengthen procedures to track money laundering, tighten border controls, and provide a broader counterterrorism role for EUROPOL, including intelligence sharing with the United States. A minister commented afterward that they accomplished more at that single meeting than they had during several previous years.[5]

On September 21, 2001, EU heads of government also met and declared their complete support for the United States in its counterterrorism campaign. JHA Commissioner Vitorino was able to present proposals for common policies on immigration and asylum at the summit. These policies were not improvised in response to the attacks in the United States, but had been carefully crafted months earlier by the Commission. It was, however, a public relations coup for the EU to be able to announce that they were enacting timely measures to strengthen their cooperation in the field of JHA. Many EU leaders flew to Washington and met with President Bush. Belgian Prime Minister Verhofstadt, who held the EU presidency, met with President Bush shortly after the attacks and was given a five-page list of recommendations for advancing U.S.-EU cooperation against terrorist networks, including those based in Europe.

On October 19, the justice and interior ministers met again in Brussels and approved another series of JHA measures, some of which had been pending for years. The most important measures were a common definition of terrorism, a common list of organizations suspected of terrorism, a list of serious crimes that involved crossing borders, and a common search-and-arrest warrant. Because of the new sense of urgency, many of the EU's new JHA measures, including increased airport security, were implemented almost immediately.

The common definition of terrorism faced some opposition on the grounds that it was too broad and might restrict freedom of speech and assembly. The measure also prescribed prison sentences for persons convicted of planning and carrying out terrorist acts. The arrest warrant proposal, including a list of thirty-two crimes to which it applied, was almost blocked by the Italian government. Some said this was because Prime Minister Berlusconi feared he could be charged with certain crimes under the proposed measure. However, Berlusconi backed down under pressure from the leaders of Britain and Spain. Both the arrest warrant and the common definition of terrorism were approved three months after the attacks in the United States, much faster than JHA matters are usually dealt with in the EU.[6]

In December 2001, the EU expanded its list of terrorist organizations to include Irish, Basque, Greek, and Middle Eastern extremist groups. The significance of this action was that all EU member states were required to freeze the assets and arrest any members of these groups who were found on their territory. The eastern European candidates for EU membership were also allowed to propose the names of organizations to be included on the list. In the same month, the EU issued a list of nineteen individuals whose assets were to be frozen because they were believed to be aiding and abetting terrorism.[7]

The terrorist attacks in the United States and the new counterterrorist measures announced in Europe may have increased the political resistance in EU countries to more liberal immigration and asylum policies. Britain and Germany were the only Union governments that had made serious efforts to develop immigration policies that took account of their need for skilled workers. However, in 2002, EU leaders began to consider the need for common policies on immigration and asylum.[8]

Figure 12.2    Justice and Home Affairs Commissioner
Antonio Vitorino spearheaded the effort to enact
strong antiterror measures after the September 11
attacks. *Credit:* European Commission Audiovisual
Library.

## Political Asylum

Many European countries adopted very generous asylum policies after
World War II because so little was done to help Jews fleeing Nazi Germany during the war. However, by the end of the century, it was clear that
many people with no legitimate claim to political asylum were taking
advantage of this loophole in order to remain in Europe more or less
indefinitely. Public opinion in most EU countries favored tighter standards for granting asylum, and the focus on terrorism added political
pressure in this direction. Certain right-wing parties in Italy, Denmark,
Austria, and elsewhere in the Union were not above suggesting that all
asylum seekers should be turned away as potential terrorists.[9]

A few EU governments tightened their immigration and asylum laws after September 11, 2001, although the terrorist attacks may not have been the main reason. For example, the newly elected center-right government in Denmark proposed legislation to restrict the travel of refugees and increase the period they must wait for permanent resident status from three to seven years. The new laws would also abolish the granting of humanitarian asylum in some cases, and anyone under the age of twenty-four would be prohibited from bringing a foreign spouse to live in Denmark. In Germany, the highest court blocked a new law that would have opened the door to more skilled foreign workers.[10]

## IMPLICATIONS FOR THE EASTERN ENLARGEMENT

After the terrorist attacks on the United States, the main focus of justice and interior ministers in the EU was on creating common programs to combat terrorism, but they realized this called for a fresh look at how the eastern enlargement would affect the Union's internal security.[11] The Commission also gave special attention to JHA issues in its October 2001 report on the status of the accession process. All of the candidate countries except Romania had opened the JHA chapter in their accession negotiations by that date, but none had closed it.

The Commission said most of the candidates were making good progress on external border controls and on their implementation of visa, immigration, and asylum policies. However, some of the EU's plans for managing the eastern border were still under discussion because the Commission was anxious not to create a new iron curtain between the Union and former Soviet republics. The Commission's status report also said that judicial reform was incomplete in most of the eastern European countries, and they were told to address problems related to the conduct of their police and the treatment of prisoners.

The Commission also cited human rights problems and discrimination against ethnic minorities as major areas of concern, although it noted improvements in the way Estonia and Latvia dealt with their Russian minorities. They also noted improvement in the treatment of the Roma (Gypsies) in Hungary, the Czech Republic, Slovakia, and Romania.

### Poland

Poland would be responsible for managing long stretches of the EU's border with Belarus, Ukraine, and the Russian enclave of Kaliningrad. As the largest candidate country, Poland faced some of the most difficult tasks in meeting EU standards for JHA. For example, by the summer of 2003 it would have to implement EU visa regulations for Russia, Belarus, and Ukraine, which would mean hiring three hundred additional officials and opening new consulates in those countries. Moreover, it would inevitably lead to some reduction in Poland's trade with those countries, which was vital to eastern Poland and worth the equivalent of billions of dollars a year.[12]

In its October 2001 report, the Commission noted that Poland had made progress concerning border management and border guards, but needed to work harder in the area of customs and in the fight against organized crime. When President Kwasniewski visited Russia in June 2002, he rejected President Putin's request for a special "corridor" through Poland to allow visa-free travel by Russian citizens to and from Kaliningrad.[13]

### Czech Republic

After enlargement, the Czech Republic would be the only one of the new eastern members that would not be responsible for managing part of the EU's external border. Nevertheless, the Commission praised the Czech Republic for adopting a high-quality Schengen Action Plan and for improving the system of checks at official border crossings. However, the Commission also noted continuing problems of intercepting illegal immigrants and the need to combat organized crime. The Czech Republic's efforts to improve the status of the Roma minority were noted by the Commission, but it said that more public funding was needed for this program.

### Slovakia

After enlargement, Slovakia would be responsible for a portion of the EU's external border with Ukraine. The Commission noted that Slovakia had made some progress in regard to border controls, visa policy, and police cooperation and had also adopted a Schengen Action Plan, but much work remained to be done, particularly in strengthening administrative capacities. The Commission noted Slovakia's efforts to protect minority rights, particularly regarding the Hungarian and Roma minorities, but the Slovakian government needed to provide more money for these programs.

### Slovenia

Slovenia's borders with Bosnia and Croatia places it on a major route used by illegal migrants, refugees, and asylum seekers from many distant and poor countries. However, it was the richest and one of the smallest of the ten candidate countries, and its border problems were more easily dealt with than those of large countries like Poland and Romania. In 2001, Slovenia reinforced its staff for processing asylum applications and developed a Schengen Action Plan, but the Commission said it still needed to improve its preparations for border control and create more adequate facilities for asylum seekers. The Commission also gave Slovenia good marks for judicial reform, but said that it should address police behavior because of reported cases of ill treatment of prisoners.

### Hungary

Hungary's central location placed it on the route used by large numbers of refugees, asylum seekers and illegal immigrants trying to enter the EU from poor countries in Asia, Africa, and the Middle East. Many were smuggled across the border from Ukraine by professional traffickers, but some also entered or tried to enter Hungary from Slovakia, Romania, Serbia, Croatia, and Slovenia. The volume of people smuggled into and through Hungary doubled every year from 1995 to 2000, according to Hungarian border guards, who estimated that there were sixty thousand illegal border crossings in 2000, with forty thousand of the illegals caught.[14]

The situation was complicated by the fact that large numbers of ethnic Hungarians were living in the neighboring countries. Some, particularly those in Ukraine, depended on what income they could earn by commuting to jobs in Hungary or trading across the border. In 2001, Hungary's Status Law granted special economic and social benefits to ethnic Hungarians in neighboring countries, a move that complicated Hungary's relations with several of these states. The EU has provided substantial aid to Hungary's border police under the PHARE aid program, and Hungary will follow the Union's guidelines in the way it operates its border controls, but Hungarian officials hoped they would be allowed some flexibility because the relationship with each of its neighbors was different.[15]

The Commission's 2001 assessment noted that Hungary had made considerable progress in the area of visa and asylum policy. Asylum procedures were more efficient, and better facilities were provided for people while their applications were being processed. Judicial reform had also progressed but needed better budget support, and the Commission warned that Hungary needed to address police behavior because there had been reports of ill treatment of prisoners. In regard to the large Roma minority, Hungary had adopted new policies and provided more funds to improve their access to education, employment, social policy, and legal assistance, but the Commission said Hungary must do more to eliminate widespread discrimination against this group and help them to participate more actively in public life.

## Estonia

Estonia had a common border with Russia, and relations with its huge neighbor were improving. The only deficiencies in border management noted by the Commission were in implementing customs regulations and a need to improve coordination between Estonia's law enforcement bodies. Russian leaders resented Estonia's assertion of its independence in 1991 and its refusal to grant automatic citizenship to its large Russian minority. As part of a campaign to intimidate Estonia in the early 1990s, Russian leaders accused Estonia of serious human rights violations and of allowing people-smugglers and criminal gangs to transit its territory.[16] Nevertheless, relations improved toward the end of the decade, and Estonia's progress in integrating its Russian minority, including changes in its naturalization procedures, received mainly positive comments by the Commission. The Russian government even relaxed its opposition to Estonia, Latvia, and Lithuania joining NATO.

## Latvia

Like Estonia, Latvia had a common border with Russia and a large Russian minority. Its relations with Russia have followed much the same pattern as Estonia's, going from very bad in the early 1990s to near normal by 2002. Latvia also has a common border with Belarus and a much smaller Belarusian minority. The Commission's comments on Latvia's naturalization procedures and other efforts to integrate these minorities into Latvian society were generally positive and similar to its comments regarding Estonia. The Commission also noted Latvia's progress on visa policy and border control, and its adoption of an action plan to prepare to join the Schengen system of open internal borders. However, the Commission said the alignment of Latvia's laws with EU laws on migration and asylum should be completed. Upgrading border management was another important priority, and Latvia was told to increase its efforts to combat organized crime, drug trafficking, money laundering, fraud, and corruption.[17]

## Lithuania

Lithuania had borders with Latvia, Belarus, Poland, and the Russian enclave of Kaliningrad. Because its Russian minority was much smaller than those in Estonia and Latvia, Lithuania adopted much easier procedures for naturalization than those two countries, and consequently it had a less acrimonious relationship with Russia. For example, in the early 1990s, an arrangement was negotiated whereby a limited number of unarmed Russian troops could cross Lithuania by train to the Russian enclave of Kaliningrad.[18] Under EU rules, however, Russian citizens would be required from mid-2003 on to have a "facilitated transit document" (which amounted to a visa) to enter or transit Lithuania. The issue was resolved in November 2002 after lengthy negotiations between the EU and Russia.

Lithuania had a Schengen Action Plan, and the Commission noted that the country had strengthened its external border. In addition to sustaining these efforts, the Commission also told Lithuania to give priority to judicial reform and anticorruption measures.

### Romania

Bordered by Bulgaria, Serbia, Hungary, Ukraine, and Moldova, Romania was a natural corridor for refugees and illegal immigrants. For this reason, during the height of the illegal immigration problem in the 1990s, the EU required Romanians and Bulgarians seeking to enter the Union to obtain visas, but this requirement was canceled in 2001. In its 2001 review of the accession process, the Commission noted that Romania had made progress in its own visa policy and border control, but still needed to upgrade its facilities for border management.[19]

The Commission also took note of the fact that new legislation was approved extending the use of minority languages, and a national strategy for improving the condition of the large Roma minority was also adopted. The Roma gained greater access to education in Romania, but efforts were still needed to combat widespread discrimination and improve their living conditions.

Reform of Romania's childcare system was well under way for the large number of orphans and abandoned children, but the living conditions in orphanages still needed to be improved. Important legislation had been passed by Romania regarding the treatment of asylum seekers and refugees; penal reforms had been adopted; and during 2001, Romania's Regional Center for Combating Transborder Crime reportedly arrested 106 persons involved in trafficking human beings.[20]

### Bulgaria

Surrounded by Balkan states (Turkey, Greece, Macedonia, Serbia, and Romania), Bulgaria had a major stake in promoting stability and the rule of law in this traditionally unstable region. The Commission noted Bulgaria's strong support for efforts to promote better relations among Balkan states, including the EU's Stability Pact for southeastern Europe and a Bulgarian initiative to create a Southeast Europe Brigade.[21] Some progress was also noted in Bulgaria's control of its external borders, but the EU still regarded Bulgaria as a major transit country for illegal immigrants attempting to enter the Union.

The Commission mentioned Bulgaria's adoption of national strategies for judicial reform and combating corruption, but it noted that Bulgaria still needed to implement these plans. Some progress had been made on the training of police in human rights and combating trafficking of human beings, but police behavior still needed considerable improvement. The situation of children in orphanages and homes for children with mental disabilities was criticized by the Commission, which also noted that the Roma continued to suffer from widespread discrimination. Therefore, in spite of making important progress, Bulgaria had its work cut out in order to reach EU standards in justice and home affairs. Bulgaria and Romania would not be in the group of countries joining the Union in 2004, but they were considered to be on track to join in 2007.

## CONCLUSION

For years, most public discussion of the eastern enlargement began with a series of pessimistic assumptions about the costs and risks involved, particularly in the area of JHA. In 2002, Enlargement Commissioner Verheugen argued that enlargement would broaden the area of freedom, security, and justice that the EU was trying to create. A few EU leaders began to echo Verheugen's optimistic statements, while insisting that the candidate countries must be held to the highest possible standard in the area of JHA. Commissioner Verheugen assured them that the new countries would be required to do an even better job of implementing EU laws and policies than the existing member states.[22]

## NOTES

1. Desmond Dinan, *Ever Closer Union*, 2d ed. (Boulder, Colo.: Lynne Rienner Publishers, 1999), pp. 439–40. Dinan notes that the interior ministers also expanded their scope to cover the growing problem of soccer hooliganism.

2. Ibid., pp. 446–47.

3. Heather Grabbe, "Breaking New Ground in Internal Security," in Edward Bannerman and others, *Europe After September 11th* (London: Centre for European Reform, 2001), pp. 68–69. Since September 11, EUROPOL has been given greater powers to obtain information from EU member governments and to coordinate arrests, but it has not so far been granted the power to work independently of national governments. EUROPOL also has been given a mandate to work with its U.S. counterparts on terrorism and to be the central point for exchanging information with the U.S. agencies.

4. Emek M. Ucarer, "Justice and Home Affairs in the Aftermath of September 11: Opportunities and Challenges," European Union Studies Association, *EUSA Review* (spring 2002): pp. 1, 3–5.

5. Heather Grabbe, "Breaking New Ground in Internal Security," pp. 63–75.

6. Ibid., pp. 63–66. Grabbe considers the common arrest warrant a giant leap for the EU, because it will require the member states to trust each other's judicial systems.

7. "European Union Expands Its List of Terrorist Groups, Requiring Sanctions and Arrests," *New York Times* (December 29, 2001).

8. "Blair Urges Unity among Europe's Moderate Parties," *Financial Times* (May 13, 2002).

9. "Fischer Warns against Coalitions with Rightwing, Populist Parties," *Financial Times* (May 8, 2002).

10. "Danish Immigration Policy Attacked," *Financial Times* (May 28, 2002).

11. "Europe Ponders Uniform Security for Its Borders," *New York Times* (October 7, 2001).

12. "Worried in Warsaw," *Financial Times* (January 10, 2002).

13. "Serious Business for the EU and Russia," *Financial Times* (May 29, 2002), and "Status of Baltic Enclave Overshadows Summit," *Financial Times* (May 30, 2002).

14. "Asian Migrants Head for Europe's Eastern Gateway," *Financial Times* (October 11, 2000): p. 3.

15. Of Hungary's seven neighbors, Austria is an EU member, and Slovakia, Romania, and Slovenia will be eventually, so the borders with them will be "internal" Union borders. Nevertheless, these countries will all have to continue to be on the alert for illegal immigrants trying to use their countries as corridors to go further west. While Ukraine has no prospects for joining the EU, Croatia and Serbia, Hungary's other two neighbors, may eventually join the Union.

16. Patrick Heenan and Monique Lamontagne (eds.), *The Central and East European Handbook* (Chicago: Fitzroy Dearborn, 1999), pp. 27–30.

17. European Commission, *Making a Success of Enlargement,* October 2001, p. 46.

18. Heenan and Lamontagne, *Central and East European Handbook,* p. 33.

19. European Commission, *Making a Success of Enlargement,* October 2001, pp. 54–56.

20. Ibid. In his October 2001 speech at Johns Hopkins University School for Advanced International Studies, Washington, D.C., Prime Minister Nastase said the FBI group seconded to the Romanian center had been very helpful in these arrests.

21. European Commission, *Making a Success of Enlargement,* October 2001, pp. 32–33.

22. "EU Entrants Not Equipped to Fight Corruption, Says Report," *Financial Times* (June 6, 2002).

# CHAPTER 13

# Enlargement and the EU's Security and Defense Policy

The eastern enlargement is closely linked to the EU's security and defense policy, as well as its internal security (JHA) regime. As the EU and NATO struggle to define their defense roles, most of the central and eastern European states will be full members of both organizations by 2004. They will bring the EU close to the arc of unstable countries from the former Soviet republics through the Middle East to North Africa and the Balkans. During the cold war, the eastern European states were a buffer zone separating western Europe from the Soviet Union and allowing little contact between the two regions. They do not want to play that role again when they join the EU. Instead, they want to be involved in developing policies to stabilize and trade with these neighboring regions.[1]

## PREPARING FOR THE NEXT ENLARGEMENT

The EU's Copenhagen summit in December 2002 not only welcomed eight new central and eastern European members (and two strategic islands in the Mediterranean), but also set the stage for a further enlargement of the Union to include all of southeastern Europe, the region that has been an important seedbed of EU foreign and security policy.

Romania and Bulgaria were reaffirmed to be on track for full EU membership by 2007. Turkey was told that accession negotiations would proceed "without further delay" if they met the Copenhagen criteria for membership by December 2004. In return, Turkish leaders promised to try to resolve the divided status of Cyprus, and they agreed to let the EU make use of NATO assets in support of its security and defense policy. This cleared the way for an important expansion of the EU's security role in the Balkans, where it will take charge of police training in Bosnia and a small peacekeeping operation in Macedonia. EU leaders also hope to assume responsibility for the much larger peacekeeping operation in Bosnia.[2]

In this chapter, we look first at how the EU's Common Foreign and Security Policy (CFSP) has evolved, note how the central and eastern European countries have sought increased security through membership in European regional organizations, and examine the state of transatlantic relations. Finally, we consider how membership in the EU and NATO will enhance the security of the central and eastern European countries while also contributing to the development of those two institutions.


## THE EU'S FOREIGN AND SECURITY POLICY

For many years, the European Union was an economic giant with little clout in foreign affairs, except in the area of trade policy. Although the fifteen EU member states had an astonishing total of forty thousand diplomats serving in their embassies abroad, they were mostly concerned with promoting their own governments' interests, seldom with broader Union affairs. During the 1970s and 1980s, a process called European Political Cooperation led to the formation of many working groups to draft position papers, and EU leaders issued statements on hundreds of issues worldwide. This helped to bring their national positions closer together, but the requirement for unanimity meant the EU's pronouncements were often bland and ineffective.[3]

From the early 1990s, the ethnic wars in the Balkans and former Soviet Union finally drove home the lesson that Europe faced serious security threats and needed to be able to defend itself against them, not least because the U.S. government's interest in Europe seemed to be declining. Figure 13.1 lists key steps in the evolution of EU foreign and security policy.


### Common Foreign and Security Policy

The European Union treaty of 1992 called for the creation of a Common Foreign and Security Policy (CFSP), but at first this was hardly more than a name with little to back it up. Gradually, however, it began to have some meaning as the EU responded by trial and error to the continuing crises and ethnic wars in the Balkans. As EU External Affairs Commissioner Chris Patten put it,

The Balkans...taught us that Europe needed to be capable of mounting large-scale peace enforcement operations and sustaining them. They taught us that we needed a policing capacity...to keep the order after fighting is over...And they taught us

**Figure 13.1**
**Development of EU Foreign and Security Policy**

---

1969    European Community launches European Political Cooperation (EPC).

1992    EU Treaty calls for a Common Foreign and Security Policy (CFSP) and adds a commissioner for external affairs.

1997    Amsterdam Treaty creates the High Representative for CFSP with a small staff in the Council of Ministers.

1998    Franco-British St. Malo initiative calls for European defense force that can supplement NATO or act alone.

1999    Kosovo war demonstrates huge disparity between U.S. and European military capabilities and diverging security policy concerns.

1999    At their Cologne and Helsinki summits, EU leaders agree to create a rapid reaction force that can act alone.

2001    United States initially declines, and then accepts European offers of military support in battle against Taliban in Afghanistan. Europeans eventually play a major role in peacekeeping and reconstruction in Afghanistan.

2003    EU takes over NATO's peacekeeping role in Macedonia as well as UN police-training program in Bosnia.

---

that we must be better at designing and delivering post-conflict assistance to consolidate the peace.[4]

The French and British governments, which had the largest numbers of troops involved in Balkan peacekeeping, began to discuss the need for an EU defense force, and found they agreed on many issues. In a 1998 meeting in the French town of St. Malo, the heads of the two governments issued a joint statement on the role and possible composition of such a European force.[5]

In their June 1999 summit at Cologne, EU leaders chose Javier Solana, the highly respected secretary general of NATO, to be the main focal point of their Common Foreign and Security Policy. Supported by a very small policy unit of only twenty-six diplomats with offices in the Council of Ministers, Solana concentrated on a few key issues in the EU's "near abroad," particularly the Balkans, the Middle East, and relations with Russia. His small staff and a budget equivalent to $35 million a year were even less than the foreign minister of Luxembourg had to work with, but by concentrating on a few key issues, rather than reacting superficially to many, he was able to produce results.

EU leaders had begun to face the fact that they must be able to back their security policy with force if necessary, so at their Helsinki summit in December 1999, they agreed to form a rapid reaction force of up to sixty thousand troops by 2003 to carry out humanitarian and peacekeeping missions. They also created a Political and Security Committee (PSC) composed of ambassadors from the fifteen member states to channel proposals to senior ministers for decision.

The PSC meets regularly in Brussels, is chaired by Solana (particularly when they are dealing with a serious crisis like an outbreak of fighting in the Balkans). They are advised by a Military Committee and Military Staff located in the Council of Ministers, where Solana serves as secretary general.

In 2001, the EU achieved its first important success through its more focused approach. It managed to stave off a potential civil war in Macedonia between the ethnic Slav majority of the population and the ethnic Albanian minority who formed about a quarter of the population. By offering aid and the possibility of eventual EU membership, Solana coaxed the Macedonian government into accepting the Albanian minority's most urgent demands for autonomy. NATO provided a peacekeeping force of seven hundred European troops to assist in disarming Albanian insurgents, and as noted earlier, the EU assumed responsibility for this operation in 2003.[6]

In March 2002, Solana succeeded in persuading Serbia and Montenegro (the only remaining pieces of the former Yugoslav federation) to stay together in a new union. The EU was concerned to prevent further fragmentation of the western Balkans, including demands by ethnic Albanians in Kosovo for independence from Serbia, and was also worried that a split-up of Serbia and Montenegro could destabilize neighboring Macedonia.[7]

### Paying for Defense

Were the EU governments willing to support the European Security and Defense Policy (ESDP) by paying the costs it would entail? This question was important because the defense budgets of most Union countries declined in real terms throughout the 1990s, and defense spending generally had much lower priority than social programs in EU member states. In Poland, Hungary, and the Czech Republic, defense spending also tended to decline after those countries were admitted to NATO in 1999, and it was probably realistic to expect the same to happen after seven more former communist states join the alliance. However, a study by an American think tank concluded that the EU could afford its rapid reaction force without larger defense budgets if member states were willing to transfer funds from their national defense programs.[8]

## Pooling Resources

By the end of 2002, EU leaders were beginning to talk seriously about the need for increased sharing of their considerable diplomatic and military assets. Plans to create an EU diplomatic service and a network of EU embassies were said to have wide support, and EU leaders were beginning to realize they could have much better equipped defense forces without increased spending if they were willing to share training, transport, and logistical services.[9] However, even if these plans materialize, EU countries will continue for the foreseeable future to have their own foreign ministries and military forces to serve purely national interests.

## Too Many Chiefs

In the EU's quest for a more effective foreign and security policy, another key problem was the number of people trying to serve as the EU's official spokesman. Javier Solana's appointment as High Representative for foreign and security policy left him with many competitors in this area. The prime minister of the country holding the EU's rotating presidency often represented the EU in bilateral dialogues with other governments and in international organizations, and the Commission president and heads of other EU governments also undertook diplomatic missions. The commissioner for external relations controlled an EU foreign aid budget equal to nearly $10 billion a year and headed a staff of some eight hundred Commission officials, which was many times larger than Solana's staff. By the end of 2002, the EU's constitutional convention had failed to reach a consensus on whether the Union's "foreign secretary" should be a member of the Commission or the Council of Ministers.

## CENTRAL AND EASTERN EUROPEAN STATES' QUEST FOR SECURITY

Ideally, each of the central and eastern European states wants to be surrounded by countries that are democratic, peaceful, and prosperous. This means not only avoiding conflict with their neighbors, but also helping the less-advanced ones achieve political and economic stability.

As figure 13.4 shows, the eastern European states have followed a practice of joining every important European regional organization, regardless of whether or not it had a security and defense role. For example, the Council of Europe serves as a gatekeeper for other organizations by admitting only those countries that have achieved a certain level of political development and protection for the rights of its citizens. Eastern European leaders reasoned that the more links they had with the West, the more likely it was that western powers would come to their aid if they were again threatened by a hegemonic power such as Russia.

Figure 13.2  Javier Solana, the EU's High Representative for
Common Foreign and Security Policy, has focused mainly on the
Balkans and Middle East crises. *Credit:* European Commission
Audiovisual Library.

After regaining their independence in 1989, some leaders of former
communist states considered following the example of Finland and Austria and adopting a policy of neutrality, but they abandoned this idea and
applied for NATO membership after Soviet interior ministry troops killed
civilian demonstrators in Lithuania and Latvia in early 1991. As soon as
they were allowed to, the eastern European states also began to apply for
membership in the EU and Western European Union (WEU), an alliance
with almost the same membership as the EU. However, joining NATO
was their first priority, because they viewed the U.S. commitment to
defend Europe as essential to their own security. As figure 13.4 shows,
NATO responded by inviting them to join a newly created North Atlantic
Cooperative Council.

Figure 13.3   External Affairs Commissioner Chris
Patten had a large staff and aid budget and concen-
trated much of his attention on former Soviet republics.
*Credit:* European Commission Audiovisual Library.

## The Western European Union

The WEU was created in 1954, largely as a device to get Germany into
NATO. For the next forty years, it played a very marginal role in European
security to avoid competing with NATO, but in the early 1990s, some EU
leaders favored making it the EU's defense arm. The WEU gave the eastern European states most of the privileges of full membership, while
NATO initially offered them the same limited status it gave the former
Soviet republics in its Partnership for Peace program. Therefore, some
eastern European leaders may have hoped the WEU would provide a
back door to early membership in NATO or the EU. However, the United
States made it clear that it wanted to choose the countries it was responsi-

**Figure 13.4**
**Central and Eastern European States and the European Regional Organizations**

---

1975   Eastern European states join the Conference on Security and Cooperation in Europe, which includes NATO and Warsaw Pact states.

1990–95   Most of the eastern states are admitted to the Council of Europe.

1991   Warsaw Pact Organization is disbanded, and most Soviet troops are withdrawn from central and eastern Europe.

1991   NATO creates the North Atlantic Cooperation Council (NACC), and invites all eastern European states to join.

1992   WEU establishes Forum for Consultation, exclusively for the central and eastern European states.

1994   NATO launches its Partnership for Peace, including almost every nation in Europe and central Eurasia.

1999   Hungary, Poland, and the Czech Republic join NATO two weeks before the start of the air war in Kosovo.

2000   The WEU is incorporated into the EU by the Treaty of Nice.

2002   At the NATO summit in Prague, Estonia, Latvia, Lithuania, Slovakia, Slovenia, Romania, and Bulgaria are invited to join the alliance.

2002   At the EU summit in Copenhagen, Estonia, Latvia, Lithuania, Poland, Hungary, the Czech Republic, Slovakia, Slovenia, Cyprus, and Malta are invited to join the Union. Turkey agrees to allow the EU to use NATO assets for humanitarian and peacekeeping missions.

---

ble for protecting, and EU leaders were equally determined to control access to the Union.[10]

### Eastern Europe and NATO

NATO membership continued to be the priority of many eastern European leaders because the effectiveness of NATO intervention in Bosnia in 1995–96 contrasted with EU diplomatic efforts that failed to resolve the conflict. In addition, while EU leaders made it plain that joining the Union would be a lengthy and difficult process, the United States seemed to support a relatively rapid expansion of NATO. In 1999, Poland, Hungary, and the Czech Republic became full members of the alliance just two weeks before the air war began in Kosovo. The war demonstrated a widening gap between U.S. and European defense capabilities, and was thus a major catalyst for the EU leaders' decision to develop an independent Union defense force. However, for the eastern Europeans, the main lesson of the war in Kosovo was that they had been right in viewing NATO as the primary and essential organization for European defense.[11]

## TRANSATLANTIC SECURITY RELATIONS

During the decades of the cold war, the United States and its European allies often had serious disagreements about security policy, but they rarely questioned the basic necessity for the alliance until the Soviet Union collapsed. A dozen years later, transatlantic arguments about security issues had become almost a daily occurrence, and Defense Secretary Rumsfeld made it clear that he saw little need for the advice or support of allies. U.S. and European officials increasingly focused on different threats to their security or different dimensions of the same threats.

### At Cross-Purposes in the Middle East

European leaders feared the political and economic repercussions of war and instability in the Middle East because of their dependence on Middle Eastern oil and because of the millions of unassimilated Muslims living in Europe. For these reasons, the European governments strongly supported the U.S. campaign against terrorism by sharing intelligence and countering international efforts at money laundering. EU leaders also assumed major responsibilities for peacekeeping and reconstruction in Afghanistan, even though the United States initially refused their offers of military support against the Taliban.

To attack the root causes of Islamic terrorism, European leaders tried to contain the conflict between Israel and the Palestinians. They urged the United States to continue its longstanding efforts in that regard and to support the cause of democratic reform throughout the Muslim world. However, the Bush administration seemed to prefer the opposite approach, supporting Israel's effort to crush the Palestinian resistance with military force and allying itself with repressive Muslim leaders for an invasion of Iraq to depose Saddam Hussein. Despite U.S. efforts to portray its campaign against Saddam as part of the "war on terrorism," many Europeans saw it as a distraction from the counterterrorism struggle and one that was likely to breed greatly increased support for Islamic terrorist organizations.[12]

### A Troubled Partnership in the Balkans

From 1990 to 2002, U.S. administrations tried to limit American involvement in the Balkans, and even when the Clinton administration mounted bombing campaigns in Bosnia and Kosovo, it tried to leave most of the peacekeeping and reconstruction tasks to the Europeans, who tended to resent this division of labor.

However, EU leaders have gradually recognized that keeping the peace in former Yugoslavia is a responsibility that they can and must accept. Despite their initial failures, the Balkan region has been the seedbed for the creation of an increasingly successful security policy. The EU has paid most of the costs of reconstruction in the former Yugoslav states, and it is taking over most of the military tasks of peacekeeping. Moreover, the EU has used the prospect of eventual membership in the Union to persuade these countries to begin to adopt EU political and economic standards.

### Trade Tensions Weaken the Alliance

During the cold war, trade disputes between the United States and the EU were common, but both sides were usually willing to compromise to avoid weakening the security relationship. However, since the collapse of the Soviet Union, these disputes have often led to prolonged and bitter wrangling, with each side inclined to go to bat for narrow domestic interests. Thus, haggling between the United States and the EU over farm subsidies held up a world trade agreement for several years in the early 1990s. More recently, the U.S. administration raised tariffs on imported steel by as much as 30 percent in an obvious bid for political support in the steel-producing states of Ohio, Pennsylvania, and West Virginia. The EU responded by threatening to impose sanctions on exports from those states.[13]

## ENLARGEMENT AND THE COMMON FOREIGN AND SECURITY POLICY

How will the eastern enlargement affect the EU's Common Foreign and Security Policy? Every enlargement of the EU has brought new ideas and new national interests that have been factored into EU foreign policy, and certainly the eastern enlargement will be no different. As we have seen, the original reason the new democracies sought to join the EU and NATO was to enhance their own security, and there is still some fear in these countries of a revival of Russian imperialism. However, a more immediate concern has been the widening gap between U.S. and European views on security issues, notably in the case of Iraq. The eastern states want the United States and Europe to repair their differences on security policy as soon as possible.

Since most of the eastern European states are strongly oriented toward the United States, they will resist any weakening of the Atlantic alliance and any tendency by its members to downgrade it to a political forum. To take the example of Poland, one of the most pro-American countries in

Europe, Warsaw's main security concern is that NATO might be weakened by policy conflicts between the United States and its European allies. When such conflicts have arisen, for example over Iraq, Polish officials have instinctively sided with the United States. When President Chirac said they should have remained silent on the issue, they reminded him that Polish foreign policy was made in Warsaw.

What military and other assets will the new member states bring to the EU? They have contributed military units to peacekeeping operations in the Balkans, which has taught them how to work with the military forces of the EU states. The addition of their territory and bases to the Union will probably be an even more important contribution. For example, Hungary has allowed NATO forces to use its bases to support peacekeeping in Bosnia and Kosovo, and Slovenia's port at Koper has also been important for logistical operations in the Balkans. The EU will undoubtedly find the same facilities useful when it takes over from NATO in the Balkan region.

Because the eastern European members of the EU will manage the Union's eastern and southern borders, they will be involved in shaping EU policy toward Russia, Ukraine, and other former Soviet republics. The eastern Europeans have many reasons for wanting good relations with these countries, including a mutual interest in trade. The new Union members are also helping to prepare some of the former Yugoslav republics such as Croatia for membership in the EU and NATO, so they are determined that the Union's borders will not become a new iron curtain.

## NOTES

1. The analytical views expressed in this chapter are the author's unless otherwise noted.

2. Judy Dempsey, "EU to Deploy Troops After Deal with NATO," *Financial Times* (December 16, 2002).

3. Steven Everts, *Shaping a Credible EU Foreign Policy* (London: Centre for European Reform, 2002), pp. 55–61.

4. Speech by Commissioner Chris Patten, "A Voice for Europe? The Future of the CFSP," Institute of European Affairs, Dublin, March 2001.

5. Anthony Forster and William Wallace, "Common Foreign and Security Policy," in *Policy-Making in the European Union*, ed. Helen Wallace and William Wallace, 4th ed. (Oxford: Oxford University Press, 2000), pp. 485–87.

6. "Spain Urges EU to Take Over NATO Military Operations in Macedonia," *Financial Times* (February 2, 2002), and "EU to Take Over Police Operations in Bosnia," *Financial Times* (January 29, 2002).

7. "Montenegro and Serbia Agree to Remain Together," *Financial Times* (March 15, 2002).

8. Charles Wolf, Jr. and Benjamin Zycher, *European Military Prospect, Economic Constraints, and the Rapid Reaction Force* (Santa Monica, Calif.: RAND, 2001), pp. 25–34.

9. Tim Garden and Charles Grant, "Europe Could Pack a Bigger Punch by Sharing," *Financial Times* (December 18, 2002); and George Parker and Daniel Dombey, "Support Grows for an EU Embassy Network," *Financial Times* (December 10, 2002).

10. Stuart Croft and others (eds.), *The Enlargement of Europe* (Manchester, U.K.: Manchester University Press, 1999), pp. 90–105.

11. Hungarian officials were reassured by the fact that the United States and other NATO members warned Serbian leader Slobodan Milosevic not to attack the large Hungarian minority in Serbia's Vojvodina province.

12. *The Economist*, "Special Report: America and Europe: Who Needs Whom?" (March 9, 2002): pp. 30–32.

13. David Broder, "Europe's Fury," *Washington Post* (March 27, 2002).

# CHAPTER 14

# Looking Beyond the EU's Eastern Enlargement

European public opinion strongly opposed the new U.S. doctrine of pre-emptive war and the invasion of Iraq without a clear UN mandate. The deep split in Atlantic relations and in the EU raised serious questions about the future of European integration:

- Would the Iraq crisis upset the eastern enlargement?
- What would the impact be on EU plans to expand into southeastern Europe?
- How will the war and transatlantic tensions affect the prospects for European integration?

## PROSPECTS FOR ENLARGEMENT

In February 2003, President Chirac warned the eastern states that France might block their entry into the EU unless they abstained from supporting U.S. policy on Iraq. He had the power to make good on his threat, but this would carry an enormous risk of destroying the European Union, and France would be one of the main losers if this happened.

Leaders of the eastern countries were angered by President Chirac's effort to silence them, but they were careful to avoid making the situation worse. They had no desire to contribute to friction within the EU or risk failing to become full members. They concentrated on the immediate task of building support in their countries for ratification of the accession treaties. In most of the candidate countries, polls showed the treaties were very likely to be ratified. Iraq was not an issue. The main opponents of EU membership were usually farmers who felt their interests were being neglected. A key factor would be the level of voter turnout, especially in Poland.

No referendum was scheduled in Cyprus, but talks aimed at uniting the island broke down in March 2003. The newly elected Turkish government was distracted by the Iraq crisis and failed to press the Turkish Cypriot negotiators to agree to a unified island. However, elections in the Turkish Cypriot community in December 2003 could produce new leaders who are more willing to unify Cyprus before it enters the EU.

## SOUTHEASTERN ENLARGEMENT

The eastern enlargement has begun to lay the groundwork for the EU's next major expansion into southeastern Europe. At the Copenhagen summit, Turkey's prime minister was told that Turkey could begin accession negotiations in 2005 if it met the basic criteria for EU membership. The Iraq crisis underscores the fact that the EU and Turkey have a strong mutual interest in working together to help stabilize the Middle East.

At Copenhagen, EU leaders also confirmed that Romania and Bulgaria were on track to join the Union in 2007. The support those two countries showed for the U.S. war in Iraq was criticized by some EU officials, but it would be impossible for the Union to pursue its goal of stabilizing southeastern Europe without the active involvement of Romania and Bulgaria. In fact, the foreign ministers of Greece, Turkey, Romania, and Bulgaria were working together for their countries' common interests, and Greece had become one of the main supporters of Turkey's membership in the Union.

Hungary and Slovenia were helping their neighbors in the western Balkans prepare for eventual membership. Croatia and Macedonia already had agreements with the EU covering many issues, and Croatia was likely to apply for membership soon, but first it would have to cooperate more fully with the War Crimes Tribunal in The Hague and improve its record on refugee resettlement.

The assassination of Serbia's prime minister in March 2003 was a reminder that the western Balkans were still awash in crime and corruption, which limited their access to foreign investment and condemned them to high unemployment. The EU would need to make skillful use of the prospect of membership, as it did in eastern Europe, to encourage these countries to make reforms.

## COMMON FOREIGN AND SECURITY POLICY

During the 1990s, EU leaders learned from their mistakes in former Yugoslavia, and they are now assuming responsibility for peacekeeping as well as reconstruction throughout the Balkan region. Turkey's agreement

Figure 14.1    Recep Tayyip Erdogan led his Justice and
Development Party (AKP) to a decisive victory in
Turkey's November 2002 election. He promised to institute the democratic reforms required by the EU in order
to qualify for membership in the Union. *Credit:* Embassy
of Turkey in Washington, D.C.

to allow the sharing of NATO assets cleared the way for EU peacekeeping
in Macedonia and Bosnia, and the EU's Balkan template for a common
foreign and security policy was being applied to other regions. While
Britain and France fought over Iraq at the UN, officials of the two governments were discussing how to make the EU's rapid reaction force more
effective. Europe's vital interests in the Middle East would compel it to
play an active role in the political and economic reconstruction of Iraq and
in the peace process between Israel and a Palestinian state.

## ENLARGEMENT AND INTEGRATION

The basic theme of this book has been that enlargement encourages integration. Much important work remained to be done in the final year before the new states were due to enter the Union. The preparation of a constitutional treaty was one of the most obvious tasks that should not be delayed by quarreling over Iraq policy. Monetary union had been rushed into place before enlargement made the process more difficult, but reforms of the Stability and Growth Pact were urgently needed to make the system more flexible. Rapid progress in the area of Justice and Home Affairs remained necessary—both the shaping of new EU policies and their implementation by the candidates—in order to make the EU safer and more secure after enlargement. Finally, the diplomatic train wreck that preceded the Iraq war showed that the EU needed to greatly strengthen its Common Foreign and Security Policy to protect its vital interests worldwide.

# Appendix

# "From Confederacy to Federation: Thoughts on the Finality of European Integration"

### EXCERPTS FROM A SPEECH BY JOSCHKA FISCHER
### AT THE HUMBOLDT UNIVERSITY IN BERLIN
### 12 MAY 2000

Fifty years ago almost to the day, Robert Schuman presented his vision of a "European Federation" for the preservation of peace. This heralded a completely new era in the history of Europe. European integration was the response to centuries of a precarious balance of powers on this continent which again and again resulted in terrible hegemonic wars culminating in the two World Wars between 1914 and 1945. The core of the concept of Europe after 1945 was and still is a rejection of the European balance-of-power principle and the hegemonic ambitions of individual states that had emerged following the Peace of Westphalia in 1648, a rejection which took the form of closer meshing of vital interests and the transfer of nation-state sovereign rights to supranational European institutions.

Fifty years on, Europe, the process of European integration, is probably the biggest political challenge facing the states and peoples involved, because its success or failure, indeed even just the stagnation of this process of integration, will be of crucial importance to the future of each and every one of us, but especially to the future of the young generation. And it is this process of European integration that is now being called into question by many people; it is viewed as a bureaucratic affair run by a faceless, soulless Eurocracy in Brussels—at best boring, at worst dangerous.

...Allow me, if you will, to cast aside for the duration of this speech the mantle of German Foreign Minister and member of the Government—a mantle which is occasionally rather restricting when it comes to reflecting on things in public—although I know it is not really possible to do so. But what I want to talk to you about today is not the operative challenges facing European policy over the next few months, not the current intergovernmental conference, the EU's enlargement to the east or all those other important issues we have to resolve today and tomorrow, but rather the possible strategic prospects for European integration far beyond the coming decade and the intergovernmental conference.

So let's be clear: this is not a declaration of the Federal Government's position, but a contribution to a discussion long begun in the public arena about the "finality" of European integration, and I am making it simply as a staunch European and German parliamentarian. I am all the more pleased, therefore, that, on the initiative of the Portuguese presidency, the last informal EU Foreign Ministers' Meeting in the Azores held a long, detailed and extremely productive discussion on this very topic, the finality of European integration, a discussion that will surely have consequences....

Quo vadis Europa? is the question posed once again by the history of our continent. And for many reasons the answer Europeans will have to give, if they want to do well by themselves and their children, can only be this: onwards to the completion of European integration. A step backwards, even just standstill or contentment with what has been achieved, would demand a fatal price of all EU member states and of all those who want to become members; it would demand a fatal price above all of our people. This is particularly true for Germany and the Germans.

The task ahead of us will be anything but easy and will require all our strength; in the coming decade we will have to enlarge the EU to the east and south-east, and this will in the end mean a doubling in the number of members. And at the same time, if we are to be able to meet this historic challenge and integrate the new member states without substantially denting the EU's capacity for action, we must put into place the last brick in the building of European integration, namely political integration.

The need to organize these two processes in parallel is undoubtedly the biggest challenge the Union has faced since its creation. But no generation can choose the challenges it is tossed by history, and this is the case here too. Nothing less than the end of the cold war and of the forced division of Europe is facing the EU and thus us with this task, and so today we need the same visionary energy and pragmatic ability to assert ourselves as was shown by Jean Monnet and Robert Schuman after the end of the Second World War. And like then, after the end of this last great European war, which was—as almost always—also a Franco-German war, this latest stage of European Union, namely eastern enlargement and the completion of political integration, will depend decisively on France and Germany.

Two historic decisions in the middle of last century fundamentally altered Europe's fate for the better: firstly, the USA's decision to stay in Europe, and secondly France's and Germany's commitment to the principle of integration, beginning with economic links.

The idea of European integration and its implementation not only gave rise to an entirely new order in Europe—to be more exact, in Western Europe—but European history underwent a fundamental about-turn. Just compare the history of Europe in the first half of the 20th century with that in the second half and you will immediately understand what I mean. Germany's perspective in particular teaches a host of lessons, because it makes clear what our country really owes to the concept and implementation of European integration.

This new principle of the European system of states, which could almost be called revolutionary, emanated from France and her two great statesmen Robert Schuman and Jean Monnet. Every stage of its gradual realization, from the establishment of the European Coal and Steel Community to the creation of the single market and the introduction of the single currency, depended essentially on the alliance of Franco-German interests. This was never exclusive, however, but always open to other European states, and so it should remain until finality has been achieved.

European integration has proved phenomenally successful. The whole thing had just one decisive shortcoming, forced upon it by history: it was not the whole of Europe, but merely its free part in the West. For fifty years, the division of Europe cut right through Germany and Berlin. And on the eastern side of the Wall and barbed wire an indispensable part of Europe, without which European integration could never be completed, waited for its chance to take part in the European unification process. That chance came with the end of the division of Europe and Germany in 1989/90.

Robert Schuman saw this quite clearly back in 1963: "We must build the united Europe not only in the interest of the free nations, but also in order to be able to admit the peoples of Eastern Europe into this community if, freed from the constraints under which they live, they want to join and seek our moral support. We owe them the example of a unified, fraternal Europe. Every step we take along this road will mean a new opportunity for them. They need our help with the transformation they have to achieve. It is our duty to be prepared."

Following the collapse of the Soviet empire the EU had to open up to the east, otherwise the very idea of European integration would have undermined itself and eventually self-destructed. Why? A glance at the former Yugoslavia shows us the consequences, even if they would not always and everywhere have been so extreme. An EU restricted to Western Europe would forever have had to deal with a divided system in Europe: in Western Europe integration, in Eastern Europe the old system of balance with its continued national orientation, constraints of coalition, traditional interest-led politics and the permanent danger of nationalist ideologies and confrontations. A divided system of states in Europe without an over-arching order would in the long term make Europe a continent of uncertainty, and in the medium term these traditional lines of conflict would shift from Eastern Europe into the EU again. If that happened Germany in particular would be the big loser. The geopolitical reality after 1989 left no serious alternative to the eastward enlargement of the European institutions, and this has never been truer than now in the age of globalization.

In response to this truly historic turnaround the EU consistently embarked upon a far-reaching process of reform:

- In Maastricht one of the three essential sovereign rights of the modern nation-state—currency, internal security and external security—was for the first time transferred to the sole responsibility of a European institution. The introduction of the euro was not only the crowning-point of economic integration, it was also a profoundly political act, because a currency is not just another economic factor but also symbolizes the power of the sovereign who guarantees it. A tension has emerged between the communitarization of economy and currency on the one hand and the lack of political and democratic structures on the other, a tension which might lead to crises within the EU if we do not take productive steps to make good the shortfall in political integration and democracy, thus completing the process of integration.

- The European Council in Tampere marked the beginning of a new far-reaching integration project, namely the development of a common area of justice and internal security, making the Europe of the citizens a tangible reality. But there is even more to this new integration project: common laws can be a highly integrative force.

- It was not least the war in Kosovo that prompted the European states to take further steps to strengthen their joint capacity for action on foreign policy, agreeing in Cologne and Helsinki on a new goal: the development of a Common Security and Defence Policy. With this the Union has taken the next step following the euro. For how in the long term can it be justified that countries inextricably linked by monetary union and by economic and political realities do not also face up together to external threats and together maintain their security?

- Agreement was also reached in Helsinki on a concrete plan for the enlargement of the EU. With these agreements the external borders of the future EU are already emerging. It is foreseeable that the European Union will have 27, 30 or even more members at the end of the enlargement process, almost as many as the CSCE at its inception.

Thus we in Europe are currently facing the enormously difficult task of organizing two major projects in parallel:

1. Enlargement as quickly as possible. This poses difficult problems of adaptation both for the acceding states and for the EU itself. It also trig-

gers fear and anxiety in our citizens: are their jobs at risk? Will enlargement make Europe even less transparent and comprehensible for its citizens? As seriously as we must tackle these questions, we must never lose sight of the historic dimension of eastern enlargement. For this is a unique opportunity to unite our continent, wracked by war for centuries, in peace, security, democracy and prosperity.

Enlargement is a supreme national interest, especially for Germany. It will be possible to lastingly overcome the risks and temptations objectively inherent in Germany's dimensions and central situation through the enlargement and simultaneous deepening of the EU. Moreover, enlargement—consider the EU's enlargement to the south—is a pan-European programme for growth. Enlargement will bring tremendous benefits for German companies and for employment. Germany must therefore continue its advocacy of rapid eastern enlargement. At the same time, enlargement must be effected carefully and in accordance with the Helsinki decision.

2. Europe's capacity to act. The institutions of the EU were created for six member states. They just about still function with fifteen. While the first step towards reform, to be taken in the upcoming intergovernmental conference and introducing increased majority voting, is important, it will not in the long term be sufficient for integration as a whole. The danger will then be that enlargement to include 27 or 30 members will hopelessly overload the EU's ability to absorb, with its old institutions and mechanisms, even with increased use of majority decisions, and that it could lead to severe crises. But this danger, it goes without saying, is no reason not to push on with enlargement as quickly as possible; rather it shows the need for decisive, appropriate institutional reform so that the Union's capacity to act is maintained even after enlargement. The consequences of the irrefutable enlargement of the EU is therefore erosion or integration.

Fulfilling these two tasks is at the heart of the current intergovernmental conference. The EU has pledged to be able to admit new members by 1 January 2003. Following the conclusion of Agenda 2000, the aim now is to put in place the institutional preconditions for the next round of enlargement. Resolving the three key questions—the composition of the Commission, the weighting of votes in the Council and particularly the extension of majority decisions—is indispensable for the smooth continuation of the process of enlargement. As the next practical step these three questions now have absolute priority.

Crucial as the intergovernmental conference is as the next step for the future of the EU, we must, given Europe's situation, already begin to think beyond the enlargement process and consider how a future "large" EU can function as it ought to function and what shape it must therefore take. And that's what I want to do now.

Permit me therefore to remove my Foreign Minister's hat altogether in order to suggest a few ideas both on the nature of this so-called finality of Europe and on how we can approach and eventually achieve this goal. And all the Eurosceptics on the other side of the Channel would be well advised not to immediately produce the big headlines again, because firstly this is a personal vision of a solution to the European problems. And, secondly, we are talking here about the long term, far beyond the current intergovernmental conference. So no one need be afraid of these ideas.

Enlargement will render imperative a fundamental reform of the European institutions. Just what would a European Council with thirty heads of state and government be like? Thirty presidencies? How long will Council meetings actually last? Days, maybe even weeks? How, with the system of institutions that exists today, are thirty states supposed to balance interests, take decisions and then actually act? How can one prevent the EU from becoming utterly intransparent, compromises from becoming stranger and more incomprehensible, and the citizens' acceptance of the EU from eventually hitting rock bottom?

Question upon question, but there is a very simple answer: the transition from a union of states to full parliamentarization as a European Federation, something Robert Schuman demanded 50 years ago. And that means nothing less than a European Parliament and a European government which really do exercise legislative and executive power within the Federation. This Federation will have to be based on a constituent treaty.

I am well aware of the procedural and substantive problems that will have to be resolved before this goal can be attained. For me, however, it is entirely clear that Europe will only be able to play its due role in global economic and political competition if we move forward courageously. The problems of the 21st century cannot be solved with the fears and formulae of the 19th and 20th centuries.

Of course, this simple solution is immediately criticized as being utterly unworkable. Europe is not a new continent, so the criticism goes, but full of different peoples, cultures, languages and histories. The nation-states are realities that cannot simply be erased, and the more globalization and Europeanization create superstructures and anonymous actors remote from the citizens, the more the people will cling on to the nation-states that give them comfort and security.

Now I share all these objections, because they are correct. That is why it would be an irreparable mistake in the construction of Europe if one were to try to complete political integration against the existing national institutions and traditions rather than by involving them. Any such endeavour would be doomed to failure by the historical and cultural environment in Europe. Only if European integration takes the nation-states along with it into such a Federation, only if their institutions are not devalued or even made to disappear, will such a project be workable despite all the huge difficulties. In other words: the existing concept of a federal European state replacing the old nation-states and their democracies as the new sovereign power shows itself to be an artificial construct which ignores the established realities in Europe. The completion of European integration can only be successfully conceived if it is done on the basis of a division of sovereignty between Europe and the nation-state. Precisely this is the idea underlying the concept of "subsidiarity," a subject that is currently being discussed by everyone and understood by virtually no one.

So what must one understand by the term "division of sovereignty"? As I said, Europe will not emerge in a political vacuum, and so a further fact in our European reality is therefore the different national political cultures and their democratic publics, separated in addition by linguistic boundaries. A European Parliament must therefore always represent two things: a Europe of the nation-states and a Europe of the citizens. This will only be possible if this European Parliament actually brings together the different national political elites and then also the different national publics.

In my opinion, this can be done if the European parliament has two chambers. One will be for elected members who are also members of their national parliaments. Thus there will be no clash between national parliaments and the European parliament, between the nation-state and Europe. For the second chamber a decision will have to be made between the Senate model, with directly-elected senators from the member states, and a chamber of states along the lines of Germany's Bundesrat. In the United States, every state elects two senators; in our Bundesrat, in contrast, there are different numbers of votes.

Similarly, there are two options for the European executive, or government. Either one can decide in favour of developing the European Council into a European government, i.e. the European government is formed from the national governments, or—taking the existing Commission structure as a starting point—one can opt for the direct election of a president with far-reaching executive powers. But there are also various other possibilities between these two poles.

Now objections will be raised that Europe is already much too complicated and much too intransparent for the citizen, and here we are wanting to make it even more complicated. But the intention is quite the opposite. The division of sovereignty between the Union and the nation-states requires a constituent treaty which lays down what is to be regulated at European level and what has still to be regulated at national level. The majority of regulations at EU level are in part the result of inductive communitarization as per the "Monnet method" and an expression of interstate compromise within today's EU.

There should be a clear definition of the competences of the Union and the nation-states respectively in a European constituent treaty, with core sovereignties and matters which absolutely have to be regulated at European level being the domain of the Federation, whereas everything else would remain the responsibility of the nation-states. This would be a lean European Federation, but one capable of action, fully sovereign yet based on self-confident nation-states, and it would also be a Union which the citizens could understand, because it would have made good its shortfall on democracy.

However, all this will not mean the abolition of the nation-state. Because even for the finalized Federation the nation-state, with its cultural and democratic traditions, will be irreplaceable in ensuring the legitimation of a union of citizens and states that is wholly accepted by the people. I say this not least with an eye to our friends in the United Kingdom, because I know that the term "federation" irritates many Britons. But to date I have been unable to come up with another word. We do not wish to irritate anyone.

Even when European finality is attained, we will still be British or German, French or Polish. The nation-states will continue to exist and at European level they will retain a much larger role than the Lander have in Germany. And in such a Federation the principle of subsidiarity will be constitutionally enshrined.

These three reforms—the solution of the democracy problem and the need for fundamental reordering of competences both horizontally, i.e. among the European institutions, and vertically, i.e. between Europe, the nation-state and the regions—will only be able to succeed if Europe is established anew with a constitution. In other words: through the realization of the project of a European constitution centred around basic human and civil rights, an equal division of powers between the European institutions and a precise delineation between European and nation-state level. The main axis for such a European constitution will be the relationship between the Federation and the nation-state. Let me not be misunderstood: this has nothing whatsoever to do with a return to re-nationalisation, quite the contrary.

The question which is becoming more and more urgent today is this: can this vision of a Federation be achieved through the existing method of integration, or must this method itself, the central element of the integration process to date, be cast into doubt?

In the past, European integration was based on the "Monnet method" with its communitarization approach in European institutions and policy. This gradual process of integration, with no blueprint for the final state, was conceived in the 1950s for the economic integration of a small group of countries. Successful as it was in that scenario, this approach has proved to be of only limited use for the political integration and democratization of Europe. Where it was not possible for all EU members to move ahead, smaller groups of countries of varying composition took the lead, as was the case with Economic and Monetary Union and with Schengen.

Does the answer to the twin challenge of enlargement and deepening, then, lie in such a differentiation, an enhanced cooperation in some areas? Precisely in an enlarged and thus necessarily more heterogeneous Union, further differentiation will be inevitable. To facilitate this process is thus one of the priorities of the intergovernmental conference.

However, increasing differentiation will also entail new problems: a loss of European identity, of internal coherence, as well as the danger of an internal erosion of the EU, should ever larger areas of intergovernmental cooperation loosen the nexus of integration. Even today a crisis of the Monnet method can no longer be overlooked, a crisis that cannot be solved according to the method's own logic.

That is why Jacques Delors, Helmut Schmidt and Valery Giscard d'Estaing have recently tried to find new answers to this dilemma. Delors' idea is that a "federation of nation-states," comprising the six founding states of the European Community, should conclude a "treaty within the treaty" with a view to making far-reaching reforms in the European institutions. Schmidt and Giscard's ideas are in a similar vein, though they place the Euro-11 states at the centre, rather than just the six founding states. As early as 1994 Karl Lamers and Wolfgang Schauble proposed the creation of a "core Europe," but it was stillborn, as it were, because it presupposed an exclusive, closed "core," even omitting the founding state Italy, rather than a magnet of integration open to all.

So if the alternative for the EU in the face of the irrefutable challenge posed by eastern enlargement is indeed either erosion or integration, and if clinging to a federation of states would mean standstill with all its negative repercussions, then, under pressure from the conditions and the crises provoked by them, the EU will at some time within the next ten years be confronted with this alternative: will a majority of member states take the leap into full integration and agree on a European constitution?

Or, if that doesn't happen, will a smaller group of member states take this route as an avant-garde, i.e. will a centre of gravity emerge comprising a few member states which are staunchly committed to the European ideal and are in a position to push ahead with political integration? The question then would simply be: when will be the right time? Who will be involved? And will this centre of gravity emerge within or outside the framework provided by the treaties? One thing at least is certain: no European project will succeed in the future either without the closest Franco-German cooperation.

Given this situation, one could imagine Europe's further development far beyond the coming decade in two or three stages:

First the expansion of reinforced cooperation between those states which want to cooperate more closely than others, as is already the case with Economic and Monetary Union and Schengen. We can make progress in this way in many areas: on the further development of Euro-11 to a politico-economic union, on environmental protection, the fight against crime, the development of common immigration and asylum policies and of course on the foreign and security policy. In this context it is of paramount importance that closer cooperation should not be understood as the end of integration.

One possible interim step on the road to completing political integration could then later be the formation of a centre of gravity. Such a group of states would conclude a new European framework treaty, the nucleus of a constitution of the Federation. On the basis of this treaty, the Federation would develop its own institutions, establish a government which within the EU should speak with one voice on behalf of the members of the group on as many issues as possible, a strong parliament and a directly elected president. Such a centre of gravity would have to be the avant-garde, the driving force for the completion of political integration and should from the start comprise all the elements of the future federation.

I am certainly aware of the institutional problems with regard to the current EU that such a centre of gravity would entail. That is why it would be critically important to ensure that the EU *acquis* is not jeopardized, that the union is not divided and the bonds holding it together are not damaged, either in political or in legal terms. Mechanisms would have to be developed which permit the members of the centre of gravity to cooperate smoothly with others in the larger EU.

The question of which countries will take part in such a project, the EU founding members, the Euro-11 members or another group, is impossible to answer today. One thing must be clear when considering the option of forming a centre of gravity: this avant-garde must never be exclusive but must be open to all member states and candidate countries, should they desire to participate at a certain point in time. For those who wish to participate but do not fulfil the requirements, there must be a possibility to be drawn closer in.

Transparency and the opportunity for all EU member states to participate would be essential factors governing the acceptance and feasibility of the project. This must be true in particular with regard to the candidate countries. For it would be historically absurd and utterly stupid if Europe, at the very time when it is at long last reunited, were to be divided once again.

Such a centre of gravity must also have an active interest in enlargement and it must be attractive to the other members. If one follows Hans-Dietrich Genscher's tenet that no member state can be forced to go farther than it is able or willing to go, but that those who do not want to go any farther cannot prevent others from doing so, then the centre of gravity will emerge within the treaties. Otherwise it will emerge outside them.

The last step will then be completion of integration in a European Federation. Let's not misunderstand each other: closer cooperation does not automatically lead to full integration, either by the centre of gravity or straight away by the majority of members. Initially, enhanced cooperation means nothing more than increased intergovernmentalization under pressure from the facts and the shortcomings of the "Monnet Method." The steps towards a constituent treaty—and exactly that will be the precondition for full integration—require a deliberate political act to reestablish Europe.

This, ladies and gentlemen, is my personal vision for the future: from closer cooperation towards a European constituent treaty and the completion of Robert Schuman's great idea of a European Federation. This could be the way ahead!

# Selected Bibliography

Amato, Giuliano, and J. Batt. *The Long-Term Implications of EU Enlargement: The Nature of the New Border,* Final Report of a Reflection Group. Florence: European University Institute, 1999.

Avery, Graham, and Fraser Cameron. *The Enlargement of the European Union.* Sheffield, U.K.: Sheffield Academic Press, 1998.

Bannerman, Edward, and others. *Europe After September 11th.* London: Centre for European Reform, 2001.

Baun, Michael J. *A Wider Europe: The Process and Politics of European Union Enlargement.* Lanham, Md.: Rowman and Littlefield, 2000.

Bond, Martin, Julie Smith, and William Wallace (eds.). *Eminent Europeans: Personalities Who Shaped Contemporary Europe.* London: Greycoat Press, 1996.

Brenner, Michael. *Terms of Engagement: The United States and the European Security Identity.* The Washington Papers, 176. Westport, Conn.: Praeger for the Center for Strategic and International Studies, 1998.

Cafruny, Alan, and Glenda Rosenthal (eds.). *The State of the European Community, Volume 2: The Maastricht Debates and Beyond.* Boulder, Colo.: Lynne Rienner, 1993.

Cockfield, Arthur. *The European Union: Creating the Single Market.* Chichester, U.K.: John Wiley and Sons, 1994.

Corbett, Richard. *The European Parliament's Role in Closer European Integration.* Basingstoke, U.K.: Macmillan, 1998.

Cowles, Maria Green, and Michael Smith. *The State of the European Union: Risks, Reform, Resistance, and Revival.* Vol. 5. New York: Oxford University Press, 2000.

Croft, Stuart, John Redmond, G. Wyn Rees, and Mark Webber. *The Enlargement of Europe.* Manchester, U.K.: Manchester University Press, 1999.

Curzon Price, V., A. Landau, and R. Whitman (eds.). *The Enlargement of the EU.* London: Routledge, 1999.

Dehousse, Renaud. *The European Court of Justice: The Politics of Judicial Integration.* New York: St. Martin's Press, 1998.

Dickinson, David G., and Andrew W. Mullineux (eds.). *Financial and Monetary Integration in the New Europe: Convergence between the EU and Central and Eastern Europe.* Northhampton, Mass.: Edward Elgar, 2002.

Dinan, Desmond. *Ever Closer Union: An Introduction to European Integration.* 2d ed. Boulder, Colo.: Lynne Rienner Publishers, 1999.

Duchene, Francois. *Jean Monnet: The First Statesman of Interdependence.* New York: Norton, 1994.

*The Economist, Pocket Europe in Figures.* London: Profile Books, Ltd., 2000.

Emerson, Michael. *Redrawing the Map of Europe.* London: Macmillan, 1998.

George, Stephen. *An Awkward Partner: Britain in the European Community.* 2d ed. Oxford: Oxford University Press, 1996.

Gower, Jackie, and John Redmond (eds.). *Enlarging the European Union: The Way Forward.* Aldershot, U.K. and Burlington, Vt.: Ashgate, 2000.

Grabbe, Heather. *Profiting from EU Enlargement.* London: Centre for European Reform, 2001.

Grabbe, Heather, and K. Hughes. *Enlarging the EU Eastwards.* London: Printer for the Royal Institute of International Affairs, 1998.

Grabbe, Heather, and Wolfgang Munchau. *Germany and Britain: An Alliance of Necessity.* London: Centre for European Reform, 2002.

Grant, Charles. *Delors: Inside the House that Jacques Built.* London: Brealey, 1994.

Hallstein, Walter. *Europe in the Making.* London: Allen & Unwin, 1972.

Hauf, K., and B. Soetendorp (eds.). *Adapting to European Integration: Small States and the European Union.* London: Addison-Wesley, 1998.

Hayes-Fenshaw, Fiona, and Helen Wallace. *The Council of Ministers.* New York: St. Martin's Press, 1996.

Heenan, Patrick, and Monique Lamontagne (eds.). *The Central and East European Handbook.* Chicago: Fitzroy Dearborn, 1999.

Henderson, Karen. *Back to Europe: Central and Eastern Europe and the European Union.* London: Taylor and Francis, 1999.

Hunter, Robert E. *The European Security and Defense Policy: NATO's Companion or Competitor?* Santa Monica, Calif.: RAND, 2002.

Hurwitz, Leon, and Christian Lequesne. *The State of the European Community: Policies, Institutions and Debates in the Transition Years.* Boulder, Colo.: Lynne Rienner, 1991.

Ingersent, K. A., A. J. Rayner, and R. C. Hine. *The Reform of the Common Agricultural Policy.* Basingstoke, U.K.: Macmillan, 1998.

Jenkins, Roy. *European Diary, 1977–1981.* London: Collins, 1989.

Jones, Erik. *The Politics and Economics of Monetary Union.* Boston, Mass.: Rowman and Littlefield, 1999.

Kaldor, M., and I. Vejvoda (eds.). *Democratization in Central and Eastern Europe.* London: Cassell, 1998.

Laurent, Pierre-Henri, and Marc Maresceau (eds.). *The State of the European Union.* Vol. 4. Boulder, Colo.: Lynn Rienner and Longman, 1998.

Lavanex, S. *Safe Third Countries, Extending the EU Asylum and Immigration Policies to Central and Eastern Europe.* Budapest: Central European University, 1999.

Leonard, Dick. *Guide to the European Union*. 7th ed. London: The Economist/Profile Books, Ltd., 2000.

Leonard, Mark. *Network Europe: The New Case for Europe*. London: Foreign Policy Centre, 1999.

Lippert, Barbara, K. Hughes, H. Grabbe, and P. Becker. *British and German Interests in EU Enlargement: Conflict and Cooperation*. London: Continuum/Royal Institute of International Affairs, 2001.

Maresceau, Marc (ed.). *Enlargement of the European Union: Relations between the European Union and Central and Eastern Europe*. London: Longman, 1997.

Marjolin, Robert. *Architect of European Unity: Memoirs: 1911- 1986*. London: Weidenfield & Nicolson, 1989.

Mattli, W. *The Logic of Regional Integration: Europe and Beyond*. Cambridge, Mass.: Cambridge University Press, 1999.

Mayhew, A. *Recreating Europe: The European Union's Policy toward Central and Eastern Europe*. Cambridge, Mass.: Cambridge University Press, 1998.

McCormick, John. *Understanding the European Union*. New York: St. Martin's Press, 1999.

Michalski, Anna, and Helen Wallace. *The European Community: The Challenge of Enlargement*. London: RIIA, 1992.

Miles, Lee (ed.). *The European Union and the Nordic Countries*. New York: Routledge, 1996.

Monnet, Jean. *Memoirs*. Garden City, N.Y.: Doubleday, 1978.

Moravcsik, Andrew *The Choice for Europe: Social Purpose and State Power from Messina to Maastricht*. Ithaca, N.Y.: Cornell University Press, 1998.

Nello, Susan Senior, and Karen E. Smith. *The European Union and Central and Eastern Europe: The Implications of Enlargement in Stages*. Burlington, Vt.: Ashgate, 1998.

Neunreither, K. H., and A. Wiener. *European Integration After Amsterdam: Institutional Dynamics and Prospects for Democracy*. Oxford: Oxford University Press, 2000.

Nicholson, Frances, and Roger East. *From Six to Twelve: The Enlargement of the European Communities*. Chicago: St. James Press, 1987.

Peterson, John. *Decision-Making in the European Union*. New York: St. Martin's, 1999.

Peterson, John, and Helen Sjursen. *Common Foreign Policy for Europe? Competing Visions of the CFSP*. London: Routledge, 1998.

Pinder, John. *The European Community and Eastern Europe*. London: Royal Institute of International Affairs, 1991.

Preston, Christopher. *Enlargement and Integration in the European Union*. London: Routledge, 1997.

Redmond, John (ed.). *The 1995 Enlargement of the European Union*. Aldershot, U.K.: Ashgate, 1997.

Redmond, John, and Glenda Rosenthal (eds.). *The Expanding European Union: Past, Present, Future*. Boulder, Colo.: Lynne Rienner, 1998.

Rhodes, Carolyn (ed.). *The European Union in the World Community*. Boulder, Colo.: Lynne Rienner, 1998.

Rhodes, Carolyn, and Sonia Mazey (eds.). *The State of the European Union: Building a European Polity?* Vol. 3. Boulder, Colo.: Lynne Rienner, 1995.

Ross, George. *Jacques Delors and European Integration.* Oxford: Oxford University Press, 1995.

Smith, Karen E. *The Making of EU Foreign Policy: The Case of Central and Eastern Europe.* London: Macmillan, 1998.

Spence, D. "Enlargement without Accession: The EC's Response to German Unification," Royal Institute of International Affairs Discussion Paper No. 36. London: RIIA, 1991.

Sperling, J. (ed.). *Two Tiers or Two Speeds? NATO and EU Enlargement Compared.* Manchester, U.K. and New York: Manchester University Press, 2000.

Thatcher, Margaret. *The Downing Street Years.* New York: HarperCollins, 1993.

Thorhallsson, Baldur. *The Role of Small States in the European Union.* Aldershot, U.K. and Burlington, Vt.: Ashgate, 2000.

Torreblanca, Jose Ignacio. *The European Community and Central Europe.* Aldershot, U.K. and Burlington, Vt.: Ashgate, 2000.

Ungerer, Horst. *A Concise History of European Monetary Integration: From EPU to EMU.* Westport, Conn.: Greenwood Press, 1997.

Van Oudenaren, John. *Uniting Europe: European Integration and the Post-Cold War World.* Boston, Mass.: Rowman & Littlefield, 1999.

Wallace, Helen (ed.). *Interlocking Dimensions of European Integration.* Basingstoke, U.K.: Palgrave, 2001.

Wallace, Helen, and William Wallace (eds.). *Policy-Making in the European Union.* 4th ed. Oxford: Oxford University Press, 2000.

Westlake, Martin. *The Commission and the Parliament: Partners and Rivals in the European Policy-Making System.* London: Butterworth, 1994.

Westlake, Martin (ed.). *The European Union Beyond Amsterdam.* London and New York: Routledge, 1998.

Young, Hugo. *This Blessed Plot: Britain and Europe from Churchill to Blair.* London: Macmillan, 1998.

## EU-RELATED WEB SITES

www.europa.eu.int—official server of the European Union
www.europarl.eu.int—European Parliament's web site
www.ecb.int—European Central Bank's web site
www.useu.be—web site of the U.S. Mission to the EU
www.eurosceptic.com—web site of U.K. Euroskeptics
www.eustudies.com—The European Union Studies Association
www.euractiv.com—Belgian information source focused on EU news, policy positions, and actors

# Index

**About the Author**

PETER A. POOLE is a former foreign service officer who has served in Brussels. Dr. Poole was the founding director of the M.A. in International Studies program at Old Dominion University and currently serves as an instructor at George Mason University's Learning in Retirement Institute. Among his earlier books are *Profiles in American Foreign Policy* (1981) and *Eight Presidents and Indochina* (1988).